THE WAY OF
THE HUMAN

THE QUANTUM
PSYCHOLOGY NOTEBOOKS

OTHER BOOKS BY STEPHEN WOLINSKY

Trances People Live
Healing Approaches in Quantum Psychology
ISBN 0-9626184-2-X, The Bramble Company

Quantum Consciousness
The Guide to Experiencing Quantum Psychology
ISBN 0-9626184-8-9, Bramble Books

The Tao of Chaos
Essence and the Enneagram
ISBN 1-883647-02-9, Bramble Books

The Dark Side of the Inner Child
The Next Step
ISBN 1-883647-00-2, Bramble Books

Hearts on Fire
The Tao of Meditation
ISBN 1-884997-25-2

THE WAY OF THE HUMAN

THE QUANTUM PSYCHOLOGY NOTEBOOKS

VOLUME I

DEVELOPING MULTI-DIMENSIONAL AWARENESS

SPECIAL SECTION:
TRANCES PEOPLE LIVE REVISITED

STEPHEN H. WOLINSKY, PH.D.

For information write to:
Stephen H. Wolinsky, Ph.D.
Quantum Institute®
101 Grand Avenue, Suite 11
Capitola California 95010
(831) 464-0564

ISBN: 0-9670362-0-8

First printing 1999
Printed in Canada

THE AUTHOR

Stephen H. Wolinsky, Ph.D., began his clinical practice in Los Angeles, California in 1974. A Gestalt and Reichian therapist and trainer, he led workshops in Southern California. He was also trained in Classical Hypnosis, Psychosynthesis, Psychodrama/Psychomotor, and Transactional Analysis. In 1977 he journeyed to India, where he lived for almost six years studying meditation. He moved to New Mexico in 1982 to resume a clinical practice. There he began to train therapists in Ericksonian Hypnosis and family therapy. Dr. Wolinsky also conducted year-long trainings entitled: Integrating Hypnosis with Psychotherapy, and Integrating Hypnosis with Family Therapy. Dr. Wolinsky is the author of *Trances People Live: Healing Approaches in Quantum Psychology*®, *Quantum Consciousness: The Guide to Experiencing Quantum Psychology*®, *The Tao of Chaos: Quantum Consciousness Volume II, The Dark Side of the Inner Child* (Bramble Books) and *Hearts on Fire: The Roots of Quantum Psychology*. He is presently completing a three volume set entitled *The Way of the Human: The Quantum Psychology Notebooks*. He is the founder of Quantum Psychology®. Dr. Wolinsky presently resides in Capitola, California. He can be reached for workshop information by calling (831) 464-0564 or by FAX at (831) 479-8233.

Finding out who you are is not about being or becoming something, it is about first realizing your humanness. . . .

Stephen Wolinsky

TABLE OF CONTENTS

SPECIAL SECTION

INTRODUCTION

To put together these three Volumes required an inordinate amount of organizational work. For this reason, to give myself more leeway, and as a way to have the book available sooner to the public, I decided to use the subtitle of *The Quantum Psychology Notebooks*.

This "took me off the hook" in trying to produce a manuscript of great literary value, and gave me the possibility of releasing the material sooner. I did not want to go over *all* of the material in the last five books. I wanted this work to stand on its own, hence the idea of calling the three Volumes *notebooks* seemed like a good idea. These books are therefore designated as notebooks, to be used as notebooks, with the assumption that the reader will study them and go back to the earlier Quantum Psychology Volumes since this present work in many respect might require some previous background.

I decided to place the introduction prior to the dedication and acknowledgments because I wanted to be clear about who and in which "book" (of the three) the dedications should go. In other words, each Volume has different dedications and major influences.

When this Quantum event "began" to solidify, the possibility of writing a three Volume series called the *Way of the Human* had not quite occurred to "me." In this, the first of three Volumes, *Developing Multi-Dimensional Awareness*, I wanted to encapsulate a major focus of Quantum Psychology the development of multi-dimensional awareness as a "possible" step in the discovery of *Who You Are*.

MAJOR INFLUENCES

As I was writing the introduction to *The Way of the Human* trilogy, I recalled that shortly after *Trances People Live: Healing Approaches in Quantum Psychology* was released in 1990, I received a phone call from Peter Madell, a doctor in Northern California. Peter was with my teacher, Nisargadatta Maharaj, just around the time that he died. We talked for a while about him and I asked Peter if he knew where I could get an audiotape of the chanting that took place in his room. Peter said that he had such a tape and that he would send a copy with arati (chanting) and some questions and answers taped in Maharaj's room.

I used to listen to the tapes while I was driving to and from Albuquerque and Santa Fe. One day I heard Nisargadatta Maharaj say something which *shocked* me:

> In the beginning there was **NOTHING**, absolutely. The **I AM** appeared (condensed) within that **NOTH-INGNESS**. And one day, the **I AM** will disappear (thin-out) and there will be **NOTHING** again and that is all it is."

What shocked me was not that he had said it. What shocked me was that even though I had been with Nisargadatta Maharaj, I had never heard him saying anything like that. What was even more shocking was that I had been presenting this exact material in Quantum Psychology workshops for years and I did not know that he had ever said it. All "I" could imagine was that at some level, Nisargadatta Maharaj had *planted seeds* and that Quantum Psychology was the fruit of those seeds.

I recall that when "I" was writing *Trances People Live* in 1985, "I" thought I had come up with this incredibly brilliant idea called *associational networks*. I thought, "What an incredible discovery," that inside the mind there are associational networks. Even the term made sense to me. I remembered Freud having written that the mind organizes itself in chains of earlier similar events, but "my" idea of *associational networks* seemed even clearer. I picked up one of Milton Erickson's books shortly thereafter which I think was called, *Experiencing Hypnosis.* And right there, was exactly the same phrase, *Associational Networks.*

What exactly does this mean? Did I come up with it? Did Erickson come up with it? Had I read it? Had I not read it? I don't know. When I completed the original book, *The Way of the Human*, I realized that parts of it (dimensions) were somewhat similar to G. I. Gurdjieff's Fourth Way idea of the different centers. Now, Quantum Psychology does not see it as centers in the body like Gurdjieff and I was never a Gurdjieff person but certainly I had read Gurdjieff's material. I had read it years ago, I had sat with it. I had even attended a Gurdjieff movement workshop. But I would not consider myself a Gurdjieff student. Still, parts of the Multi-Dimensional Awareness approach which arose within me had similarities. Did it come from Gurdjieff? Did it come out of "me?" Did I read it and forget about it? Did I have what a therapist once termed *source amnesia* and it later came back to "me?" I don't know. Either way, I want to acknowledge Gurdjieff *also* as a source, either directly or indirectly in the understanding of multi-dimensional awareness as an approach.

What does seem clear, however, is that certain knowledge around the development of consciousness and the discovery of "**WHO YOU ARE**" is universal and that there is, and has to be, an overlap.

Quantum Psychology will focus shortly on nine major points which I have selected out from "my time" with Nisargadatta Maharaj and which will be discussed later.

The purpose of Quantum Psychology is to find out **WHO YOU ARE** The question is, how can you use the material in this trilogy in a way that you can "facilitate such a process?" To begin with, this trilogy can be considered and used as a *de-programming guide*. In other words, the two statements by my teacher Nisargadatta Maharaj which underscore this are:

1. "Question everything, do not believe anything."
2. "In order to find out who you are—you must first find out who you are not."

With this understanding as a major context for the Quantum work and the discovery of **WHO YOU ARE**, it is important to begin by exploring how you organize the "you" you call yourself—and bring into question everything you imagine "yourself" to be. The notions that you have about yourself are just that, notions and concepts about who you are, which is not who you are. Alfred Korzybski, the father of General Semantics, would say it this way: "The idea is not the thing it is referring to." What begins to occur is that upon inquiry not only does the imaging and the notions disappear but so does the imag*er* the notion*er* and ultimately the know*er*.

For this reason, Quantum work asks readers to question and "look at" the concepts and psychic structures by which you define, organize and justify the "you" "you" call "yourself," be they spiritual or psychological, and to go beyond them.

Questioning is not an irreverent sin or a sacrilege—rather, it is the duty and responsibility of every sincere "seeker."

We need to question the underlying assumptions of psychological and spiritual practice to see how they might re-enforce, mask or hide much deeper structures which lie beneath the surface. Questioning is imperative to understanding "why am I not getting much out of my psychological or spiritual practice even after years." Maybe, the practices are not right for you maybe they re-enforce deeper patterns, or maybe their effects and limitations have been overstated or understated respectively. But once you begin to explore, you might be surprised how these practices which are supposed to "liberate" actually re-enforce self-fulfilling concepts thus continuing our underlying presuppositions about who we think we are. Once discarded these concepts are seen as just that, concepts, and then **WHO YOU ARE** *naturally* emerges and is revealed. However, you must have a willingness to question everything and not believe anything. It is a process whereby you find out who you are by finding out who you are not.

The Quantum work is both a map and a de-programming guide to hopefully enable people to wake-up and go-beyond all they think they are to find out **WHO THEY REALLY ARE**.

In the later stages both the question*er* and question*ee* dissolve. What is beyond this? Nisargadatta Maharaj answered this question. When a student asked, "Who are you?" he said, "Nothing perceivable or conceivable."

Enjoy the ride.
    With love
        Your brother,
            Stephen

DEDICATION

To the memory of my teacher and the Grandfather of Quantum Psychology, Shri Nisargadatta Maharaj

ACKNOWLEDGMENTS

To the memory of Alfred Korzybski, the Father of General Semantics

To the memory of G. I. Gurdjieff, the Father of the Fourth Way

Special thanks to Allen Horne for his editorial assistance.

And thanks to Marylu Erlandson and Susan Briley for word processing the manuscript.

To Alfred Schatz—the Brain Baba.

To my divine Leni.

A man is three things:
What people think he is,
What others think he is
and
What he really is.

Anonymous

CHAPTER I
AN INTRODUCTORY CHAPTER

I n December 1995, *The Way of the Human* was finally completed and scheduled for publication in May. However, publishing problems prevented its release. At first, this seemed disastrous, but a year and a half later, "I"[1] saw the much larger picture. Quantum Psychology, like the Quantum itself, is an ongoing "quantum event." In other words, in the unseen "quantum world", the book you are reading appears solid; but it is actually a condensation of *THAT UNDIFFERENTIATED CONSCIOUSNESS* which IS and always appears to be changing (condensing-thinning out) instant-to-instant. Unfortunately, our eyes, through the vehicle of the nervous system cannot "see" this and hence organizes the book as solid with the appearance of permanence rather than its being the movement of atoms and electrons within the **EMPTINESS** of **UNDIFFERENTIATED CONSCIOUSNESS**. Rather, our nervous system "later" creates and imagines the **EMPTINESS** of **UNDIFFERENTIATED CONSCIOUSNESS** as a solid book. In this way, Quantum Psychology is not static, but rather mirrors the Quantum (unseen) world as on-going event and process.

---

[1] Please note personal pronouns have quotation marks around them. This is an attempt to denote them as moving Quantum events which arise and subside. They (I, me, she, him, her) are an appearance as the **VOID OF UNDIFFERENTIATED CONSCIOUSNESS** condenses and thins-out, and represent only a facsimile of the nervous system. This suggests that each arising I is made of the same substance as the **VOID OF UNDIFFERENTIATED CONSCIOUSNESS**; but from the space-time limitations of the nervous system the I appears to be made of a different substance than the "no-I" **VOID** background. I should also note that the **VOID** is **UNDIFFERENTIATED CONSCIOUSNESS** (i.e., consciousness without distinctions). The "you" you call yourself (i.e., like a thought, chair, air, the observer, etc.) is differentiated consciousness. The **VOID OF UNDIFFERENTIATED CONSCIOUSNESS** *appears* to be differentiated when actually it has not.

For this reason, "Quantum Psychology" as well as the "me," the "you", "this book," "your last thought," is an event (i.e., a coming together or a moving apart of **THAT ONE SUBSTANCE.**).[2]

I AM NOT ME

"Nothingness is the building block of the Universe."

John Wheeler

The "I" is not a "me," the "I" cannot be a specific something because this "I" is a condensation and solidification of the **EMPTINESS** or **NOTHINGNESS** which is continually condensing and thinning out, while never losing its nature as the **EMPTINESS** or **UNDIFFERENTIATED CONSCIOUSNESS**. For this reason (as will be discussed later), the "I" I think I am is very temporary, arising and subsiding in and as that ONE SUBSTANCE only to re-appear again "later" while the nervous system records and acts "as if" it were always there in time and had never left (see Volume III, Appendix: Vishnu's Demon).

MULTI-DIMENSIONAL AWARENESS

In order to understand "the self" and its connection to the underlying unity, I realized that "we" must first acknowledge that we are human. Understanding first and foremost our full human nature becomes important if "we" wish to stabilize our awareness of the **VOID** which is the underlying unity of our Quantum Nature.[3]

All too often in the past, I first sought my Quantum nature by following psycho-spiritual disciplines, only to be "pulled out" or "forward" into and by my human nature. In fact, many paths of knowl-

---

[2]It should be noted that the Nervous System too is a condensation of **that ONE SUBSTANCE.** Therefore, just as a wave (Nervous System) in the ocean (**THAT ONE SUBSTANCE**) cannot influence the ocean, the Nervous System can only imagine it can influence the ONE SUBSTANCE. This, as will be discussed later, is a grandiose illusion.
[3]Please note, this is not the only way, nor a must, rather it is a possibility. As will be discussed later, we oftentimes lose the awareness of **ESSENCE, I AM**, etc., because we are "pulled" out into unprocessed material. To illustrate, unprocessed psychological material can be likened to undigested food. Undigested food sits in our intestines making us sick and pullling our attention and awareness. In the same say, unprocessed or undigested psychological material sometimes can pull our attention out of the awareness of WHO WE ARE.

edge suggest that it is our human nature which gets in the way of discovering and experiencing the underlying unity of our Quantum Nature. In Yoga-land, for example, emotions such as anger, jealousy, greed, lust, and hatred are referred to as the five enemies. In the Christian tradition oftentimes those and others like envy, pride, sloth, gluttony, avarice, vanity, lust, etc., are considered vices which should be converted into virtues. According to Buddha, all pain arises because of desire. The dilemma seems to be that it is human nature to desire. In fact, more pain is caused by resistance to desiring. After all, what is desire but an impulse that comes as the **EMPTINESS** or underlying unity pulsates and contracts to become something. Quantum Psychology sees pain as being caused by substituting biological desires, which are "have to's", for psychological "wants" (see The Biological Dimension).

However, in many-spiritual systems, the body's myriad emotions and basic human experiences (which are wired into the fight/flight nervous system) are seen as undesirable, even bad and something to be gotten rid of, transformed or healed, thus implying that they take us further away from our universal nature, commonly called **God**, the **VOID, UNDIFFERENTIATED CONSCIOUSNES** or the **SELF**.

What I discovered, however, is quite the opposite. Emotional and psychological states are part of being human. States of compassion and unconditional love are qualities of **ESSENCE**. This understanding led me to see that within the underlying unity of **EMPTINESS** there are different dimensions of manifestation, all with different functions. And although each dimension is connected to, and can influence other dimensions, each has its own function.

Quantum Psychology (1999) suggests that there are eight dimensions of manifestation which comprise being fully human (the ninth, the **VOID OF UNDIFFERENTIATED CONSCIOUSNESS**, and the tenth, the **NAMELESS ABSOLUTE**, are beyond dimensions, and will be discussed in Volume III). When awareness of all of these eight dimensions are included and their functions understood, we can experience our full humanity. Briefly these eight dimensions are: One, the external world; two, the thinking world; three, the emotional world; four, the biological or animal dimension; five, **ES-**

SENCE; six, the no-state state of **I AM**; seven, Archetypes of the **COLLECTIVE UNCONSCIOUS**; and eight, the "**NOT-I-I.**"

How are some problems created? Unfortunately, our awareness of the different functions of these dimensions get confused. When this occurs, we confuse one dimension's function with another dimension's function. This causes confusion and pain. For example, attempts to change the thinking or emotional dimensions—i.e., trying to make them more unconditionally loving, compassionate, and forgiving—confuses the functions of these dimensions. In the above example, unconditional love or compassion are not qualities of the biological animal, thinking or emotional dimensions. Rather, these are the qualities of **ESSENCE**. Therefore, we must understand the different dimensions of consciousness and their functions.

In this way, we can allow each dimension of humanness to have its function, without trying to change, override, overcome, or trade in one in favor of the other. To illustrate, it is the function of my right hand to write. It is the function of my mouth to take in food. Obviously my hand and my mouth are connected as they are part of my body but they have different functions. In the same way, we often try to "reform" our animal nature (lust) or emotional dimension (anger) by being celibate (if one's a yogi) or unconditionally loving (if one's a New-Ager). We can see that this rarely works. Why not? Because *being unconditionally loving is not a function of our animal or emotional nature; rather it is a function of our ESSENCE* (to be discussed in greater detail in Volume III).

COLLAPSING AND CONFUSING THE LEVELS

In Quantum Consciousness we call this confusion "collapsing the levels." Problems arise, for example, when we try to change and make our thinking level, emotional level or animal nature, unconditionally loving (which is a function of **ESSENCE**). Instead, we should let the psychology be and do psychology, and let **ESSENCE** be and do **ESSENCE**. Moreover, these qualities we seek, like peace or unconditional love, are not the *only* part of our human nature but represent just one of its dimensions, namely **ESSENCE**. No dimension can be overcome or gone beyond in favor of another dimension if "you" wish to stabilize awareness in the underlying unity. For now, we can say that our **ESSENCE** has essential qualities, like unconditional love, or love with no object. This is, however only one part of human nature. For that reason, to try to deny our animal nature, or try to reprogram or recondition our thinking or emotional nature, is not to realize that our animal nature, or our thinking or emotional nature, has a different function than does **ESSENCE**. This trying to deny our animal human nature and make it more like **ESSENCE** is a distortion which leads to more confusion (i.e., like the body is bad), intra-psychic war, dichotomy, and more importantly, it keeps us from being fully human.

In other words, to be fully human means to be aware of the external world while being aware of our animal nature with its sexual desires, etc., our thinking and emotional dimensions with its pain and pleasure, **ESSENCE** with its qualities of love, peace, etc., the **I AM**, the **COLLECTIVE**, and the "**NOT-I-I**". This is the development of Multi-Dimensional Awareness, which is the Way of the Human, and which might or may hopefully aid in the discovery of **WHO YOU ARE**.

Quantum physics has shown us beautifully that everything is made of the same substance. With this knowledge, how could anything be inherently bad, something to be gotten rid of, or something which can lead us away from our true nature? We must therefore appreciate all of the dimensions of being human with the understanding that each dimension has a function, and allow each dimension to work according to its nature. This means not substituting or trying to overcome one dimension, like using **ESSENCE** to overcome the emotional dimension, or the thinking dimension to overcome the biological dimension. This is *The Way of the Human*, to understand and allow all dimensions to function, *without resistance*, the way they were meant to function. This can be called the development of a **FUNCTIONAL AWARENESS**. **FUNCTIONAL AWARENESS** can be defined as the ability to place awareness on any single dimension, all dimensions simultaneously, or no dimensions, until awareness itself disappears in the **VOID** rather than having awareness habitually fixated and placed on only one or two dimensions.

Nisargadatta Maharaj once asked a man, "Why are you coming here to see me?" "Because the guru takes away the negative and gives us our true nature," he said. Maharaj replied, "There is nothing that anyone can take away from you or give to you which you are not already since there is only **THAT ONE CONSCIOUSNESS**."

All this considered, I am proposing that as humans we have an animal nature, a thinking nature, an emotional nature which contains feelings, and an **ESSENCE** with its essential qualities, etc. Awareness "unfortunately" seems to get fixated in one or more dimension. These dimensions need to BE without interference in order to liberate awareness which might help in the discovery of who you are.[4] Stated another way, since *Quantum Psychology defines spirituality as the realization that there is only ONE SUBSTANCE*, then true spirituality must include everything from emotions to thoughts and from fantasies to the physical body—*since there is only THAT ONE SUBSTANCE*. Actually, as will be discussed later, what we are ultimately looking at is a biological spirituality whereby biology and psychology are included within spirituality, and the underlying unity of *THAT ONE SUBSTANCE*.

WHY MULTI-DIMENSIONAL AWARENESS?

In the early 1990s, Quantum Psychology continued to grow and expand through books such as *Quantum Consciousness*, Volume I, *The Tao of Chaos: Quantum Consciousness,* Volume II. The question that continued to emerge from workshop participants as "I" traveled throughout the United States and Europe was no longer, "Who Am I?" but rather, "How do we as human beings live our lives and still maintain the awareness of the underlying unity of Quantum Consciousness?"

This question both intrigued and motivated me to complete what Quantum Consciousness Volumes I and II had begun, namely, how to be fully human and how to actualize and realize who we are on all dimensions.

---

[4]It should be noted that ultimately the concept of a path also disappears in the **VOID** (see Volume III).

What seemed clear to me was that to meditate and taste the "EMPTINESS" or "FULLNESS" or even to be emerged in the no-me state or samadhi was not enough.

What interested me more was what takes us out of the awareness of the underlying unity and, more importantly, how do we stabilize that awareness while we live our lives, work, have sex, etc.

In a word, how can "we" "stabilize" awareness in the underlying unity while being fully human?

COMPLETING THE HUMAN POTENTIAL MOVEMENT

In the 1960s and early 1970s, the human potential movement, led by noted psychologist Abraham Maslow, inspired many of us to reach for the heights of **SELF-ACTUALIZATION**. However, by the mid-1970s, I saw that this was not enough. my life had changed through psychology and certainly I no longer felt self-defeating but much more powerful and in touch with my body and feelings—but still I felt unfinished. I had not found out **WHO I WAS**.

For years I put aside psychology since I saw that **SELF-AC-TUALIZATION** was the end point of psychology and was not all that I had hoped it would be. I decided to go to India to seek **SELF-REALIZATION**.

By 1976 I was headed for India and **SELF-REALIZATION ("NOT-I-I")** and **WHO I WAS.** In India, and later on in the United States, through yoga and Buddhist practices, many of us were able to experience quite readily the empty-mind (no-mind), pure **WITNESS-ING**, and the underlying unity I now call Quantum Consciousness.

Unfortunately, in India it was stated both overtly and covertly that to attain and live in **THAT VOID OF UNDIFFERENTIATED CONSCIOUSNESS** required a giving-up of the world. At first, this seemed romantic, noble, and super-spiritual; but in the end I saw that this was both impractical and unrealistic. After all, most of us live, work, have relationships, and interact with the world.

In the late-1970s, I felt split. I had compartmentalized the spiritual or quantum world, on the one hand, and the thinking, emotional and biological, on the other. It was "as if" one dimension of manifestation negated the other. If I were in one dimension—for example, the emotional—the awareness of the EMPTINESS or underlying unity or interconnected fullness was lost or, at best, became a memory. I soon realized that I was compartmentalizing, separating the "spiritual" from the material.

Multi-dimensional Awareness, therefore, is where self actualization meets self-realization. It is where the external, thinking, emotional and biological-animal are no longer separate from the underlying unity. In short, *Quantum Psychology incorporates and includes the self-actualization of the West with the self-realization of the East through Multi-dimensional Awareness.*

For this reason it is important to let go of idea of "health" at a thinking or emotional dimension—such as always being unconditionally loving or always forgiving—and understand that this is a not a quality or function of the thinking or emotional dimensions but is a quality of **ESSENCE**. In this way, we can begin to accept our biological-animal, our thinking and emotional dimensions and their "limitations." This will enable us to develop a multi-dimensional *functional awareness* which leads to the underlying unity which "I" call our *quantum nature*.

How does one fully integrate, develop, and reach what is so adamantly sought by the human potential movement and the spiritual aspirants of the East? Simply stated: *Where do self-actualization and self-realization meet*? They meet in the development of multi-dimensional awareness as a possible aid to discovering "**WHO YOU ARE**" without negating or losing any part of human nature which includes the world which is made of **THAT ONE SUBSTANCE**.

The challenge is in being human as both a biological and psychological (thinking) emotional being, without losing our loving **ESSENCE** or the *awareness* of the underlying unity of the **VOID** (**NOT-I-I**) which is Quantum Consciousness. *The Way of the Human* asks us to do just that, to be fully human and develop our multi-dimensional awareness as a possible aid to discovering **WHO WE ARE**; in other words, to maintain awareness at all levels without exclusion but with total inclusion. *The Way of the Human* is where **SELF-REALIZATION** and **SELF-ACTUALIZATION** meet.

Throughout all three books, "I" will talk about dimensions of awareness. The purpose of these maps is not to lose sight of your ultimate goal, but rather to use them so you can identify where your own attention and awareness might be stuck or fixated, thus inhibiting "your" awareness of the underlying unity of Quantum Consciousness.

Awareness, once it has been freed from habitual fixation, leads to the liberation of awareness. In short, this first Volume in the trilogy is about multi-dimensional awareness and functional awareness.

QUANTUM PSYCHOLOGY PRINCIPLE:

The greater the functional awareness, the greater the "subjective" experience of freedom.

The exclusion of any part of your human nature does not reflect worship of **THAT ONE SUBSTANCE**—but shows denial and hatred (misunderstanding) of its manifestation. In this way, to be fully human is to have your consciousness and awareness free and liberated. This could be the answer to the question of where the human potential movement and Eastern traditions of self-realization meet— *the liberation of your awareness at all dimensions of manifestation.*

This current Volume assumes previous understanding. With this in mind, the earlier two Volumes, *Quantum Consciousness Volume I* and the *Tao of Chaos*: *Quantum Consciousness Volume II* should be used as references. Although they are not mandatory to explore this book, they would certainly build a greater context and experience for developing an answer to, What does it mean to be fully human?

The purpose of this first book of the trilogy is to provide just that: An overview of the liberation of "you," as pure awareness, in all dimensions and then ultimately to even go beyond that. This is *The Way of the Human.*

NEW AGE GRANDIOSITY

In ego psychology, also known as Psychoanalytic Developmental Psychology, it is the letting-go of our grandiosity and realizing our limitations that free us at the level of individuality, and enables us to dismantle our narcissism (our tendency to think we are the center and source of the universe). This narcissism can manifest as some combination of, "I create my reality," "The universe is my reflection and reflects back to me what I need," or "I co-create with *(fill in the blank)*, etc., etc.

In an introductory workshop I did in Seattle, much to the chagrin of some of the participants, I suggested that (contrary to what many seminar leaders insist and present in their training), you cannot get everything you want. I suggested that you can have what you want, *given your personal limitations* like IQ, talents, the external context and abilities. For example, if you were born with no vocal cords, no matter how much you want to be a professional singer, you probably won't be able to make it as one.[5] If your IQ is low, the probability is that you won't become a nuclear scientist, no matter how much you want to be one. In the movie, *Chariots of Fire*, Harold Abrahams (one of the runners) is told by his trainer, "There's an old expression in this business, you can't put in what God left out!" In the same way, don't be bummed-out reading this. Rather, the work is simple: to study and go beyond who you "think," "feel," etc. you are. In this way, you can explore what *is* rather than live in a world of illusory dreams where nothing can be actualized.

Another aspect of *The Way of the Human* and discovering who you are by acknowledging and being willing to include and experience your animal and psycho-emotional nature as part of being human, understanding that since there is only **ONE SUBSTANCE**, that *they are just as important as ESSENCE* since they are made of the same underlying substance and therefore must be included in order to *possibly stabilize* in our Quantum nature.

Human nature (as I will continue to repeat, much to the irritation of my editors), I discovered, is part of our Quantum nature and cannot be ignored or excluded. What happened to me was that my

---

[5]Of course, there are exceptions to the rule. Please note, Quantum Psychology like Quantum Physics is talking about probabilities.

attempts to enter into my Quantum nature, and somehow discard or trance-end my animal, thinking or emotional nature led me into more pain, more suffering, more fragmentation because it separated and divided me into parts. It was often a spiritualized denial of my animal nature. In other words, I used spiritual philosophy to re-enforce the denial of the animal (biological) as well as the psychological.

This self-defeating tendency to divide yourself by "taking on" psycho-spiritual belief systems, techniques, philosophies and identities has, more often than not, created more divisions externally, i.e., us and them, and internally, i.e., spiritual or higher parts trying to subdue "lower" parts and emotions.

With this in mind, *The Way of the Human* asks us not to get rid of anything but to study and appreciate everything, not to destroy but to enjoy, not to disembody but to embody and be present. *The Way of the Human* starts with where you are as the link that connects to the underlying unity. Simply stated, to be human and embody is a form of biological spirituality. It is the way to connect to humanity, which is here and now and which *is* the underlying unity.

The purpose of Quantum Psychology can be summarized as the development of multi-dimensional awareness as a vehicle that *might* help you discover **WHO YOU ARE**. Incidentally, I underlined *might* since there are no guarantees nor can an individual promise that there will be. Ultimately, even the "individual" doing the process along with awareness itself disappears as you find out **WHO YOU ARE** by finding out *who you are not* (see Volume III).

To venture onto such a "path"[6] requires a different kind of discipline and focus of attention. In order to explore *The Way of the Human* we must first be willing to look at our *limitations*, the ways we deny, pretend—or in the words of *Trances People Live—*"trance-out" to avoid the experiences of that which make us human. This approach asks us to look clearly and precisely at how we disembody or dissociate from our bodies, our minds, the world, and the universe. It can be noted that the degree to which we deny our connection to our body and our animal nature is the degree by which we

---

[6]The path is used to denote a road, such as, I am going from New York to London. However, as will be discussed later, there is no path or as Krisnamurti said, "Truth is a pathless land."

deny our connection to the world. This disconnection from our body and our animal nature leads us into more isolation, aloneness, alienation and misunderstandings—in short, our False Core (to be discussed in Volume II).

Ultimately, to deny our connection to our body denies our connection to the world. To deny our connection to the world is to deny our connection to the universe and to the underlying unity of Quantum Consciousness. In the past, oftentimes yoga in the form of mantras, yantras, and tantras has taken us out of the world. Spiritual philosophies have claimed, "You are not your body," and that sex and emotions are to be avoided. Yet, as many a fallen guru and spiritual master might now finally concede, this is not possible. The question is why would anyone want to? If there is only **THAT ONE SUBSTANCE**, what is there to get rid of? Why would you even want to get rid of your animal or psycho-emotional nature, or as you might say, "As you judge, so shall you be judged." Or in Quantum Psychological terminology, "As you judge yourself, so shall you judge others."

In *The Way of the Human*, the body is not to be excluded but included; emotions are not to be judged as bad, but as a vehicle to deepen our realization of **THAT ONE SUBSTANCE**. Many an ancient scripture contends everything is ONE, or as Quantum Psychology states, everything is made of **THAT ONE SAME SUBSTANCE**. This means also that the body, with its thoughts and feelings, is the same substance as everything else and is **THAT ONE SUBSTANCE**.

Spiritual philosophies (as we will explore later) are oftentimes spiritual trances which prevent us from experiencing the present moment; and more often than not, reinforce our internal psychological structures and developmental arrests, blocks, gaps and conflicts.

This Volume is dedicated to humanity, with the understanding that our animal- and psycho-emotional nature must be included and seen as important as our essential nature so that ultimately the underlying unity of our Quantum nature can become stabilized and remain in our awareness.

So the purpose of this Volume is 1) to present and complete the dimensions of awareness; 2) to have them written down, defined and clarified; and 3) to have closure, a completion for "me." I am sure you will notice as you go through the material, that there are overlaps from previous work. Some of the material is similar, some dissimilar. Some of it is new, some are additions, clarifications, new translations or evolutions of other materials "I've" written about. The purpose of this is a completion for Quantum Psychology at the level of awareness so that ultimately "you" go beyond even awareness itself and beyond Quantum Psychology or Quantum Consciousness (see Volume III). By delineating all of these levels you can then consider the possibility of Going Beyond Awareness, Beyond **ESSENCE**, Beyond the **I AM**, into the **VOID OF UNDIFFERENTIATED CONSCIOUSNESS** and into the **NAMELESS ABSOLUTE** and even **BEYOND**, which is beyond Quantum Psychology.

To enquire in this way you'll face a lot of new challenges. There are many concepts we hold onto to explain the universe which act as sacred cows and prevent us from reaching the deeper levels of our own psyche and, consequently, of our humanity. I hope you have not found this opening too heavy-handed. Actually, when I realized that I only had to look at the "I" and the "self" I thought I was, I felt relieved. I hope we can continue to have the willingness to explore and dismantle whatever stands in our way, to hold any belief system open to enquiry, and to appreciate the words of the 10th century *Siva Sutras* which say "All bondage is caused by sound." Why? Because sound creates letters, letters create words, words create ideas and ideas create concepts and belief systems which, by their very nature, can only bind. In this way, hopefully, we can join humanity in its divine quantum splendor. This is the Way of the Human.

With love,
Your brother,
Stephen

CHAPTER II
OVERVIEWING THE NOTEBOOKS

E ntering into a three Volume set, for the reader as well as the writer, is no easy task. To start off, these Volumes represent a culmination of years of research and study in the quest to discover and answer the question, "**WHO AM I?**" Naturally, this **WHO AM I** quest (as mentioned in *Quantum Consciousness*, *Volume I*) began as far back as "I" can remember. So there is the organization of the material to be dealt with. Then, the reader's previous knowledge of Quantum Psychology has to be called into question as a context for the trilogy. The trilogy attempts to stand on its own; but, it is highly recommended that *Quantum Consciousness, Volume I* and *The Tao of Chaos*, *Quantum Consciousness, Volume II* be considered as aids so that readers can appreciate and expand their context and understanding of this work.

This chapter is an attempt to give an overview of some of the basic principles of Quantum Psychology and in which Volume of the Trilogy "I" will focus on what specific subject. Hopefully, this "never-ending story" does reach an end and conclusion in *Volume III, Beyond Quantum Psychology*.

Readers might be tempted to flip to the end to see "who done it," as if they were reading a detective novel but my suggestion is to go through each Volume from beginning to end because the ending is the surprise you always knew. Quantum Psychology encompasses psychology and Eastern and Middle Eastern religions along with Quantum Physics. This context permitted "me" to outline what is called Quantum Psychology in Volumes I and II of the trilogy. In Volume III, however, not only multi-dimensional awareness (Volume I) and the False Core-False Self (Volume II) are gone beyond, but also awareness itself, along with Quantum Psychology, is dismantled and gone BEYOND.

Before we get ahead of ourselves, however, it seems important, though perhaps unnecessary, to take this whole quest in stages. As we all know, this is not a linear process. On the contrary, we all get bursts of awareness, some coupled with experiences, some show us what is to come, or what is possible, and some take us beyond what we call ourselves. Hopefully, *The Way of the Human*, *Quantum Psychology Notebooks* (*Volumes I and II*) and *Beyond Quantum Psychology* (*Volume III*) can aid us in doing just that.

It is for this reason that it is important to get an overview of what material each of the three Volumes contains.

THE PURPOSE

Quantum Psychology is different from other forms of modern-day psychology because it has a different purpose, namely, to discover **WHO YOU ARE**. This is done by taking apart your False Core-False Self (Volume II) and developing multi-dimensional awareness (Volume I). Unlike most forms of psychotherapy, it is not intended to make you "better," "more virtuous" or teach you how to have great relationships, or how to make more money, or even how to feel more comfortable in your life. Rather, it is ultimately about the discovery of **WHO YOU ARE**. The vehicle used for the focus of Volume I is the Development of *Multi-Dimensional Awareness* which is the awareness of eight dimensions or manifestations of our Human Nature. This awareness *might* represent a stage or an integral part of this process.

Nisargadatta Maharaj was the teacher "I" took as "mine" and worked with in India where I lived for almost six years. According to him, "The only way to find out who you are is to find out who you are not." This is Maharaj's first and most basic principle: "Anything that you think you are, you are not." While he was alive, only one of his books was published, called *I Am That*. This was his most important work. He was into Advaita Vedanta (Advaita Sanskrit for non-duality) and Jnana yogi (Sanskrit for knowledge, the path of knowledge), but actually it is the *PATH OF UNLEARNING*. Advaita contends that there is only **ONE SUBSTANCE**, that everything is made of **THAT ONE SUBSTANCE**, not two or more substances, and that is all spirituality really is, and *YOU ARE THAT ONE SUBSTANCE* (Volume III).

Because of Quantum Psychology's relationship to Nisargadatta Maharaj, it is directed toward enquiry and dismantling, not fixing, transforming or healing, the False Core-False Self's psychology. The process is organized through internal questioning and enquiry. In Quantum Psychology, we want to reduce the amount of awareness placed on, and consumed by, "your" psychology, in this way liberating your awareness until the enquirer-enquiree and awareness itself disappear in the non-dimensionality of the underlying unity of **THAT ONE SUBSTANCE.**

Quantum Psychology is an extension and continuation of Nisargadatta Maharaj—i.e., Advaita Vedanta—and it has several premises which form its basic core.

Advaita	**Vedanta**
There is only **THAT ONE SUBSTANCE** Not two or more substances	Neti-Neti (Sanskrit for Not-This - Not This)

SUMMARY OF NISARGADATTA MAHARAJ

1. There is only **THAT ONE SUBSTANCE**.
2. What you know about yourself came from outside of you, therefore discard it.
3. Question everything, do not believe anything.
4. In order to find out who you are, you must first find out who you are not.
5. In order to let go of something, you must first know what it is.
6. The experienc*er* is contained within the experience itself.

7. Anything you think you are—you are not
8. Hold onto the *I Am*, let go of everything else[1].
9. Anything you know about you cannot be.

These nine principles form the core of Quantum Psychology.

Quantum Psychology incorporates a "Western Psychological" context to dismantle how you organize what you call "you." And it uses Quantum Physics to "prove" to doubters that there is only **THAT ONE SUBSTANCE**.

Quantum Psychology utilizes enquiry for it is through enquiry that the "mind" becomes more transparent. The presuppositions, conclusions and assumptions, the stories, and lies about who you are and who you are not are taken apart so that they can be seen for what they are: *misinformation*. Then not only do all the old presuppositions and premises disappear but also the "you" you called yourself. Nisargadatta Maharaj used to say, "What you know about yourself came from outside of you, therefore discard it."

The enquiry and questions used are the tools which provide a "way" to follow Maharaj's premise, *"Question everything—do not believe anything."* It should also be noted that many "Advaitists" feel that the use of any kind of "technique" presupposes an "I" which does it. Quantum Psychology appreciates this, however, knowing that ultimately both the enquir*er*-enquir*ee* naturally disappear. For this reason, Quantum Psychology suggests that you not give up your boat [techniques] on the sea of existence until you know how to swim.

It should also be borne in mind that Quantum Psychology is not for everybody. In fact, "I" often discourage people from taking workshops and turn people down if "I" don't think it's right for them. Sometimes "I" turn people down because for certain individuals it just is not appropriate or maybe it's the wrong time for them to be doing it. There's no implication that there's a "higher" or a "lower," it's just not for everybody. And, of course, there is *no guarantee* of a certain outcome happening. Actually Quantum Psychology suggests that people do the process without any intention of outcome (see Volume II of *Quantum Consciousness*, Chapter IV).

---

[1]#8 will not be discussed until the False Core-False Self is dismantled (see Volume II*).*

At the risk of sounding redundant, I want to emphasize that Quantum Psychology is not for everybody. It is not a quick fix or a cure-all, and there are no guarantees.

VOLUME I:
DEVELOPING MULTI-DIMENSIONAL AWARENESS

As a possible aid in the discovery of who you are, Quantum Psychology first looks toward the liberation of awareness through the development of multi-dimensional awareness. To paraphrase noted Sufi master Idries Shah, "You cannot become free until you have volitional choice over where you place your awareness." If your awareness is unknowingly fixated on re-enacting, reinforcing, resisting or re-creating your False Core-False Self structure—whether it be spiritualized or not—there's no way you can be free. Developing awareness of all eight dimensions of manifestation and appreciating what they mean will help to explain this better. Below are brief descriptions of each dimension with an in-depth explanation that includes examples and exercises, etc. (to follow later). These eight dimensions of manifestation will be talked about throughout the entire trilogy:

The first dimension is *THE EXTERNAL DIMENSION.* Here's the external world, here's my house, my room, I'm talking to you on the telephone. Here are all the objects and people in my life, and all the rules of the external dimension. For example, if I steal money from the bank, I will probably suffer the consequences. This is the first dimension. At first it seems easy because, of course, there is a person, there is a car, etc. However, can you notice that all the internal dialogues (trances) stop you from realizing and experiencing the present time external as the present time external.

The Second Dimension is *THE THINKING DIMENSION.* There is a thinking world which appears to be inside of "you." The Thinking Dimension includes thoughts, images, memories, associations, concepts, values, beliefs etc.

The Third Dimension is *THE EMOTIONAL DIMENSION.* This dimension includes sadness, anger, fear, etc.

The Fourth Dimension is *THE BIOLOGICAL OR ANIMAL DIMENSION.* This dimension is your basic biological animal nature, which is part of your nervous system and also represents survival. It includes eating, sleeping, going to the bathroom, having sex, the fight/flight, survival mechanism, including merger-separation and learning.

The Fifth Dimension is *ESSENCE* (see Volume III). **ESSENCE** is the spaciousness that your physical body organizes around and when realized becomes the **FULLNESS** of **ESSENCE**, containing "essential qualities" like love with no object, observation with no object, peace, compassion, etc.

The Sixth Dimension is *I AM* (see Volume III) which is prior to the qualities of **ESSENCE**.

The *verbal I AM* precedes the False Core-False Self; it is prior to **I AM** (*fill in the blank*), and before any definition of self.

The *non-verbal I AM* is the No-state-state; it is non-verbal pure being. It is the root, or as Nisargadatta Maharaj said, the seed of individual consciousness. Without it there can be no individual psychology, i.e., *it occurs* or is naturally realized when you do not use your thoughts, memories, emotions, perceptions or associations, and is pure being. However, there is no awareness of the **VOID**. The **I AM** is the deepest archetype of the Collective.

The Seventh Dimension is the *COLLECTIVE UNCONSCIOUS* **or** *THE ARCHETYPICAL DIMENSION* (Volume III). It contains the basic substance which connects us all. It also contains the archetypes which are made and produced by the physics dimensions and forces, i.e., energy, space, mass, time, gravity, light, electromagnetics, strong and weak nuclear forces, etc.

The Eighth Dimension is *THE NOT-I-I* (see Volume III). It is Pure Awareness. It is formless. It is aware of the **VOID OF UN-DIFFERENTIATED CONSCIOUSNESS** which surrounds us and yet is a part of it. It is pure **WITNESSING**, beyond the observer-observed dyad. The WITNESS, or Pure Awareness, rests between **I AM** and the **VOID.** Because the "**NOT-I-I**" is the WITNESS it knows and is aware of the **VOID**.

The dimensions of manifestation end here (Volume III). This occurs because in the underlying unity of **THAT ONE SUBSTANCE** also called **UNDIFFERENTIATED CONSCIOUSNESS** even *awareness itself* dissolves. This is why noted physicist, John Wheeler, said, "Nothingness is the building block of the universe."

The VOID or UNDIFFERIENTIATED CONSCIOUSNESS or the SELF is beyond Awareness, and is pure *UNDIFFERENTI-ATED* **CONSCIOUSNESS** or **THAT** (not to be confused with consciousness as in I-Thou).

The **NAMELESS ABSOLUTE** is beyond the **VOID** and is where the **VOID** itself ends.

BEYOND IS JUST BEYOND

Please note: In the following illustration, the vertical lines connect all the dimensions. This denotes that the dimensions interact and are connected even though they have different functions. The broken horizontal line indicates that there is a "relationship" above and below. But "you" cannot work on the areas below the biological dimension, i.e., **ESSENCE, I AM, COLLECTIVE,** and **NOT-I-I.** The solid line between **VOID** and **NOT-I-I** shows that the **VOID** and **THE NAMELESS ABSOLUTE** and **BEYOND** are not dimensions because everything, including awareness, disappears "there."

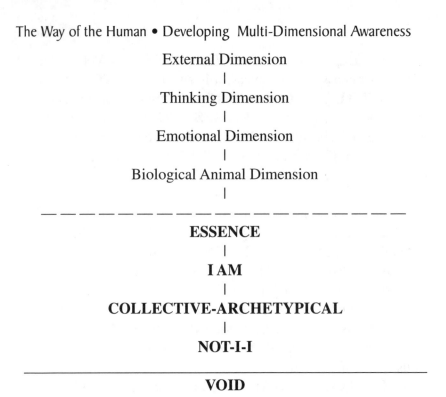

External Dimension

|

Thinking Dimension

|

Emotional Dimension

|

Biological Animal Dimension

|

— — — — — — — — — — — — — — — — —

ESSENCE

|

I AM

|

COLLECTIVE-ARCHETYPICAL

|

NOT-I-I

VOID

NAMELESS ABSOLUTE

BEYOND

THE QUESTION

The most commonly asked question is, "Why is Multi-Dimensional Awareness—and specifically, the awareness of **ESSENCE, I AM,** etc.—unknown to us?" "Why aren't they available?" The answer seems to be that if all of your awareness is fixated on thoughts and emotions around the False Core-False Self concept—for example, "I am inadequate," etc.—then there is no awareness left to be aware of **ESSENCE, I AM,** etc. In other words our awareness is gobbled up by that fixation in this one arena (dimension) and cannot become stabilized in any of the other dimensions. Simply stated, awareness that is fixated on a particular dimension cannot be liberated. But this tendency disappears and awareness which is chronically ensnared becomes liberated. When your Awareness is freed up, then **ESSENCE, I AM, "NOT-I-I,"** etc. emerge naturally. You can't work on **ESSENCE**. **ESSENCE** is always there; the **VOID** is always there. But "you" can work on dismantling your fixated Awareness.

MULTI-DIMENSIONAL AWARENESS DISMANTLING VS. TRANSCENDENCE

Nisargadatta Maharaj said, "You cannot let go of something until you know what is is."

Often spiritual systems are more into transcendence (trying to go beyond) and not dismantling. In many "Spiritual" traditions there is an idea that if I repeat my mantra enough and meditate enough, I will transcend the ego or mind, and I won't be identified with it any longer. This "Spiritual" theory is that through mantra, yantra, or tantra, you can go beyond the mind or somehow change your "vibration" in order to stabilize awareness in **ESSENCE, I AM**, etc., without having to recognize how your awareness is chronically fixated. As we will see below and in Volume I, this rarely works, is confusing and, in addition, collapses all of the dimensions.*

Quantum Psychology knows that to go beyond your psychology and stabilize awareness in **ESSENCE, I AM**, etc., you might first have to own your psychology before you can un-own it. You first have to be willing to BE it ("your" psychology) before "you" can UN-BE it. And you must be willing to have it ("your") psychology before you can un-have it. Nisargadatta Maharaj would say, "In order to let go of something you must first know what it is." Quantum Psychology says, "In order to let go of something, you must first be willing to experience it."

You also have to know and acknowledge "your" concepts so that you can then take them apart and go beyond them. Ram Dass used to say, "In order to get out of a jail your must first know you are in one." But if you do not acknowledge how your awareness is chronically fixated, then no matter what beautiful experiences you have of **ESSENCE** or the **VOID** (samadhi) during meditation, when you come out and open your eyes, talk to your relationship, your boss, etc., you are going to get smacked in the face with your own concepts. In other words, *your issues will all come up again.*

---

*As will be discussed in Volume III, all spiritual practise requires an *I* to do it.

In Quantum Psychology you cannot transcend anything if you are unwilling to experience and acknowledge it. For this reason we spell transcend, **Trance-end**, the *ending of trances*.

Transcendence by mantra, yantra or tantra is temporary; it is a temporary "high" or "hit." Somebody can achieve it for a short while if they are secluded in a retreat, workshop or Ashram. But put them on the job or in a relationship and the "uncooked seeds" (to be discussed later) sprout again. This is because each new or different external context brings up "different" uncooked seeds. If your awareness of **ESSENCE, I AM**, etc. has to be guarded (by rules and shoulds), protected (by not associating or associating only with certain people) or by isolation (retreats, Ashram, etc.), this is not Enlightenment. It is an Enlightenment prison which limits what you can or cannot do, say, think, have, experience, know, and discuss. In short, it is the maintenance of a "state" and as a basic Buddhist teaching of impermanence says—all states and everything are impermanent." Or as Nisargadatta Maharaj would say, "Who came first, you or the state?" Saying further, "What do you care what state you are in? I am not in a state."

Quantum Psychology is interested in liberating and stabilizing awareness by cooking the uncooked seeds of your False Core-False Self.

The ideal for now, but not meant as a goal to be achieved, is to live your life and have awareness of all dimensions simultaneously until naturally awareness itself disappears (Volume III). In other words, the liberation of awareness naturally becomes a function of awareness. Awareness can then be in any dimension, all dimensions or no-dimensions. Eventually awareness goes beyond awareness itself as the **VOID OF UNDIFFERENTIATED CONSCIOUSNESS** absorbs the "you" you call yourself. "Then" the **VOID** ends, or voids itself, and the **NAMELESS ABSOLUTE** is revealed.

THE FALSE CORE (VOLUME II)

"Whatever you do, you do for your own sake.

The Upanasads

QUANTUM PSYCHOLOGY PRINCIPLE:

Whatever the False Core-False Self does, it does for its own sake; i.e., its own survival.

What is the *False Core Driver*? The False Core Driver is that one concept or conclusion you hold about yourself which organizes your entire psychology—every thought, association, memory, fantasy, action, reaction, etc. It holds together your entire internal world (how you perceive yourself) and how you imagine and project how others perceive you.

The *False Self Compensator* is the way you try to overcome this primary concept.

According to Freud, "All traumas come in chains of earlier similar events." In other words, "the mind" has an associational and generalizing tendency. In short to insure its survival, it searches and scans the environment for "danger." Unfortunately, it uses the past as its reference point. In this way, the scanning-searching device, which is part of the organism's survival mechanisms, "sees" "danger" where there is none. Furthermore, the mind (the nervous system) connects events and experiences, taking "past" experiences and placing them in present time contexts where they do not belong. Hence, the saying, "You can never put your foot in the same river twice" comes into play. Your False Core Driver organizes how associations organize and interpret all of these chains of associations. The False Core is that which pulls your chain.

QUANTUM PSYCHOLOGY PRINCIPLE:

The *False Core Driver* is the glue which holds together your entire psychology.

QUANTUM PSYCHOLOGY PRINCIPLE:

The *False Self Compensator* is how you attempt to compensate, heal, or solve the problem of the False Core Driver

Quantum Psychology suggests a process whereby dismantling the False Core Driver-False Self Compensator is explored. Why? Because *you are not your False Core Driver-False Self Compensator. You are even beyond the observer* of the False Core Driver-False Self Compensator and all of its associations (uncooked seeds).

However, it should be noted that not only does the False Core Driver-False Self Compensator act at the thinking and emotional dimensions, but there is a biological component to it as well. I am talking about an energetic-genetic component which I've seen in many people I've worked with; individuals seem to have a genetic-energetic proclivity toward a particular False Core-False Self.

THE ORIGIN OF THE FALSE CORE—
THE NARCISSISTIC WOUND/INJURY STORY

Developmental psychology would say that at birth infants believe that they and their mother are one. It is only between the ages of 5-12 months that children realize they are separate from their mother. This realization comes as a huge shock to the Nervous System and causes what is called the "narcissistic wound" or the "narcissistic injury."

What Quantum Psychology would say is that at the moment of that shock, your False Core *begins* to solidify. What an infant concludes about her/himself and the situation when she/he realizes they are separate from Mom is the False Core. For example, "I am separate *because* I am worthless," or "I am separate *because* I'm inadequate," or "I am separate *means* I don't exist," or "I am separate *because* I am powerless," etc. once this conclusion solidifies. The rest of the person's life is spent "acting it out," proving that the False Core is true or trying to overcome it through a False Self. The style and way you resist the False Core, try to overcome the False Core, heal the False Core, hide the False Core, spiritualize the False Core, transform the False Core, justify the False Core, etc., represents your False Self Compensator.

As I the story goes, due to the shock of the Realization of Separation, the False Core begins to "solidify"; however, it existed in a latent form. There is an energetic-genetic proclivity to this False

Conclusion, and like cancer, diabetes or heart disease, it runs in your family. There is no "choice" because to say that you chose it would imply that you can choose a genetic proclivity towards diabetes or heart disease. The idea of that level of choice is laden with "narcissism" and the infantile grandiosity of "I create it all," and the age regressed reframe of learning lessons.

This energetic-genetic component can be likened to what Homeopathic medicine calls a miasm. If your grandfather had tuberculosis, for example, then you would have a proclivity toward the disease. Your symptoms might be a runny nose when it rains. A Homeopathic doctor would be able to make that link by analyzing and understanding your genetic lineage. In the same way the False Core Driver-False Self Compensator has a energetic-genetic lineage.

Your False Core acts as a lens and a trance through which "you" view the world and yourself and how you imagine the world views you. Once that happens, the False Core of "I am worthless" or "I am inadequate," for example, will interpret every situation through that lens. This was discussed in my first book *Trances People Live: Healing Approaches in Quantum Psychology*, Chapter 20, "The Organizing Principle."

Below is a simplified version of different False Core Drivers-False Self Compensators. Notice how each False Self Compensator tries to heal the False Core Conclusion differently.[2]

False Core Driver	False Self Compensator
I am imperfect. There must be something wrong with me	Prove there is *not* something wrong with me by being perfect
I am worthless, or have no value	Prove I am *not* worthless by proving I am Worthy or that I have value myself

---

[2]*Note:* As will be discussed in Volume III, Nisargadatta Maharaj emphasized, "Hold onto the I Am, Let go of everything else." He was trying to undercut even the False Core by just being in the **I AM** and letting go of even the False Core-False Self.

False Core Driver	False Self Compensator
I am not able to do	Proving I can do anything by Achieving and over-doing
I am inadequate	Proving I am *not* inadequate, by proving adequacy
I am non-existent, I do not exist	Prove existence
I am alone	Trying to connect
I am incomplete	I must be complete or be whole through experiences
I am powerless	I must prove how powerful I am
I am loveless	Prove I am not loveless by being extra-lovable and loving

Each False Core Driver-False Self Compensator *interprets* "life" through their lens. To illustrate, if three people got in a car accident, one might say "I'm was in a car accident, it *means* I must be worthless." Another might feel a deep sense of powerlessness about it and still a third might say "There's something wrong with me, I should have taken driving lessons." Each False Core Driver-False Self Compensator *interprets* the same trauma through a different lens. If you take off the lens (i.e., dismantle the False Core Driver and False Self Compensator) then you experience **ESSENCE** and/or the **I AM**.

This is why **ESSENCE**, the **I AM THE NOT-I I** etc. go unnoticed or are not stabilized in our awareness. Most of our attention is unknowingly focused on the False Core Driver while at the same time we try to compensate for it in some way by creating a False Self Compensator. Any attempt to reform it, transform it, reframe it, re-associate it, take the good (healthy) stuff and leave the bad (unhealthy), turn our vices into virtues, etc.—are all strategies of the False Self Compensator which tries to overcome, resist and re-solve the False Core Driver. The False Self is very insidious. (One must realize that the False Core Driver-False Self Compensator is one unit and is holographic; in other words, you cannot have one without the other.)

The False Core Driver always wins and always proves and re-enforces itself. For example, no matter how much you give to others to try to feel some sense of worth, deep down you always feel worthless. No matter how much you try to prove how adequate you are through analysis, deep down you still feel inadequate. What com-pounds the problem is that since the spaciousness of **ESSENCE** was the reference point, after the Realization of Separation trauma, you conclude that it was *because* of this now mislabeled spacious (**Es-sence**), which has become emptiness (which now has come to mean a lack) that the separation occurred. In short, **ESSENCE** is blamed for the separation. This creates a double bind—avoiding and seeking **ESSENCE** simultaneously, because it is associated with the False Core label which mislabels the spaciousness of **ESSENCE** as emp-tiness as a lack.[3]

In therapy, results are often poor because (1) you are trying to heal a reason and a made-up story; and (2) the therapy re-enforces the False Self's resistance to the False Core. The False Core-False Self is one holographic piece, it is a different side of the same coin, i.e., "You can't have one without the other."

The rest of your life then is centered around, creating a False Self Compensator to attempt to hide, overcome, resist, heal, etc. from the conclusion drawn which is the inaccurate conclusion created by the nervous system to organize and explain the shock of the Realiza-tion of Separation.

The problem is that **ESSENCE**, which contains essential qualities like love with no object, is denied while, at the same time, the False Self is seeking it. The False Self Compensator can then

---

[3]It should be noted, that the shock occurs at a neurological level. *After the experience has already occured*, the brain and nervous system create a *reason* why; i.e., "I am (*fill in the blank*)." This reason is false, and it is mis-concluded "after" the shock. In psychotherapy or even spiritual work, there is a story created even further after the fact to explain how to overcome this false conclusion.

project essential qualities onto others as if having a relationship with another or owning this or that will "get me love."

In a workshop recently, a woman told me, "Gurdjieff said that you have to grow **ESSENCE**." I think what he meant was, You have to *grow the awareness of ESSENCE*. And this requires freeing up the awareness you have fixated on your False Core-False Self.

Simply put, we deny and resist our **ESSENCE** because it is fused with the shock of the Realization of Separation and thus we blame and want to get rid of that (mislabeled) emptiness, too. Once we realize that we are resisting only our **ESSENCE**, everything shifts and the fixation on the False Core-False Self begins to soften. This is a major awakening.

If the trance of the False Core-False Self does not end, you will always unknowingly "act it out" (see Volume II). That was the piece I found missing in India. Let's say my father was an alcoholic and I try to do mantras, yantras, and/or tantras to try to transcend that. I can have a beautiful meditation and a beautiful experience of the **VOID**. I can open my eyes but within a short period of time I am back into the "uncooked seeds" of my psychology (see below). Soon I am arguing with my spouse, bickering with my father, etc. You will immediately grab onto your False Core-False Self and your uncooked seeds. Many people who are trying to transcend their psychology are in a spiritual denial. They use meditation as medication. They don't want to feel things. In this way transcendence is a trance and a resistance and hence does not work.

UNCOOKED SEEDS

The Indian metaphor I like to use is that of "uncooked seeds." Uncooked seeds are your unprocessed psychological material, i.e., your False Core and False Self. To illustrate, if I take some seeds, place them in the ground, and water them, they will grow and bear fruit. But if I take the same seeds, cook them in a frying pan and then place them in the ground, nothing will happen. In this way Quantum Psychology cooks the uncooked seeds of your psychology in the frying pan of awareness so that they can no longer sprout and bear fruit.

Now, in India you have gurus meditating their brains out, sitting somewhere in **ESSENCE, I AM NOT-I-I**, etc. most of the time. Whenever they need anything on a personal level, it is taken care of. If they're hungry, people bring food, if their clothes are dirty, people clean them. Then, they come to America or Western Europe. The context (external dimension) changes and their False Core-False Self kicks in causing their uncooked seeds to sprout. Soon they get into money, sex, creating meditation centers, etc. To explain this contradiction to their followers, bigger and better spiritual denial techniques[4] have to be employed. For example, sex is no longer sex, it is tantra; seeking fame and money is not seeking fame and money, it is having a calling or a mission from God. Soon they wind up on the front cover of Yoga Journal! They have not acknowledged their False Core-False Self (uncooked seeds). *An uncooked seed which remains unacknowledged has the potential to sprout as soon as the external dimension or context changes.* Quantum Psychology suggests utilizing awareness and dismantling your uncooked seeds so that they no longer sprout and grab your awareness and pull you out of **ESSENCE, I AM NOT-I-I**, etc.

The #1 uncooked seed of your psychology is the False Core-False Self because it drives the entire machinery of what you call the *Individual Mind*. You cannot meditate your False Core-False Self away. You cannot mantra your False Core-False Self away. You have to be willing to look at and acknowledge everything that is there. Without dismantling the False Core-False Self which drives "your" psychology, "you" can never stabilize in **ESSENCE, I AM**, etc.

THROUGH THE FALSE CORE DRIVER-FALSE SELF COMPENSATOR LENS

Let's look at this through the eyes of different False Core Drivers and False Self Compensators.

Let's say at age five, a child is molested:

One False Core would say, "There's something wrong with me, that's the reason this happened."

Another False Core would say "I'm worthless, even Uncle Henry is treating me as if I'm worthless."

---

[4]This is called the trance of Spiritualization in Chapter 14, "The Dark side of the Inner Child."

Another False Core would probably get totally frozen and feel an "inability to do" anything about it. Later they might become over-achievers to try to compensate or heal their paralyzed inability to do.

Another False Core would say, "I was molested and it really means I'm incredibly inadequate. It's my own fault, I screwed up."

Another False Core would dissociate. "After all, I am nothing, I have nothing; therefore, I don't exist anyway and maybe nothing ever happened." They have split off from the emotional dimension and their feelings associated with the event. Later they might spiritualize it. For example, a recent book came out which both spiritualized (a trance mentioned in *The Dark Side of the Inner Child*) and reframed molestation as a gift from God, an opportunity. These spiritual re-frames deny the pain of molestation.

Another False Core could think, "This means I'm alone."

Another False Core could feel, "I'm incomplete in some way, or I'm not enough. If only I were enough, had enough experience, then it wouldn't have happened."

Another False Core might feel powerless. Oftentimes, the "I am powerless" False Cores have a resistance to being powerless, so they oftentimes act overly powerful. They might say, "Actually I wasn't molested; what happened is I seduced Uncle Henry into molesting me."

Another False Core might say "See, I knew there was no love in the world."

TRYING TO HEAL THE FALSE CORE

There are many different ways to attempt to heal the narcissistic wound. Unfortunately, many False Selves do not try to heal the wound by feeling what is there. *Rather they try to heal or overcome the reason for the shock—which is not the shock itself.* However, the approach each False Self Compensator takes to heal is more false than the False Core itself. No matter how much the person tries to compensate (for "I *cannot* do") or to be perfect ("*There must be something wrong with me*") deep down they know it's merely a cover or Compensator for the False Core. Why is the False Self unable to heal or overcome the False Core and the Realization of Separation? Because they are one unit like inhaling and exhaling, that co-exist, you can't have one without the other. That's why I prefer the descriptions of each False Core-False Self to focus on the False Core driver rather than on the compensators. Somehow it feels more direct and honest.

It should be noted that some psycho-spiritual schools believe that the False Self Compensator is healthier than the False Core. Quantum Psychology feels the opposite is true, that the compensation "looks" more healthy and socially acceptable. However, it is an integrated age-regression and is insidious using tricks by the False Self, as defense against the False Core and the Realization of Separation.

For Quantum Psychology, the "decompensation" is more direct, honest, and certainly more uncomfortable. However, until the failure of the False Self is seen through along with its illusions, and the discomfort felt, it is impossible to go beyond the False Core-False Self and stabilize awareness in **ESSENCE, I AM NOT-I-I,** etc.

QUANTUM PSYCHOLOGY PRINCIPLE:

Every event and attempt to heal and compensate for the False Core *is the False Self doing it*. In this way, it only re-enforces the False Core Driver-False Self Compensator dyad.

People often respond to the False Core by saying, "If only I didn't feel *(fill in the blank)*, everything would be fine." In this way they are always trying to get rid of the False Core structure by over-compensation. For example; in order to handle *(fill in the blank)*, I'll take another lover. I'll make more money and then I won't be *(fill in the blank)*. If I have more experiences, then I'll be smart enough and I won't feel *(fill in the blank)*. This attempt to try to get rid of it, heal it, transform it, re-enforces the *False Core-False Self's Holographic nature* rather than just saying, "Hey, here's my False Core of *(fill in the blank)*, isn't that interesting? I've organized my whole life around a concept which is not true. How amazing!" And soon you begin to see that it is only a concept, and it is not true.

The paradox of this approach is that we must work with it, *without the intention of getting rid of it*. You work with it to see what occurs. The question often is, "Doesn't there have to be an intention in order to do it in the first place?" *No*. If the processes are done from a No-State State of **I AM**, there is no intention. Then, study it and dismantle it until it can begin to fall away. You might see it, observe it, the connections tracing back every thought, feeling and fantasy to see how your whole life has been organized around this one thing, and then dismantling it through enquiry. Ultimately, the enquiry continues until "you" realize that *you are neither the enquirer-questioner nor the answerer*. But this understanding occurs much "later" when you begin to see how everything is organized around one structure. It is then that you can go beyond the obsessive-compulsive fixated structure which is the False Core, thus liberating your awareness and discovering **WHO YOU ARE**.

Many psycho-spiritual systems describe the False Core tendencies. Unfortunately however, many forms of psychology and spirituality unknowingly re-enforce the client's False Core through the False Self's "imagining" it can be overcome, healed or transformed. Unfortunately these systems use the False Self to do the work or create spiritualized "Archetypical" stories like "the Fall of Man" to explain and justify this natural biological separation process. Please keep in mind that the False Core-False Self is a map, and maps are made by people—*it's not the territory* (see Volume II, *The Rise and Fall of the Enneagram*).

QUANTUM PSYCHOLOGY PRINCIPLE:

The False Core-False Self is more than just a concept you have about yourself. It represents the "I" you call yourself and, hence, it represents you and your entire experience of the "internal-external" world.

Every movement of your mind is driven by the False Core. The question that really matters is, "What is driving the movement of your psychology?" "What is the one concept you have that organizes everything in your life?" In Quantum Psychology, you learn to become clear about what the False Core is—that one underlying structure—and then to trace all of your behavior back to it. This is an internal process, and you are constantly tracking your behavior, your actions, your feelings, everything, back to your False Core. Once you get there, you have to sit in it. There's no way around it. You do not try to change it. Anytime you try to change it or get rid of it, you are resisting it, which is one of the five strategies or five *Re's* of the False Core-False Self—*re*sisting, *re*-enacting, *re*-creating, *re*-inforcing and *re*-solving.

Sitting in your False Core means you are free and are able to *BE* it or *UN-BE* but not to believe it, to merge with it and observe it simultaneously, and just be with it *without trying to get rid of it*. Then to go beyond it, "you" stay in the non-verbal **I AM** level "prior" to it (Volume III). The movement of the mind is all about the interplay of the False Core-False Self. To paraphrase Nisargadatta Maharaj, "Notice the ongoing contradictions within the mind [the False Core-False Self] and know they are not you. "In other words, the movement of the mind is to a-void the pain of the False Core. In short, the False Core-False Self deprives you of the experience of **WHO YOU ARE**. The obsessive-compulsive tendency of the False Core-False Self eats away awareness and a-voids [cancels out] the awareness of the underlying unity of the **VOID**. Once you "get" your False Core, you can trace everything back to it.[5]

NARCISSISM IN LIFE

How does the Narcissistic injury (Realization of Separation) and its ramifications pertain to life in general and, specifically in a practical way, to relationships.

Imagine an infant who has now gone through the shock of the Realization of Separation. The first thing that they would do is try to get their mother to merge with them and/or be their reflection again. Since that cannot work because on an external, thinking, emotional and biological level they are separate from Mom, the False

---

[5]It is often difficult to "get" the False Core because it is strong, defensive and very tricky. *Most descriptions of the Enneagram types, however, do not describe the driver of the type, i.e., the False Core. Rather they describe and then define the personality type by the over-compensation to the False Core.* This over-compensation is, in Quantum Psychology, the False Self and is a defense against the False Core.

Core solidifies further. The solution is a False Self Compensator. Again, since you cannot get Mom to reflect back to you and be your mirror, you decide to be your mother's mirror and reflection through mind-reading[6] what she wants and then giving it to her. This is done so that she will merge with you, and you will be in unity again.

In this way, life becomes fixated on either trying to get people to merge with you (i.e., be their reflection) or to merge with them (they become your reflection). This is done in order to achieve a unity and thus not feel the shock of the Realization of Separation. **ESSENCE** becomes mis-labeled by the False Core as a deficiency or emptiness with a lack. Please note that the False Core is a representation and a reason given for why the shock of the Realization of Separation took place. Later in life your relationships are based on the following principles: you must either 1) reflect them; 2) try to get them to reflect you in order to merge and not feel the shock of the Realization of Separation or; 3) resist them so that you can have a self, etc. Unfortunately, the greatest difficulty in "seeing" this clearly within oneself or others is tied-up in psychologizing, philosophizing, and spiritualizing.

PSYCHOLOGIZING:

A process whereby we develop an entire psychology-philosophy and lifestyle, and oftentimes a profession which justifies and defends us against and re-enforces the Narcissistic Wound.

For example, I met a psychologist in Indiana. To handle her mother's dysfunctional and unpredictable behavior she would "go into her mother's experience," (mind read), analyze and figure out "where she was" and give her an "appropriate response" in an attempt to control her mother's chaotic reactions. Years later when she became a psychologist, she was excellent at figuring out and diagnosing her clients. Unfortunately *for her,* she was really in an integrated age-regression containing transference and counter-transference issues. The problem was, she was always on automatic diagnosis. From outer to inner her layered psychology looked like this:

---

[6]In cognitive therapy, mind reading is referred as a cognitive distortion.

Layer I   Her act and the appropriate Mask.

Layer II   The analyst (psychologist) imagining, projecting
               and analyzing (this is part of the age regressed
               little girl).

Layer III   Shocked, a pained little girl

Layer IV   **ESSENCE**

In other words she was attracted to and became a psychologist to re-enforce her defenses. In this way, she used psychology to re-enforce her defenses (professional persona, analysis, diagnostic skills, etc.) against the shock.

SPIRITUALIZATION:
The process whereby infants make their parents into Gods.

If Mom and Dad are projected onto others making them God or Gurus, they will try to be the Guru's reflection (act like them) so that they are able to merge (enter the Kingdom of Heaven) with the Guru (spiritualized as Mom).

THE DIFFERENCE THAT MAKES A DIFFERENCE
Quantum Psychology differs radically from any system, be it "psychological" or spiritual, which believes you are your False Core or False Self and which attempts to heal it, reframe it, make it "better," keep the "good," get rid of the "bad," convert vices into virtues, re-associate it, rename it, re-frame it, polish it and, ultimately, even *observe* it. Quantum Psychology suggests this is just moving around furniture. The question is, Who is moving the furniture and trying to re-form the False Core? Quantum Psychology maintains that any attempt to do these things contains an underlying judgment and assumption that you are your False Core. For Quantum Psychology *you are not your False Core. Your False Core is not who you are.*

The more you identify with your False Core-False Self (even through transformation or healing), the more you reinforce it.

According to Nisargadatta Maharaj, "In order to go beyond the mind, you must look away (take your attention) from the mind and its contents." In Quantum Psychology, we do not try to change it, or to take the good stuff and leave the bad, and there is no "healthy" or "unhealthy." You are not your False Core or False Self Compensator. You can, however, use the False Core-False Self to describe who you imagine you are or were, realize you are not this and then discard it and discover *WHO YOU ARE*. Nisargadatta Maharaj said, "To discover who you are—you must first discover who you are not." Furthermore, "I" would like to note here that the *observer is part of the False Core and the False Self Compensator*. This is why observing the False Core-False Self cannot get "you" beyond them.

Ultimately, when you begin to realize that all you think you are is either the observer or the False Core-False Self and its defensive compensations, there is the realization that there is *no you*, which is normally termed a self, and then there only remains the non-verbal **I AM** or **NOT-I-I** (see Volume III).

Knowledge of the False Core-False Self is critical because wherever your mind moves—however it moves—you take your False Core with you. And wherever your mind moves, it is a movement to resist the pain of your False Core. A student of Swami Muktananda let him know he was going to take a vacation for a week. Muktananda replied, "Tell me a place where you can go and not take your mind with you and I will go there with you." The problem is, "What is driving these movements of your mind?" It is the False Core. When you "get that," you don't move. You stay just *prior* to it (the False Core) and dismantle it until it dissolves in the nonverbal "**I AM.**" When it dissolves, "you" and your subjective experience of *your* psychology dissolve. With your False Core gone, "your" psychology, and what you call "you," has no place or ground to land on; "you" have no location in space-time.

This movement of the mind to resist the False Core is a must for the "I" experiencing the False Core because anything is better than feeling the False Core structure. In *Trances People Live*, I called the False Core the *Organizing Principle* since it is the principle that organizes your entire psychology. When that False Core or Organizing Principle dissolves (a Yogi would call it "cutting the knot of the heart"), **ESSENCE**, **I AM**, **VOID**, etc., naturally emerge and are revealed. *If you do not cut the False Core (knot of the heart, i.e., the associational networks), **ESSENCE**, the I AM and the awareness of the **VOID** (NOT-I-I) can never be stabilized in your awareness.*

TRACING THE FALSE CORE DRIVER

To discover your False Core, take notice of whatever it is you are experiencing and then trace it back by asking yourself, "What is the worst of that or "what about that is so bad?" When you trace it back, you'll hit the bottom of one of them. Please note there are more False Cores than those described.

QUANTUM PSYCHOLOGY PRINCIPLE:

Who you are is beyond even the way "you" fixate your attention. The way "you" fixate attention and all "you" call "you" are part of the observer-False Core Driver-False Self Defensive Compensator complex.

QUANTUM PSYCHOLOGY PRINCIPLE:

There is not one observer but an infinite number of them. With each experience a different observer-experiencer-experience arises and subsides.

QUANTUM PSYCHOLOGY PRINCIPLE:

As in Quantum Physics so in Quantum Psychology, you cannot separate the observer from the observed or the know*er* from the known. The observer or know*er* is part of the observed or known experience; each is inseparable from the other.

THE OBSERVER IS PART OF THE OBSERVED

A pivotal part of Werner Heisenberg's theory of Quantum Physics is the fact that the observer cannot be separated from the thing being observed.

In the beginning phases, it is important to develop and observe, to realize that you are the looker and not what you are looking at, and that anything you can observe, you cannot be. Next, "you" see that the observer of the False Core Driver and the False Self Compensator itself are really one solid unit. In other words, the observer is part of that which it observes. Ultimately, you go beyond the observer-False Core-False Self complex and enter into **ESSENCE-I AM** and the **NOT-I-I**. The **NOT-I-I** is beyond the observer-observed dyad; it is Pure Awareness which a yogi would call *WITNESSING* (the observer-observed dyad). (See Volume III.)

The observer is the ego observing itself. The observer is actually a part of the structure it is observing and it too has to be gone beyond. Some systems, like Vipassana (insight), Buddhist meditation, or Gurdjieff work as it is presently being taught, think there is one observer which observes and exists "before" the observed. They don't get that the observer is part of the observed and that there are an infinite number of observers along with an infinite number of experiences.[7] In this way if "I'm" sitting here in self-observation, it often appears as though a thought comes up like "I love myself" or "I hate myself." But actually what happens—and this is the major difference in the Quantum work—is that both an observer and an observed (thought) simultaneously arise and subside together as one unit. And then a new observer or thought or experience arises and subsides together as one unit. There are an infinite number of observers which arise and subside with each experience, each experience containing a different observer.

THE ILLUSIONS OF THE OBSERVER

To explain further, there are three belief structures or illusions about the observer, or that the observer has about itself: 1) it

---

[7]Quantum Psychology actually feels that Gurdjieff's objective consciousness is a quality of **ESSENCE**, i.e., observation with no object.

observes and is separate from what it is looking at (not true); 2) it imagines that it creates what it's looking at (which it does not); 3) it imagines it came before or existed before that which it is observing (which it does not).

These are underlying structures contained within the observer which must be gone beyond. As long as the observer is there, the False Core-False Self will be there because it too is part of this holographic unit. This is why Quantum Psychology writes it using hyphens: observer-False Core-False Self, as one unit. Trying to separate the observer from the False Core would be like trying to separate the smell of a rose from the rose. You can never go beyond the False Core Driver as long as there is an observer observing it because the observer is part of the system, it observes. Therefore the observer too must be dismantled (see Volume III).

THE JUDGMENTAL OBSERVER

People often think they are simply observing something, but there is judgment, evaluation or significance placed upon the experience that is being observed. Furthermore, the observer is often either (1) in a state of dissociation caused by resisting an experience; or (2) in a state of fusion whereby the child fuses with Mom or Dad who is outside of them and observes and judges their behavior as either good or bad. In other words, children dissociate from their body-mind and see themselves through the eyes of a judgmental (this is good, this is bad) Mom or Dad, who later can be "Spiritualized" as gods.

Because Dad or Mom are the "outside" observers who are trying to reform your behavior, years later you have an observer who unknowingly is an internalized Mom and/or Dad observing and trying to reform "you" (turn vices into virtues), getting rid of the "bad" (what Mom and Dad don't want) and replacing it with good (what Mom and Dad, later spiritualized as God or Guru want) in order to merge and go to heaven. Since as an infant rewards and punishments were based on behavior judged good or bad, this fused internalized observer is actually Mom or Dad now internalized as an "observer" observing you.

QUANTUM PSYCHOLOGY PRINCIPLE:

You see and treat yourself the way Mom and Dad saw and treated you.

QUANTUM PSYCHOLOGY PRINCIPLE:

When the observer is fused with Mom or Dad, behavior, emotions, etc., are viewed as bad, vices, sins, etc. You think getting rid of the bad is "spiritual" when actually it is an internalized age-regressed re-enactment of Mom/Dad as an observer observing you as a child, which has become internalized.

In other words, the judgmental observer is part of and re-enforces the system In this way, "you" (the observer-False Core-False Self) become attracted to a system which claims you can convert vices into virtues (Christian overlay) or unhealthy into health (psychological/societal overlay).

People "act out" their False Core-False Self continually because they imagine they *are* their False Core-False Self. If you believe that you are your False Core, then you'll think that by changing this belief (transforming it in some way), you are changing yourself which is actually the *False Self* in action. When you realize that you are not your False Core, that you were there before your last thought, and after that thought leaves you will still be there—when you realize that, you can go beyond your False Core, understanding that changing thoughts and feelings don't have anything to do with changing you. In fact this approach of focusing on changing thoughts or feelings, as if they change you, is a seductively "dangerous" distraction if your wish is to find out **WHO YOU ARE**. It would be like thinking, "I am my car," and then thinking that if I buy a new car, it will change who I am.

The Observer-False Core Driver-False Self Compensator complex represents and organizes everything you call yourself, i.e., your entire psychology. But to paraphrase Idries Shah: "You can only be free if you develop volitional choice over where you put your awareness." Quantum Psychology says, "You cannot do this if you are unknowingly habitually fixated on the False Core, the compensating False Self or the

Observer. Waking up is realizing that you are not the observer-False Core-False Self complex.

THE APPROACH

The approach is through enquiry and exercises sometimes done with others. It's an ongoing enquiry into what I call *I*-dentity. *I*-dentities can be anything: I am or I *(fill in the blank)*. "I love myself," "I hate myself," "I am happy I am in a relationship," "I am miserable I am in a relationship." All of these are *I*-dentities. The goal is to take them apart through an enquiry into the assumptions and concepts you have so that eventually they and the "you" "you" call "yourself" disappear. One purpose of Quantum Psychology is that people will learn how to take these processes or ways of working, and internalize them so that they can begin dismantling their own False Core-False Self. Ultimately, the dismantl*er*-dismantl*ee* and the observer also will disappear, and *there will be no need for "me" or for Quantum Psychology any longer*. Nisargadatta Maharaj said it this way, "I am not here to accumulate students." In fact, one of the many reasons this approach is called Quantum Psychology rather than "my" name is so that whether you love me or hate me, you can still do the work. It is not personal to "me," this approach is not about winning a popularity contest.

IT TAKES TIME

The False Core is so defended and the False Self so used to distract and compensate, determining one's False Core takes time. I try never to tell anybody what False Core they are because I don't believe you can tell what somebody's False Core is by their outward behavior. I can tell what someone's behavior looks like (i.e., their False Self). Anyone can do that. I can say "you are acting as if "*(fill in the blank)*" but I don't know if that's your False Core because I don't know what's *motivating* you or what is the *driver* behind this behavior. That's why it's difficult to tell what someone's False Core is. To identify the driver of someone's entire psychology is a tough number.

Secondly, why would you want to spend time trying to figure out someone's False Core. It is oftentimes a False Self which is trying to "get" another's psychology so it does not have to feel its own False Core, or the age-regressed child trying to gain control through understanding, appreciating and then giving the appropriate response to Mom/Dad.

To illustrate, I recently met a psychologist from Florida. She was very into diagnosising people. I asked why and she said, "So I can connect to others better by understanding them." I said, "What's the worst of not understanding another and not connecting." She said, "I feel alone." I said, "What's the worst of feeling alone." She said, "I would feel worthless." I said, "What's the worst of that?" She said, "I wouldn't exist" "That's it."

Please note, all movements of the mind and justifications for actions, etc., are the False Self resisting the False Core.

STAY INSIDE IT IS ABOUT "YOU"

To illustrate this, let's say someone is a professor at the University of Washington. He works hard and is achieving and doing a lot in his field. What's driving his behavior? Is he working/doing because:

1. He feels "there is something wrong with him."

2. He feels "worthless and is trying to prove worth."

3. He feels he "cannot do" and so "overdoes."

4. He feels "inadequate"and is trying to prove he is "smart and adequate."

5. He feels "non-existent" and is trying to "prove he exists."

6. He feels "alone" and is trying to "connect" with other professionals.

7.   He feels "incomplete" and is trying to "fill in the missing pieces."

8.   He feels "powerless" and wants to be "powerful."

9.   He feels "no love" and is "seeking love" through work.

I think too much emphasis is placed on trying to analyze and figure out others. This is oftentimes yet another defense and distraction of the False Self trying to distract away from the False Core and the shock of the Realization of Separation. Emphasis could be better placed on what your False Core-False Self is and how to dismantle it and realize IT IS NOT YOU.

Quantum Psychology is an on-going internal process. In Quantum Psychology people are continually being brought back into their False Core, studying it and working in pairs or groups to dismantle it. There are two main parts to the process of dismantling the False Core-False Self (see Volume II): (1) tracing the False Core; and (2) the False Core-False Self protocols, each of which works on the False Core-False Self polarity and each protocol contains about twenty enquiry questions.

THE JOB OF THE TEACHER-THERAPIST

QUANTUM PSYCHOLOGY PRINCIPLE:

Any person who wants to be a teacher, sees themselves as a teacher or has the subjective experience of being a teacher cannot ultimately help you find out **WHO YOU ARE**."

This statement is presented up-front because when the False Core leaves, there is no subjective experience of a "you." If you think or imagine you are a teacher, your False Core-False Self is operating. Therefore you can only "act out of," and "react out of," the observer-False Core-False Self complex.

The primary job of a "teacher" is to:

1) Understand who is in front of them in all dimensions, not only the psycho-emotional but also at the level of **ESSENCE-I AM**, etc.

2) To meet the "person" where they are.

3) To know the limitations of "their" knowledge and the limitations of "their" system" and to refer people where they need to go. This is what the ancient Sufis did.

4) To know there can be no fostering of transference based on the age-regressed counter-transference issues of the teacher and no dependency allowed. In other words, I don't think it's productive to have age-regressed adults giving a teacher their power. In Quantum Psychology the "trance-ference" is seen as an age-regressed trance on the part of both the client/student and the therapist/teacher. In short, supporting trance-ference only yields more trance-ference; supporting dependence only yields more dependence.

MEDITATION

Meditation, too, has limitations. For over twelve years, I meditated 3-5 hours a day because I had been told that meditation would do it all.

I was taught and I taught 120 different meditation techniques, mostly Jnana, tantric and mantra meditations. Meditation can give you a taste of the **VOID** or **ESSENCE**, but it does not handle the thinking or the emotional level. That's why people who meditate for years are still suffering. When they "leave meditation," go out into the world, they use "spiritual philosophies" to reject the world, and re-enforce and justify the way they handle their separation shock (i.e., the False Self).[8]

Meditation does not do it all. It can open up the doorway to awareness of the **EMPTINESS**, but it will never stabilize at that level *as long as uncooked* seeds "pull you out" of that." It is important to note that *no one system does it all*. To illustrate further, a cognitive therapist, would emphasize the thinking dimension "as if" that does it all. It doesn't. If you went to an emotional release person,

---

[8]Buddha said that those who seek nirvana are ignorant and those who seek samsana are ignorant. Why? Because nirvana is samsara—samsara is nirvana. There is, after all, only one substance.

they might suggest this could do it all. It does not. If you went to an accountant, she might say that the external world does it all. It does not. Or if you went to a Rolfer, or to a Feldenkreis person, they might say bodywork can do it all, it does not.

Every system has limitations as well as a very strong suit. And it is important to acknowledge at which level your system and you are going to be working in order to use them appropriately. Feldenkreis is fantastic, as is Rolfing. Is it going to change your phobia? Probably not. Is it going to dismantle your False Core? Probably not. But it will help you to integrate your experiences more fully. When you integrate all the dimensions of manifestations, you can walk around and live your life and still keep an awareness of **ESSENCE, the I AM,** etc.

Now, let us imagine an over-emotional client who goes to a psychotherapist. If he goes into an emotional release type of therapy, he will never get better. All this will do is reinforce his False Core-False Self distractions (see Volume II). If you have somebody who is schizoid, on the other hand, they are over-observers and use thinking as a defense against feeling, and dissociate from their emotions. Now if someone like that were to do Vipassana meditation (insight meditation) or cognitive therapy, it would be the worst thing in the world because it would reinforce their structure.

For these reasons the "person" who is teaching the system has to know the systems' weak as well as its strong suits, who it is good for and who it's not good for, and then refer people out according to where they need to go. To offer a system like insight meditation to an over-observer who dissociates and observes as a defense only re-enforces the structure, as does offering the conversion of vices to virtues to somebody with a strong Christian background. It will reinforce the defensive strategy of the False Self (Compensator), unknowingly re-enforcing an age regression (False Core) or integrative age regressive (False Self). Offering a system which re-enforces the defenses of a person who is suffering can be tantamount to offering an alcoholic a drink.

Psychology and spirituality are not "one-size-fits-all." I think this is part of the problem with both of these disciplines. Recently I was doing a demonstration with a woman who had been sexually abused. Three things revealed themselves—1) she had her concepts connected to her spine and they were activated by her sitting up straight (in a meditation posture); 2), her concepts and trauma were attached around, and re-activated by, the control of her breathing and thinking (i.e., slowing her breath and stopping her thoughts); and 3) to defend herself against "feeling" the trauma she had developed an image of herself as a little girl standing in the sunlight and hanging-up clothes which relaxed her yielding safety and comfort.

If we examine this, we can easily see that if she got involved with a "spiritual" system which said you needed to sit up straight, spine erect, or watch or control your breathing or thoughts, it would only re-enforce her concepts and the trauma itself because it would ask her to unknowingly re-enforce the biological component (body position) which held the system together. If she went to a therapist who stressed a "symbol of safety" (like an Ericksonian hypnotherapist), this might make her "feel" more comfortable and relaxed. But the symbol of safety would only re-enforce the holographic nature and defense against the trauma since it was created by a "little girl" as a way of defending against a trauma and was part of the trauma itself.

If a guru has thousands of disciples, oftentimes they all get the same or similar mantras, or they all get the same or similar spiritual practice, as opposed to, "This is for you, you need this," and "This other one needs that." That requires very specific instruction. I think part of the problem is that psycho-spirituality has become a business. If a teacher refers you out to somebody else, the teacher loses dollars. That's the hard fact. Therapy, self-work, and psycho-spirituality are no longer student- or client-centered but therapist-guru-teacher- centered. The teacher *needs* the student as opposed to, "What does this particular individual student need?"

Another problem is that people involved in psycho-spirituality rarely question their own underlying assumptions and the assumptions on which the system they are involved in is based. When I was with Nisargadatta Maharaj, he often asked people to leave within a few minutes. "I fantasized" two reasons for this: (1) "He" somehow knew it was not right for them. Nisargadatta Maharaj would say, "It is not for everybody"; and (2) "I imagine" when "he" felt you got what you needed, he asked you to leave. Many times I heard him say, "I am not here to accumulate students."

Once a woman traveled all the way from Europe. Nisargadatta Maharaj asked her, "How long are you staying?" She said, "Three months." "No, stay for a week or so until you understand it. If you stay too long, you will just listen to me and not do the work." This was the mark of a "teacher" who was student-centered, not self-centered.

Everybody needs something different, something tailor-made just for them. Psychological and spiritual practices should be tailored to the individual. They should be student or client centered, not teacher centered. And teachers of each system should acknowledge the system's limitations and when called for, *refer out.*

THE DANGER OF DIAGNOSIS:
TAKING PEOPLE FOR WHAT THEY ARE NOT

There is a major problem in the world of psycho-spiritual practice. People think they can diagnose each other. Then, they think they know the person who has been diagnosed. As Korzybski said, "The map is not the territory" and "the idea is not the thing you are referring to." In this way, diagnosis and typing are not the person you are referring to. You must understand that the False Core-False Self, the Enneagram and the D.S.M. IV of Psychology are merely maps; they are constructions of the nervous system. But the nervous system does not see the underlying unity. It cannot because it is a condensation of the underlying unity. If you believe this Nervous System's construction (maps), you will never know Quantum Consciousness. Your concepts, especially your False Core Driver and False Self Compensator, have to de-constructed or disidentified from.

PSYCHOLOGY'S FAILURE

The most common trap for people is that they believe they are their False Core-False Self and that there are good parts and bad parts of it. But if you believe there is a "bad" part of the False Core-False Self and you try to focus on the "good" part, you keep the "bad" part active so you know what not to be. Again, it is a holograph and one unit.

But you are not your False Core-False Self. What does it matter if you label it as "healthy" or "unhealthy"? The False Core-False Self should be used as a tool to clarify how you fixate your awareness, so that you can stop doing it, not to believe you are this fixation and then try to make it better or virtuous. The trap is that people subtly begin to believe they are their False Core-False Self when phrases like "vices to virtues" or "healthy-unhealthy" are employed. Simply put, if I focus on how to make my False Core (bad stuff) better in some way, I am somehow believing I am my False Core. Once you fall into this trap, you begin using the False Self to handle the False Core, and you are back on the False Core→False Self→False Core→False Self wheel.

SPIRITUALIZED AGE REGRESSIONS

The False Core-False Self is not something that you assume for a lifetime in order to learn a specific lesson. The idea of "learning lessons" is rooted in age regression and infantile structures (see Volume II). Each False Self has a story which acts as both a psychological and a spiritual defense. It is an interesting story but don't believe it.

Quantum Psychology is very short on descriptions of the False Core-False Self—and very long on "how to" process through it so that **ESSENCE**, and the **"I AM"** etc., naturally become part of your awareness.

THE BIOLOGICAL CORE (VOLUME I)

Every form of psychology and spirituality has certain strong and weak suits since no one system can do it all. I think it's essential—both for clients and practitioners—to know what a particular system can and cannot do, and to acknowledge its limitations. This can sometimes be hard for teachers as well as practitioners, partly because sometimes teachers want to be able to do it all or imagine their system does it all. This is rooted in the pre-verbal identification with the omniscient magical mommy, and represents the teacher's grandiosity and counter-transeference. Likewise, a system or technique can be imagined to do it all. The occurs when the system or technique becomes magical mommy or the tranformational object (technique) of the pre-verbal nonrepresentational infant (see Volume I, The Special Section, *Trances People Live: Revisited*).

Quantum Psychology has some very clear weak suits. One of them is the external world. The other is the physical body, although the work itself does contain a lot of enquiry directed at the body.

The body needs a "hands on" approach. Body-work should deal with what Ida Rolf calls the *BIOLOGICAL CORE* (see Chapter VIII). Secondly, "bodywork" is needed in order to process and address the material in the physical body. For these reasons, Quantum Psychology recommends that people get some hands-on "body-work." For example, imagine that an incest survivor comes to me for psychotherapy and, as a therapist, I help her work through her beliefs, emotions, and memories. What happens when she goes home and has sex with her partner? The minute her body is in the same or a similar position as when the molestation happened, all the material comes back up again. You need "hands-on" work in order to liberate awareness that is unknowingly fixated in the body for the trauma to be free of the body memories. So I always recommend body-work for this reason.

Recent body-work (1996) with Alfred Schatz has also included research into the brain. For example, if you had a trauma, i.e., your father beat you, you can perhaps handle the psychological and emotional implications, but there will be a "body memory," the result being that if you hold your posture in a particular way that posture will reinforce the memory. In addition parts of your brain itself might not be "on line," thus sending "mixed messages" or not using other parts of the brain.

Physical injuries too can get tied up in the psyche in the same way. Part of the reason traumas are so intense is that there's a collapsing of the dimensions. In other words, your external thinking, feeling and biology all get collapsed and stuck together. This is why a trauma, now labeled as Post Traumatic Stress Disorder, is so powerful and hard to take apart (see *The Tao of Chaos*).

ESSENCE (VOLUME III)

ESSENCE, as was discussed in the *Taos of Chaos* appears as the spaciousness the physical body organizes around. **ESSENCE**, unlike the **I AM**, does contain essential qualities, like love with no object, compassion, observation with no object, peace, etc. These are qualities of **ESSENCE**, but there is no subject-object relationship, like observer-observed. When **ESSENCE** is fully realized and the False Core-False Self dismantled, **ESSENCE** is no longer a mislabeled emptiness, (as in a lack) experience but a fullness and spaciousness of essential qualities.

THE I AM (VOLUME III)

The **I AM** is the gift of Nisargadatta Maharaj.

The Verbal I AM is prior to the False Core-False Self. The False Core is I AM (*fill in the blank*) and can only be there if the verbal **I AM** is there first.

The non-verbal I AM is prior to the verbal **I AM,** and is prior to the essential qualities of **ESSENCE**. It is pure being. It is what your experience is or would be right now if you were without or did not use your thoughts, memory, emotions, associations or perceptions. However, it is unaware of the **BIG EMPTINESS** and this is what distinguishes it, the **I AM**, from the **NOT I-I.**

THE QUANTUM PSYCHOLOGY "SHORT-CUT"

Notice what you are experiencing. Notice what happens when I say, "Notice what observer is observing this experience. . . ." Everything might go blank for a moment because when I ask you to "notice what observer is observing that," you go beyond the observer-observed dyad, and then they both disappear. This is observation with no object and is the non-verbal **I AM**. If there is awareness too of the **BIG EMPTINESS**, it is the **NOT-I-I** (further differentiating the **I AM** and **NOT-I-I**, will follow.)

THE COLLECTIVE UNCONSCIOUS, THE ARCHETYPAL DIMENSION (VOLUME III)

The Collective Unconscious is a condensation of **THAT VOID**. It contains the physics dimensions[9] of energy, space, mass, time, gravity, strong and weak nuclear forces, light and electro-magnetics.

It is the "ground" of archetypes, and the birthplace of our "ruling" forces which lie far outside of awareness. For this reason, the physics dimensions must be processed too as we see how psycho-spirituality is a by-product of the interaction of the physics dimensions.

Finally, the key archetype, the **I AM** is in this dimension. As Nisargadatta Maharaj said, "The **I AM** comes from the collective."

THE NOT-I-I

The "**NOT-I-I**" is where the **WITNESS** WITNESSes the observer-observed dyad with no effect. At the same time, the **WITNESS** is pure awareness aware of the **BIG EMPTINESS** "Behind it." Beyond this awareness is the **VOID**, where there is no-awareness or awar*er*.

This is why the **VOID**, the **NAMELESS ABSOLUTE** and **BEYOND** are Not Dimensions.

THE VOID OF UNDIFFERENTIATED CONSCIOUSNESS: THE SOUL THING (VOLUME III)

If you follow Buddhism, Buddha's realization was that there is no individual soul which transmigrates (incarnates) again and again.

The **VOID** condenses down and becomes whatever. There is no individual separate self that incarnates. Instead the **VOID** condenses down and becomes "a thought"—"you," "me," grandma, a feeling, Coca Cola, it doesn't matter. One day that **VOID OF UN-DIFFERENTIATED CONSCIOUSNESS** will thin out and become **VOID** again. We call the condensing down of the **VOID OF UN-**

---

[9]I am using the term "physics dimensions" to differentiate it from Quantum Psychology's dimensions of manifestation

DIFFERENTIATED CONSCIOUSNESS "life," the thinning out of the **VOID OF UNDIFFERENTIATED CONSCIOUSNESS** "death." But whether it is condensed or thinned out, it is still the **VOID OF UNDIFFERENTIATED CONSCIOUSNESS** which is **UNDIFFERENTIATED CONSCIOUSNESS** and does not know itself.[10]

Thus, the Zen Patriarch said, "The Great Way is easy, except for those who have preferences." Noted Physicist, John Wheeler, said it this way, "Nothingness is the building block of the universe." To illustrate, if you put ice cubes in a bathtub, they are like condensed **VOID** but when they liquify and turn into water again, this is like thinned out **VOID** (water). Nevertheless, they are still both made of *THAT ONE SUBSTANCE*. There is no individual separate soul which incarnates again and again and again. There is only one soul, and your soul and my soul are the same soul. If you substitute the word "soul" for **SUBSTANCE,** then there is only **ONE SUBSTANCE (SOUL)**, not two or more individual souls or substances. Pure spirituality lies in understanding that there is only **THAT ONE SUBSTANCE** and that everything is made of it.

Quantum Physics has demonstrated that everything is connected to everything else. Behind all the apparent differences, there exists a unified field of interconnected wholeness. Quantum Psychology holds this unified field or background as its context.

THE NAMELESS ABSOLUTE (VOLUME III)

When the **VOID** ends the **NAMELESS** is revealed. Nisargadatta Maharaj oftentimes responded to me when I asked a question by saying, "It will be revealed to you." The **NAMELESS**

---

[10]This is not to be confused with individual consciousness. In New Age circles they say "I" as consciousness creat it all. *Undifferentiated consciousness in which there is no I creates it all.* An "I" which says I create things or even it is all, is differentiated consciousness. To imagine that **UNDIFFERENTIATED CONSCIOUSNESS** which has no awareness, no awarer and **NO-I**, creates, wants, prefers, has a will and volition—this is from the perspective of differentiated consciousness or a separate "I" which attributes human qualities of a nervous system, wanting, preferring etc., onto **UNDIFFERENTIATED CONSCIOUSNESS** which has no nervous system, this is anthropomorphic; where you project a nervous system onto something that does not have one. For example, Source wants this, Source likes that, or God wants this, the universe wants that, etc. None of these has a nervous system—but are projected onto by a Nervous System.

ABSOLUTE views the **VOID** universes as parallel universe theory in physics. It is beyond the **WITNESS** and, for purposes of language, can be called the **SUPREME WITNESS**. It is "where" there is no perception or even the ability to conceive of anything, or to conceive itself. To repeat again, when a student asked Nisargadatta Maharaj "Who are you" he replied, "Nothing perceivable or conceivable."

BEYOND

CONCLUSION

BEYOND QUANTUM PSYCHOLOGY (VOLUME III)

The False Core and False Self Compensator are a shorthand, a psycho-emotional abstraction, but ultimately this has to be looked at and gone beyond. Another thing to keep in mind is that maps are made by people. Quantum Psychology is a map, and the map is not the territory. Or as the old Zen saying puts it, "The finger that points at the moon is not the moon." **ESSENCE**, the **I AM**, the underlying unity or **VOID OF UNDIFFERENTIATED CONSCIOUSNESS** is the goal and the "how to" is the finger (in this case Quantum Psychology) must be "gone beyond" as well.

The purpose of Quantum Psychology is to find out *Who You Are*. Ultimately the enquir*ER*-enquir*EE* and the WHO AM I along with Quantum Psychology dissolve. The probability of that occurring might "hopefully" be enhanced by developing multi-dimensional awareness and by going beyond how you fixate your awareness on your False Core-False Self but there are no guarantees. Finally, it might be that through the liberation of your fixated awareness that **ESSENCE**, the "**I AM**," the underlying unity or **VOID** might become more realizable. At that point, the "you" "you" think you are disappears, and only **THAT ONE INDIVISIBLE SUBSTANCE** remains. The realization that it is all one interconnected whole, that there is only **THAT ONE SUBSTANCE** that everything is made out of, and even **BEYOND** this—and "**I AM THAT**"—is pure (no subject-object) spirituality.

Enjoy the ride!

With love,
your brother
Stephen

Personality is a mis-taken identity.

Nisargadatta Maharaj

F inding out **WHO YOU ARE** is not about being more, doing more, having more, mani festing more, creating more, being the best you can be, finding out one's imagined "mission" or "purpose" in life, or financial success.

Finding out **WHO YOU ARE** is the realization that everything is made of the same substance, and **YOU ARE THAT ONE SUBSTANCE**.

Stephen H. Wolinsky

CHAPTER III
WHY QUANTUM PSYCHOLOGY?

I
f we were to trace the history of psychology dating back to the early Greek philosophers, we could appreciate that psychology evolved from man's search to find the answer to the ultimate question: **WHO AM I**? Historically, this question of who we are has been asked for thousands of years ever since people began to recognize a sense of self, or a separate knowing. This enabled self-analysis to occur and flourish. Religions and spiritual systems emerged whereby people imagined that something larger than themselves "existed"— a supernatural source.

With the advent of psychoanalysis via Sigmund Freud, psychology developed as a path to explore this self. But the self was seen as possessing a dark and perverse unconscious whose instincts were a source of pain, conflict and problems. The ego was the mediator of these wishes, drives and desires, which Freud called the Id. The superego was the parental and societal regulator of the Id. The battle between the Id and superego drew boundaries where the "I" (or ego) could find a place to exist.

Hence, the more subtle search for who we are and our complete nature took a back seat. For many years the exploration of problem states and, of course, problem resolution have been in the driver's seat. Our search became limited to diagnosis and the treatment of problems. How do we cope with and solve the dilemmas of life?

In a real sense, the industrial revolution and technology could be seen as having dehumanized people, asking people to behave as machines. Historically, as you trace the industrial revolution, you can see how it played a major role. For example, as Europe became more industrialized, philosophy whose focus was "Who Am I?" shifted to psychology's focus of, "How can I survive, cope and handle today's problems and conflicts?" The question, "Who Am I? What is my nature?" was abandoned and in its place came "How can I cope?" "How can I survive?" And when someone could not fit into the fast-paced industrial world, rather than asking what was wrong with the system, it became "What is wrong with me?"

The industrial revolution made technology our god and own-ership of possessions our demi-god. Even in modern society the idea of discovering **WHO YOU ARE** is now confused with what you do or have. The sickness of our society was the giving-up of our con-nection to humanity for technological advances. This was deemed progress and healthy. And *the individual that could not fit in or cope was unhealthy.*

It could be said that people no longer had the time or energy to explore the question of "Who Am I?" The assembly line increased productivity and "progress" but the price was high. Stress escalated and anxiety rose to new heights as we were taken out of our natural environment and placed in an industrial complex—in a sense, an anti-human situation. It could be said that, as technology and indus-try grew and became dehumanized, so did psychology as we pres-ently know it. In fact, we can easily see the correlation.

When I embarked on "my" journey in the late 1960s, psy-chology still had a shred of light—people in search of themselves. But when "I" returned from India in 1982 the field had become an industry. "Getting" what you want or what you imagine will make you happy" were now part of the industrial complex. How to survive by looking good, feeling good, or developing strategies of "making it," was the focus. "Who Am I?— the mother and father of psychol-ogy—was lost.

QUANTUM PSYCHOLOGY

Quantum Psychology came into being to answer the ques-tion, "Who Am I?" and to bring us back to the roots of psychology.

To do this, Quantum Psychology uses physics as its philosophical context, individual psychology as its foundation, and Eastern and Middle-Eastern religions as its cornerstones. It developed the concept of multi-dimensional awareness as a possible aid to the discovery of **WHO YOU ARE.**

In today's world, people unfortunately no longer have the luxury of broader-based exploration. Instead, as the world has become more intensified time-wise and industrialized, people are forced into a narrower and more constrictive sense of "their" life and self. The questions of life and of psychology have become a search for answers to specific problems. Painful emotional states are seen as obstacles to be overcome. Patients or clients are seen as problems themselves by therapists, psychologists, and psychiatrists. Following the lead of the industrial revolution, over the last century, psychology has become a tool with a standard to measure health. Psychology has turned into a solution-focused product to be sold in the marketplace with coping, problem solving and resolution and having more as the primary goals for therapists and clients thus (con)fusing even more WHO YOU ARE from what you do and have.

Rapid change, forced adjustments, lack of insurance, the impact of the media and our standards of health, success and good looks—all have made the handling of life and problem-solving as the focus of psychology, instead of the discovery of **WHO YOU ARE.** Recently, I was shocked to find an article on the cover of the nagazine The Family Therapy Networker all about the most important psychologists of this era. I had never heard of these people. These "psychologists" were concerned about how they as a profession could survive with the HMO problem. Nothing about serving people in pain, no mention of the search for **WHO AM I**?—only health care and how and what the industry of psychology must do in order to survive.

THE CONTEXT

What psychology has forgotten is that the context is larger than the individual. For example, a heroin addict can be taken out of the context of his environment and he will stop shooting heroin. But put the junkie back and he begins to shoot drugs again.

In our society, the context and continual media bombardment make our context even larger. Image has become more important than personal fulfillment, and what we possess and do more important than the discovery of **WHO WE ARE.** Even the strongest of us gets hypnotized and tranced-out by society and in the process we lose touch with our own human nature. In short the sizzle has become more important than the steak.

In the 1970s, a terrifying film about violence and gangs forecasted the future. It was called *A Clockwork Orange*. I was fascinated when I read the book to finally understand the title: A Clockwork Orange is a person who appears human or organic (orange) but has actually become a machine (clock). This is the context in which we live. *Waking up* out of this context and the automatic reactions to it are part of becoming fully human.

We cannot know what we need to look for to become human until we first "explore" where we are. Second, we need to learn to see the subtle nuances which prevent us from being human. In the next few chapters we will explore multi-dimensional awareness. In the Special Section the focus will be on trances and spiritual pitfalls. We will look at the most frequently misunderstood trances (psychological and spiritual as well as mundane) which take us out of our body, out of relationships, out of the world, out of present time and out of humanity. And, ultimately, out of **ESSENCE** and the Underlying Unity of Quantum Consciousness.

In the words of my teacher, Nisargadatta Maharaj, "You cannot let go of something until you know what it is." Quantum Psychology takes this one step further: "You cannot let go of something until you are willing to experience it." The Special Section may seem difficult but I ask you to stay with it and persevere. For it is here that you will find a discussion of these machine-like automatic trances which are our deepest, most resistant problem, the ones most difficult to confront. This is the nature of our inner work: confronting, dismantling and waking up to the larger context of who we are on all dimensions of reality and then going beyond them. This is *The Way of the Human.*

CHAPTER IV
THE DIMENSIONS OF "MANIFESTATION"

From a Quantum Psychology perspective, it can be said that the Emptiness/Fullness of **THAT ONE SUBSTANCE** contracts or condenses. **THAT ONE SUBSTANCE** has been called the **VOID**, the **EMPTINESS** by Einstein and Buddha; **GOD**, in the Judaic tradition; and Shiva or pure (**UNDIFFERENTIATED**) consciousness by Hindu Yogis. It should be noted at this point that pure spirituality ends with the realization of **THAT ONE SUBSTANCE—I AM THAT (ONE SUBSTANCE)**. **BEYOND** is even beyond this and can no longer be called spiritual or spirituality as it is normally considered (see Volume III).

THAT ONE SUBSTANCE (UNDIFFERENTIATED CONSCIOUSNESS or **EMPTINESS**) condenses down forming the pure Awareness or Witness also called the **NOT-I-I.** Further contraction of the "**NOTHING**" forms what Carl Jung called "the collective unconscious." This Collective Dimension which contains Archetypes is that which comes "after" the pure awareness or the **WITNESS** (called the **NOT-I-I.**)

"When" **THAT ONE SUBSTANCE** contracts you get the universal concept of archetypes a by-product of the physics divisions which is that which archetypes of the collective unconscious are made (Volume III).

The Collective Dimension forms and creates our deepest Archetype, the Archetype and concept of the *I AM.* As the No-State

State of **I AM** contracts further **ESSENCE** appears. With further contraction the personal unconscious, the body (nervous system), the external world, and the personal conscious mind are made manifest.

QUANTUM PSYCHOLOGY PRINCIPLE:

What is true at one level may not be true at another level.

So let's begin by differentiating so that we can go beyond each dimension of manifestation in order to liberate awareness (which had become fixated) within each dimension and then to go beyond even awareness and the awarER itself (to be discussed later).

DEVELOPING MULTI-DIMENSIONAL AWARENESS

As mentioned earlier the most frequently asked question is, "How do I maintain my humanness and awareness of my body while keeping spiritually connected?" The possible answer might lie in the ability to develop and maintain multi-dimensional awareness. This means first becoming aware of how and where you place your awareness. For example, if you place your attention solely on an object, then you are using one-dimensional awareness. When "you" split awareness, dividing it half inward (noticing your thinking process) and half outward, "you" are exhibiting two-dimensional awareness. If "you" split attention 1/3 outward, 1/3 on thinking and 1/3 on your emotional dimension, you are exhibiting three-dimensional awareness. If "YOU" split attention 1/4 outward, 1/4 on thinking, 1/4 on your emotional nature, and 1/4 biologically, "you begin to enter into **ESSENCE-I AM**-or-**NOT-I-I**" which is beyond the observer-observed dyad. Then "you" are experiencing four-dimensional awareness. The next step is when awareness is split 1/5 on the external world, 1/5 on the thinking, 1/5 on the emotional process, 1/5 on your animal nature, and1/5 on the **ESSENCE.** Finally, we go beyond into the **I AM** and eventually into the "**NOT-I-I**", which is not observing—but **WITNESSING** the observer-observed dyad while being aware of the **VOID** and as pure awareness.

The question then emerges: "How do we become aware of and maintain all of these dimensions simultaneously?" This next section deals with just this issue. How to deepen and cultivate awareness of these different dimensions so that we can become aware of all eight dimensions of our humanness.

COLLAPSING THE LEVELS

In the early chapters of *The Way of the Human* "I" discussed eight levels or dimensions of manifestation and awareness.

The purpose of Quantum Psychology is to find out **WHO YOU ARE.** The *possible* first step is to liberate your awareness by first developing the ability to maintain multi-dimensional awareness and then to ultimately go beyond awareness itself. The liberation of awareness could be an aid in the discovery of *"WHO YOU ARE."* Unfortunately, this discovery is greatly inhibited because awareness gets habitually fixated and shrunken. Awareness can be fixated at the external dimension, thinking dimension, emotional dimension, and at the biological dimension. Awareness can even become fixated at the level of **ESSENCE.** Although being fixated on **ESSENCE** might at first seem wonderful, it can lead to problems on different dimensions. For example, being unconditionally loving, an essential aspect, is great, but if you lack awareness of the external world, then people could rip you off.

I recently met a woman in Germany who was going through a divorce. Her husband was angry, abusive and trying to "steal" their shared valuables. She said to me, "I am trying to stay in **ESSENCE,**" but I suggested a basic Quantum Psychology Principle: Meet the problem at the level of the problem. In this case, yes, stay in **ESSENCE** and on an external level, hire a lawyer.

QUANTUM PSYCHOLOGY PRINCIPLE:

Meet the problem at the level of the problem.

QUANTUM PSYCHOLOGY PRINCIPLE:

When one level is confused with another, it can yield problems.

QUANTUM PSYCHOLOGY PRINCIPLE:

What is true at one level of awareness is not necessarily true at another level of awareness.

To illustrate, because I believe (thinking dimension) I am a great singer or surgeon does not mean I can sing at Lincoln Center or perform surgery at John Hopkins (External Level). The belief that I am a surgeon is a true belief at the thinking dimension, but it is not true in the external dimension.

If I experience flying in a dream (Collective Dimension), it does not mean *my body* can fly. If I am at the level of **VOID**, it does not mean that there will no longer be feelings at the emotional level. As will be demonstrated, confusing levels can cause misunderstanding and pain.

What I have seen is that *any habitual fixation of awareness in any dimension creates an experiential limitation from the full spectrum of humanity*. One of the purposes of Quantum Psychology, therefore, is to develop a *functional awareness*. This means that in the beginning stages, while awareness is still there, developing the ability to place awareness in any dimension. To paraphrase, noted Sufi Master Indries Shah, "In order to be free, we must be able to gain choice over where we place our awareness."

SUMMARY OF THE DIMENSIONS

Please note, the line connects all dimensions showing that they are connected and influence each other; however, they do have different functions:

EXTERNAL DIMENSION
|
THINKING DIMENSION
|
EMOTIONAL DIMENSION
|
BIOLOGICAL DIMENSION
|

— — — — — — — — — — — —

ESSENCE
|
I AM
|
COLLECTIVE ARCHETYPAL DIMENSION
|
"NOT I-I"

_____

THE VOID OF UNDIFFERENTIATED CONSCIOUSNESS

THE NAMELESS ABSOLUTE

BEYOND

What is
true at the
External Dimension
may not be
true at
other Dimensions.

CHAPTER V
THE EXTERNAL DIMENSION
OF MANIFESTATION

"You never put your foot in the same river twice"

DIMENSION I: THE EXTERNAL WORLD

At first glance, we would say, "Oh, that's easy. Just be aware of what's happening around you." The ability to experience the external is to see people, situations, objects, etc., without using your thoughts, memories, emotions, associations or perceptions. To illustrate the difficulty of this, let's say I meet someone who reminds me of someone I once knew. "I" begin to relate to "my" internal memory and go "self" to "self," in the process losing my sense of present time reality. In other words, (as mentioned *in Trances People Live*), I go into a trance. I lose the external *NOW* and present time reality.

This problem of going self to self can be seen when I say that "you remind me of (*fill in the blank*)" or "this (situation, event, therapy, etc.,) is just like (*fill in the blank*)." The tendency to imagine that the present time is the same as the past is a generalizing survival function of the nervous system, and in Quantum Psychology we call this process the Associational Trance. The Associational Trance occurs when the scanning and searching device of the nervous system generalizes automatically in order to maintain its survival by assuming that the past is exactly like the present. "You" are no longer able to see differences between people, situations, or events. What the Associational Trance does is to shift the chaos of "not knowing" the present time reality onto a past associational reality, so that the present time is no longer a problem. For example, let's say Dad was mean, as well as tall, and I had to defend myself against him. The nervous system automatically goes into defense against tall men whether they are mean or not. Thus the associational trance robs the person of present time experience.

To further illustrate, a psychologist from New York kept on assuming I was *just like* her husband. When she talked about Quantum Psychology she thought it was "*just like*" the training she was receiving. Thus, her present time chaos of "not knowing" what to do or say or what was appropriate was temporarily ordered. "I" was like her husband and "my" work was the same as hers.

And so the intention in developing the first dimension of awareness of the external world is so that you can experience present-time reality without being burdened by past experiences or associations. This is quite difficult because our minds at this level are a by-product of the nervous system and continually create associations, over and over again

The external world is the dimension of reality which deals with people, objects and things. For example, the reality that if I jumped out of my apartment window, the *probability* is that my physical body would be badly hurt. That is a high *probability* in the external world, regardless of what I believe. Another *probability* is, if I want to buy something, I have to have enough money to pay for it. If I walk out of a store without paying, then there *probably* will be consequences. The external world *is* the external world. It exists. It is the lack of the acknowledgment, the fixating on one dimension or confusing it for another or trying to overcome and even heal one dimension with another which can cause the loss of awareness and pain.

The external world is simply—there's a chair, there's a person, understand there's a context which rules each culture. In this world, we often don't experience things as they really are. Rather we experience our ideas or associations about who or what we're dealing with (thinking dimension). For example, you meet somebody and you find there is an enormous lack of communication. Why?

Because you do not treat them in present time, nor are they treating you in present time. You are relating to them out of an image, idea or trance from the thinking or emotional dimension. Simply put, you are treating the present time external world and people "as if" they were the past. *Worse yet, you do not know it.* This was the crux of *Trances People Live* and *The Dark Side of the Inner Child*, namely, losing a sense of what is happening in the present time external level, and *trancing-out.*

Relationships generally begin with the external world because you usually meet people in the context in which you live, work, play, and where your interests lie.

THE EXTERNAL CONTEXT RULES

Different contexts or external circumstances pull out different internal responses. To illustrate, imagine everything is going well in your life. You are not in a relationship, but work, friends, etc., are fine and you are feeling good about yourself. Soon you meet someone and it gets sexual. All of a sudden your psychological and emotional issues begin to come up. Why? *Different externals pull up different unresolved internals.*

EXERCISES FOR THE FIRST DIMENSION OF AWARENESS THE EXTERNAL WORLD

Exercise #1

Step I: Eyes open. Slowly look around the room at people and objects. Notice the memories, internal voices, and associations which automatically "pop up" for you.

Exercise #2

Step I: Now without using your thoughts, memory, emotions, associations or perceptions, look around the room.

Step II: Notice the difference in your experience between Exercise #1 and Exercise #2.

Practice:

Take some time to explore for a few hours a day being with people in your life *"without using your memory, mind, associations or perceptions."*

THE EXTERNAL DOMINATES

The external is dominant. People in the healing arts and in the New Age sometimes negate the external. They "believe" (thinking dimension) that they can master or control the external through their internal thoughts, beliefs, or images (see thinking dimension). This, as will be discussed throughout, is not only trying to overcome one dimension with another, but it also demonstrates what is labeled in psychoanalytic developmental psychology as *Infantile Grandiosity.*

To illustrate this, imagine you want to open up a shirt shop on *this* street where there are 47 shirt shops. No matter how clear you are, no matter how much you work with your beliefs or your issues around your mother and father, or how much you've prayed or visualized, the *probability* of success is greatly reduced. The external context is dominant. *Whatever you have not processed (uncooked seeds), the external context will oftentimes bring it up.* (Its connection to, and unity with, other dimensions will be discussed in Volume II, The False Core and the False Self.)

At each age, the external world will bring up different developmental issues. As you go through different external contexts with different challenges they will bring up different *uncooked seeds*. For example, in one Quantum Psychology training, after the first or second day of the workshop there was a man who said, "I don't know what's going on, I feel like I'm age-regressed. Normally I don't feel this way." I asked him how he felt and he said, "I feel like I'm in school, like I'm five years old and just starting school." He was withdrawn, he was trying to disappear, he was not aware that he was trying to accumulate information. In fact, he was always complaining about about there being "no hand-outs." He was "acting out" the False Core of, "I do not exist" (to be discussed later) and he was age-regressing back to being a five-year old facing the challenge of beginning school. It's when you start your social life, when you leave home and start going to school.

In this way each age has a different context and a different developmental challenge to deal with, one in which you unknowingly bring your past *uncooked seeds* to meet (unsuccessfully) that new challenge. In other words, (see *Volume II, Quantum Psychology and the False Core-False Self*), your *uncooked seeds* are taken with you to meet each new context. For that reason, each new external is not seen anew. Rather it is seen through the lens of the past. The seed of the past forms the *root* of your present time subjective experience. The saying, "You can never put your foot in the same river twice," clarifies that the Associational Trance of the False Core makes you believe it is the same river (situation). No matter what the situation, you find yourself acting the same way "as if" it were the same. Because of this you cannot experience Suzuki Roshi's *Zen mind—a Beginner's Mind.*

In spiritual circles the external world is often negated entirely for the "inner" world. In India, I would often hear gurus say that "inner bliss is greater than outer bliss." In many psychology and New Age circles, the external world is really underrated or is seen as a problem to be solved. There is oftentimes a presupposition that if you handle "your" psychological beliefs (thinking dimension), you are going to have what you want in your external life. That statement is only true given the context. As I said before, if I solved all "my psychological problems" and wanted to open a clothing store on a street where there are many other stores, even if my psychology is clear and I'm focused, it might be a total flop.

The old saying, "Do what you love and the money will come," demonstrates both the collapsing of the levels and a neglect for the external context. A more accurate saying would be, "Do what you love and if the external context supports it the money *might*(?) follow." The distortion is, *"If I am clear about it and I want it, then I will get it," fuses together "wanting equals getting,"* as if wanting something had something to do with getting it. It's nice to be clear about what you want, but you need to look at the context in which you are trying to manifest this since context is the major component in manifestation. In other words, *your perceptions must be grounded in physical reality* otherwise you will be misled by the infantile understanding which collapses the levels and manifests as the distortion—"If I control my internal (beliefs, images, etc.), I can control my external" (the world). This can be related back to a child who, when they control their feelings, actions, thoughts, etc., mom or dad gives them what they want. They are told by mom and dad they got what they wanted because they deserved it for being good. Years later, they trance-fer mom and dad onto the world or God, imagining if they control their internal, and are good and virtuous, according to mom/dad's standards, they will get what they want from the world or God (mom/dad). because they *deserve* it.

If you don't handle the external world and pay attention to the context in which you are living, at some point it will come up and bite you. You'll be blind-sided. The external world will pull up that which is unprocessed (*uncooked seeds*). Gurus come to America or to Europe and all of a sudden, their biology is ignited or their images (thinking dimensions) come up and they want money and power. Initially a Guru wears rags but soon they have to *have* silk, they have to *have* people waiting on them. Thus the external which is holographically related to the other dimensions brings up their *uncooked seeds*. So, ultimately, whether you think the external context is crazy or not crazy, you still have to acknowledge it.

NOTICING THE DIFFERENCE[1]

The following two exercises are open-eyed. The first one involves practice with objects in the room. When you try this exercise, you might want to practice with a small group since it is often clearer when you make eye-contact with a partner, then switch in the middle to another partner.

Stabilizing Awareness:

---

[1]The following exercises are in *Quantum Consciousness* and *Hearts on Fire*. If you've done them and do not need a review—skip these pages

74

Look at an object in the room and then withdraw your energy from it, thus, eliminating the knowledge of the object along with the thought or impression (Vijnana Bhairava, Jaideva Singh).

Practice:
First, pick an object in the room. Now I'd like you to begin to pull back your attention. In other words, your attention is moving forward, going out toward a particular object, like the couch, for instance. Pull your attention back. As you look at an object, pull your energy back *prior* to having the impression or knowledge of the object.

A student commented that she could get beyond the knowledge of the object except for its color. "You will continue to see the color," I said, "but it will no longer register as, say, the rug in the living room. In other words, the color is still there, it's not going to disappear, but you're moving, withdrawing your energy prior to the thought and impression, even the knowledge of it.

I'd like you to pair up with a partner for this next practice.

Practice:
Let your eyes close for a second, then make eye contact with your partner. Let your attention withdraw, *prior to* any knowledge or information or any impressions or thoughts you have about that person. Turn your attention backward, withdrawing it backward. Next, let your eyes close again. Make eye contact with another person, and again gently withdraw your attention *prior to* any thoughts or impressions or information you have about that person. Find the space prior to any thought information; withdraw your attention *prior to.*

"Everything went out of focus," one student said, "And my partners began to become less solid. It was really interesting because what I noticed was, the more I looked from back there, the less solid she became and that there was this great big light around everything and then the moment of complete detachment came."

Another student commented, "The focusing happened very

fast for me and I lost the boundaries of objects." In response to this student, "I" said, "Everything loses its form because we (the nervous system) make a form like a chair appear solid by the concept we hold of it. In other words our Nervous System makes the unseen Quantum World solid by seeing ideas and images of the object, not the object itself

This is a good method to use if you're in a relationship and you're in the middle of a heated discussion—*if you can remember* to do this with them, to drop all of your concepts and move *prior* to any impressions, information or knowledge about that other person. If used, this method of seeing and experiencing from "back there" trains you to do it all the time. In this way, each moment can be experienced right now, in present time, rather than experiencing the present in terms of past explanations you (the nervous system) created about the present.

A student commented, "I felt as if nobody was there, so it feels as if you really end up with nothing. All of a sudden, my partner wasn't there." "I" asked this student if she was here. She said "No, I was getting lost too."

I asked her to do the exercise again with me. "I" said, "Withdraw your attention as you breathe and look at me. What happens?" She said, "I guess I'm constantly seeking meaning, and this strips everything of meaning."

I pointed out to her, "When you say 'meaning', what you are really saying is that you want things to have meaning in life—meaning and purpose. That's the nature of the mind, to seek meaning and purpose. But the mind is not you. Now, I'm not saying you shouldn't look for meaning, but let your mind do it. You **WITNESS.** If you jump in there, and try to figure it out, you'll get burned out. I'm saying let your mind do whatever it does." She said, "I guess I'm looking for a state of peace or happiness." I repeated Nisargadatta Maharaj's reply when someone said, "I want to be happy": "That's nonsense," he said, "Happiness is—where the *I* isn't."

W hat is true
at the Thinking
Dimension may
not be true
at any other
dimension.

CHAPTER VI
THE THINKING DIMENSION OF MANIFESTATION

The Second Dimension of Manifestation represents the development of awareness at the Thinking Dimension.

It involves not only our thoughts and images but also fantasies, values, beliefs, concepts, ideas and perceptions. In order to understand this dimension, it is necessary to deepen "our" internal focus and develop our awareness of what is happening inside our psyche. Otherwise we will never see present time, never experience people or situations or objects in the here-and-now.

Thoughts and images do not create external reality, a point often misunderstood. However, they do create our interpretation and our internal subjective experience of our external reality, if we believe them. And hence our subjective experience of the internal gets projected onto the external. For example, if I change my thought called "You do not like me" to "You like me," "I" internally might have the experience of, "You like me" but whether *you* like me or not might not be affected. Why is it important to know how the internal thinking world works?

Nisargadatta Maharaj was once asked, "Why should we meditate (enquire)?" He replied,

> Of the outer world, we know a lot. Of the inner world,
> we know very little. Anything that you do not know
> about, you are the slave of; anything you know about

you can be free of. Therefore, we meditate to know and be free of the unknown material in our consciousness.

UNCOOKED SEEDS

The external world is oftentimes neglected in both psychological and New Age spiritual circles. It is imagined and *thought* to be dominated by our beliefs, traumas, etc., hence the New Age expression, "Our thoughts create reality." But thoughts are on one dimension and the external world is on another. They are connected but they have different functions. Remember, *thoughts help to create our subjective internal reality* but not necessarily our external reality.

This represents the collapsing and confusing the thinking dimension with the external dimension. Imagine a guru who sits in a protected external world where all his needs are met, food, clothing, etc., He is able to sit somewhere in **ESSENCE, I AM**, etc., Change the context (the external) and his unprocessed psychology (thoughts, etc.,) comes up for him. For example, when gurus come to America or Europe, they get into money and sex. As mentioned before, you might be living your life and have everything going well for you. But then you get involved with somebody sexually and all of a sudden the external context changes and all your unresolved issues (uncooked seeds) come up.

The best metaphor "I" know to describe this phenomenon is from India and it is called *Uncooked Seeds*. To explain, if I have seeds and I put them in the ground and water them, I will soon get plants which bear fruit. But if I first take the seeds, put them in a frying pan and *cook them*, and then put them in the ground, they won't grow or bear fruit. *Awareness is the heat that cooks uncooked seeds (unprocessed) concepts.* In this way, Quantum Psychology uses awareness as the stove to cook the uncooked seeds (beliefs, concepts, points of view, etc.,) so that they no longer sprout.

Going back to our guru, this is what happens. If they sit alone somewhere in a cave, there is no issue. It's really easy to be pure awareness with your eyes closed while people bring you whatever you need. But if you put them back into a relationship or into the world making a living, I don't care who it is, their *uncooked seeds* are going to sprout. That's why, when gurus come to the West, all of sudden they want money, sex, meditation centers, brochures and have a mission (from God). Unfortunately, most teachers or gurus rather than acknowledging their "uncooked seeds" go into the trance of spiritualization, (*Dark Side of the Inner Child*, Chapter 14). Sex becomes tantra, and desiring fame and money become a *mission* from God. In short, before you know it, all their *uncooked seeds pop-up* and then get spiritualized. So as you can see, it's easy for some gurus to say, "I am not the doer" when everything is being done for them. In other words, *their philosophy matches the context.*

There is a famous Sufi story about Sheik Nasudin. He was tending his flower garden and went inside for a moment. A goat chewed through the rope in the garden and began to eat the flowers. Nasudin came out of the house, saw this and began to beat the goat with a stick. A man passing by yelled at Nasudin, "Stop, how can you beat a poor defenseless goat?" Nasudin replied "I am not the doer, God does everything, I do nothing." The passerby fell to his knees, touching Nasudin's feet. "Oh I am so sorry, I did not realize you were an enlightened saint, please forgive me. By the way," the passerby continued, "This is a beautiful garden, who made such a beautiful garden?" Nasudin replied "*I DID.*"

The external context brings up your uncooked seeds. Each new context will yield different uncooked seeds. It should be noted that the nervous system contains an associational trance which has a scanning-searching-seeking device which has a generalizing tendency which serves as a survival mechanism of the nervous system, which makes the past into the present and represents a major defense against an unpleasant external which can bring up unwanted or denied uncooked seeds. For example, I saw a client whose sexual relationship with her husband was non-existent. She responded in the following ways: First, when she met a man she was turned on to, she treated him just like her husband, so there was no sexual charge. Second, she took medication to repress her sexual feelings. And, third, she held a past time concept of no sexual feelings being allowed outside of her marriage which further repressed her present time sexual feelings.

MEDITATION AND UNCOOKED SEEDS

You can get into a great state of meditation, but unless the psychological and emotional issues are really clear, you will immediately identify with your issues and move out of **ESSENCE-I AM NOT-I-I**, etc., We have all been hypnotized and, actually, the whole game is about becoming dehypnotized or "getting," in the words of Nisargadatta Maharaj, that "whatever you think you are—you are not."

Quantum Psychology explores the liberation of awareness which is *DE*-**HYPNOSIS**. Someone asked me a question about meditation. "Doesn't it help?" Yes, meditation can lead to Samadh which means "no me." But that awareness can rarely be stabilized as long as other dimensions are not looked at and gone beyond.

It is like the story told by Swami Muktananda about people who bathe in the Ganges. In India it is believed that if you bathe in the Ganges your sins are washed away. But sins (uncooked seeds), according to Mukananda, go up into the trees so that after you come out of the water (meditation), they jump back on you.

This is the problem with refusing to look at issues that arise in the thinking or emotional dimension and stabilizing in the no-state state. In meditation, "I" could sit quietly and enter into the **NOT-I-I** or disappear in the **VOID**. However, like the Ganges, "I" would be bathed and my sins (uncooked seeds) would disappear. But shortly after "I" arose from meditation (the Ganges) my mind with all its issues would come back.

The next step after **the first dimension of awareness of the external** is to develop a *two-dimensional awareness* by incorporating the thinking dimension. Often, in relationships we lose ourselves by focusing on our partner. Others lose their connection because they remain distant and aloof. Thus the double-bind of either "I have a relationship and lose myself," or "I have myself and don't have a relationship." This creates some of the conflicts that constantly arise in relationships. I am often asked in workshops, "How can I have myself [my own space] and still have a connection with another [a relationship]?"

This exercise suggests you can have both by splitting your attention inside and outside so that they are equally balanced. To repeat the approach given by Fourth Way teacher, G. I. Gurdjieff to his well-known student, P. D. Ouspensky,

> When I pay attention to the external world, I am like an arrow pointing outward. When I close my eyes and sink into myself, my attention becomes an arrow pointing inwards. Now, I try to do both at once—to point the arrow in and out at the same time—I immediately discover that this is incredibly difficult. After a second or two, I either forget the outside world, and sink into a daydream, or forget myself and become absorbed in what I am looking at (Ouspensky, 1949).

This approach asks the practitioner to do precisely this technique of self-remembering: To focus on the thinking dimension (inside) and the external world (outside), simultaneously, and in a balanced way. Ultimately in Quantum Psychology, we will later ask much more, i.e., to focus on three or more dimensions simultaneously.

The thinking world contains our beliefs, trances, assumptions, decisions, and values at a thinking level. It comprises not only what we think and believe, but also the world of images. For example, imagine you are sitting and all of a sudden you have an image of the beach, or you have an image of the mountains, or you have an image of the relationship that you want, or you have an image of your mother, or your father, or a past event, or a future event—all those different images are part of the thinking world. Of course, emotions are involved and connected with beliefs, but as we see the levels, we realize that they have different functions.

Unfortunately, we often favor one dimension of reality over another. For example, we might be in a conversation with somebody, let's say a lover, and all of a sudden we go into a fantasy about their breaking up with us. That fantasy moves us from a present time relationship of the external dimension into our thinking dimension. We lose our present time reality. In *Trances People Live: Healing Approaches in Quantum Psychology,* I call that going into a trance and losing present time reality. What happens when we do that is we *no longer see the person in present time, but rather we have, and relate to, an idea we have about them.*

We (the nervous system) infer and abstract, omitting certain things and selecting out others, becoming ultimately dominated by the thinking world over the present time experience of the external world. The noted father of General Semantics, Alfred Korzybski, would have said, "The map is not the territory." In Quantum Psychology terms, this means you have an idea or an inference about the external world which is not the external world. For example, if I suddenly imagine the person I am with is going to leave me and fixate on those thoughts and images, then not only do I lose the present time now and who they are in present time; but I also begin to make certain *inferences*. I select out certain things from the situation and their behavior and decide what their behavior might *mean*. Creating and adding meaning to situations is a resistance to chaos, created by the nervous system (to be discussed later).

QUANTUM PSYCHOLOGY PRINCIPLE:

Any dissociation or loss of awareness from *any* dimension of reality causes a loss in the experience of the multi-dimensional universe.

QUANTUM PSYCHOLOGY PRINCIPLE:

Any dissociation from any dimension causes a loss in our humanness.

QUANTUM PSYCHOLOGY PRINCIPLE:

Any dissociation from, or fixation on, any dimension creates an accompanying loss of present-time reality.

QUANTUM PSYCHOLOGY PRINCIPLE:

The more awareness of dimensions that is available, the greater the "subjective" experience of freedom. The less dimensions of awareness available, the less the "subjective" experience of freedom.

The thinking dimension contains our thoughts, fantasies and images. If, without warning, the memory of your mother pops up, this image is at the thinking dimension. The emotion you feel is on the emotional dimension. When a trauma occurs, there is a fusion or collapsing of the dimensions. This is why traumatic experiences are so difficult to deal with because all the dimensions are merged together.

In the following section, we will introduce several exercises to develop awareness of the thinking dimension.

THINKING DIMENSION
EXERCISE #1[1]

Focus:
When a thought arises, ask "From where does that thought arise?"

When we ask ourselves, "From where does that thought arise?" we soon learn that a thought arises and subsides and that there is a space in between. Asking ourselves after each thought, "From where does that thought arise?" brings us back to that space so that we can observe the rising and subsiding of each thought, acknowledging what it is, how it impacts our subjective experience and letting it go.

Imagine waking up in the morning lying next to the person you love. A thought comes into your mind, "This is far out, I really like this." Then, all of sudden your mind thinks," I like the way they look," or "I like how they are," or "I like the way he/she sleeps next

---

[1]Many of these exercises are in *Quantum Consciousness* and *Hearts of Fire*. If you do not need a review—skip them.

to me," etc. Two or three days later, you wake up and look at your lover and a thought goes by, "Oh, no, what am I doing with her/him?" The next thing you find yourself thinking, "I really would like to go out with somebody else," or "Maybe I should get a divorce," or "What a mistake, I am wasting my time."

An even more common experience is to wake up in the morning feeling very good; a thought goes by your awareness called "I feel good" and you identify with that thought. Your mind will then start coming up with reasons why you feel good: "I feel good *because* I got a lot of sleep." "I feel good *because* I didn't sleep very much." "I feel good *because* I meditated this morning." "I feel good *because* I had a lot for dinner." "I feel good *because* I didn't' have a lot for dinner."

Around noon, a thought goes by which says, "I'm tired," and if you identify with that thought, you might say, "I'm tired, why do I have to go to work? It's such a drag. I knew I slept too much—or I didn't sleep enough," or whatever the sequence of events you might be experiencing. What happens is, a thought arises and subsides, and there's a space. This is the way thoughts occur: they arise, and subside—and there's space.

The purpose of this practice is to bring you back into the space between two thoughts or *prior* to your last thought. Understand that anything you identify with yields a limiting experience.

For example, a thought goes by called "I feel good," or "I feel bad, I wish I were there, I'm here, I wish I weren't here." If a thought comes by that says, "I don't understand," you identify with it and then begin a chain of associations like "I don't understand," "I never understood anything," "This is my story."

But anything you identify yourself with as "I" will limit you. The nature of the mind is to always change its mind; that's why one minute you like your job, the next you don't. One minute you like your relationship, the next you don't. One day you're really happy with the course of your life, the next day you're not. If you fall in love today, tomorrow you won't like the person so much. Therefore, you can't depend on your thoughts.

And so there is no answer to the question, "From where does this thought arise." But notice what happens if you ask that question and look for the space from which each thought arises The thing to remember is—who is the knower of "your" thoughts (to be discussed in Volume III).

I once worked with a married couple in a workshop. The couple had paired up with one another, asking each other, "From where does that thought arise?" The woman stopped her inquiring, looked at me, and said "I'm trying to think of something to say—I'm always trying to think of something to say." I replied, "That's the story of your life," and she answered, "Yes." That thought "I should say something" went by and she identified it as herself. She would then run all her trips about how and why she never knew what she should say.

So as thoughts arise, keep asking yourself, "From where does that thought arise?"

If there is a thought called "I'm afraid," you identified with it and feel like "That's me." Then suddenly your mind said, "I'm afraid because I don't have enough money." "I'm fearful because my relationship is screwed up," "I afraid because *(fill in the blank)*." The minute you identify with any thought, you have all of the *associated* psycho-emotional reactions, such as "I'm afraid," and your mind will give you a thousand reasons why you're afraid, or why you should be afraid three weeks from now. Such as, "What if I lose my job," or "What if the person I'm living with leaves me." One of the basic principles of Jnana Yoga is that you are not your thoughts. Please note that the *reason* or idea you have about why you are afraid comes after the experience has passed. If you try to solve the problem presented like "I am afraid because I am unloved," by getting your spouse to do more "loving" things, you are creating a solution to a False conclusion which means the solution must also be False (Volume II).

Nisargadatta Maharaj once asked Jean Dunn, who was taping his most recent talk and planning to write a book, "What is the name of my next book?" (As if he cared!) She replied, "Beyond Consciousness." He said, "No, no. The name should be *Prior to Consciousness, prior* to your last thought, *prior* to the thought that you're having, stay there."

Practice:
Watch the thoughts coming into your awareness. Each time a thought comes through, ask yourself, "From where does this thought arise?

I was once sitting with Nisargadatta Maharaj when a psychiatrist and his wife who were visiting from France came over to him. The psychiatrist asked a very long-winded question about birth and death, going on and on. Maharaj looked at him, then asked, "Who told you that you exist?" The psychiatrist looked at his wife and his wife looked at him (I was sitting behind them) and Nisargadatta said, "Your mind tells you 'you' exist. Consciousness tells you 'you' exist and you believe it. If you understand just that, it's enough."

In relationships a thought comes by called "I'm angry with you," and suddenly I believe it. The next thing I know, I've identified with the thought called "I'm angry with you." My mind will then come up with reasons why. For example, I'm angry with you because you're too tall or you're too short or I need less affection or I need more affection. So if I'm in a relationship with you, and I identify with the thought called "I want you to be taller," you might say, "Okay I'll wear high heels and do my hair up in a bun!" When you buy into my thoughts of you, you may try to resist them as a way to a-void your False Core (Volume II).

A basic teaching might therefore be stated as turning your attention to the changeless space that's always there.

THINKING DIMENSION EXERCISE #2

Focus:
When a thought arises, ask yourself, "To whom does this thought arise?" Answer: "To me." Then ask, "Who is this 'I'?" (Ramana Maharshi)

One of the purposes of this method is to separate the transient "I thoughts" of the thinking dimension. In this way we can observe them, see how they impact our life by constructing our internal subjective reality so that we can "let it go" or in Nisargadatta Maharaj's words "discard it." The process is as follows: *Only when a thought arises* ask yourself, "To whom does this thought arise?" Answer to yourself, "To me." Then ask, "Who is this I?" This approach moves the "I" thought from being the subject (you), to making the "I" thought an object to be observed. The "I thought" will disappear and another "I thought" will appear and take its place.

This process can be done with a partner. Pair up with partner. Make direct eye contact with them. Whenever a thought comes into the mind, the first person says it out loud. For example, "I don't like it," "I do like it," "it's hot," "it's cold," "I wish I weren't here," whatever the thought is. The second person, sitting opposite asks the question, "To whom does this thought arise?" The first person responds "To me," and the second then asks "Who is this I?"

A student asked, "Is there an answer to the question, 'Who is this I?'" "I" replied, "To whom does that thought arise called, Is there an answer to the question?" "To me," she replied. I then asked, "Who is this I?" She said, "The thought disappeared." When a thought comes into your mind, ask, "To whom does that thought arise?" Answer, "To me." Ask, "Who is this I?" A student once said, "I don't think I know what I'm doing." "I" asked him, "To whom does that thought arise?" He answered, "To me." I asked, "Who is this I?" and continued, "Notice that there is a space that opens up after the question, Who is this I?'"

To repeat, anything that you believe about yourself is limiting: "I feel good," "I feel bad," "I'm tall, short, fat, thin, ugly." Whatever thought comes into mind that you identify with will limit you, it doesn't matter what the content is. "I like it here," "I love myself," "I hate myself"—they are all thoughts. When a thought arises like, "I feel good," ask, "To whom does this thought arise?" Answer, "To me." Then ask, "Who is this I?" Begin to notice that there's a space at the end of that question. Notice that space.

When "I" was in India, "I" used to start meditation at 3:00 a.m. One morning "I" was meditating in the cave and a thought came by, "It's an uphill battle all the way." It arose very gently. "I" looked at it and "I" asked, "Who is this I?" and it disappeared. The truth was that I had experienced my whole life as an uphill battle all the way, which is what my mother had always told me. This assumption about life had been outside of my awareness and I had never questioned it. But once I questioned this thought—it disappeared. I would say that one of the major things Nisargadatta Maharaj has taught "me" is how to enquire.

Meher Baba once described the ego—or the "I"—as being like an iceberg. All you can see is 10% of the iceberg and the other 90% is under water (outside of "your" awareness) so you can't see it. As you begin to enquire what is underneath, the water starts to come up. You don't have to do anything with it, just notice that it's there, how it constricts your internal subjective reality and impacts your life—then "discard it."

If a thought goes through your awareness called "It's difficult" and you identify with it, your mind will work out a whole story to validate the "I" thought you identified with. "I was never able to do it," "I never could do it," "I knew I shouldn't have come here," "I knew I should have gone to the movies," and on and on. The content of your story doesn't matter. The minute you identify with "It's difficult," then the whole chain of associations begins and that's what your experience will be. Suppose you had an opposite reaction—that "this is great," and you identify and fuse with that. Then you have an experience of its being great. To repeat an earlier story, a student came to Nisargadatta Maharaj and said "I want to be happy." Nisargadatta Maharaj replied, "That's nonsense. Happiness is where the 'I' isn't."

You are not your associations or patterns. That's not who you are. Stay *prior* to it.

Practice:
Again, you don't have to think of an answer. I'd like you to let your eyes close very gently. Notice the way you're sitting. As thoughts arise in your consciousness, I'd like you to ask yourself, "To whom does this thought arise?" Answer, "To me." Then ask, "Who is this I?" and notice what happens.

THINKING DIMENSION EXERCISE #3

Focus:
When a thought arises ask, "Who told you that?" then answer, "The mind."

The purpose of this practice is to cultivate the understanding that all information comes from the mind. To emphasize this, since it is the nature of the mind to always change its mind, it is apparent that one must understand that thoughts are the mind. By practicing this meditation, the identification with the "mind stuff" loosens its grip. Nisargadatta Maharaj used to say, "To go beyond the mind you must look away from the mind and its contents."

This practice can be done with a partner. Each time a thought arises, ask yourself, "Who told you that?" Then answer, "The mind." Whenever anything comes into your awareness, the question will be asked of you by a partner, "Who told you that?" and the answer is, "The mind." The only way you could possibly know what you are feeling or experiencing is if the voice in the back of your head says, "I'm happy" or "I'm sad"or whatever.

A student asked, "Why is it *the* mind?" I replied, "Because it's made of thoughts. Thoughts that are identified with, become my thoughts. So, really, it's *the* mind and *the* thoughts. Also, for the seeding for future understanding, there is only one mind, not many minds (to be discussed in Volume III).

Practice:
I'd like you to sit for about seven to ten minutes and notice each thought as it comes through your awareness. Say to yourself, "Who told you that?" Then answer, "The mind."

The aim is to not identify with anything that comes through your mind. There's a book by a woman saint, Ananda Mayi Ma, who died about 1980. When people asked her a question, she always said "The body thinks or the mind thinks," rather than "I think."

THINKING DIMENSION EXERCISE #4

Focus:
Each time a thought arises ask, "Where does that thought subside to?"

This teaching is from Ramana Maharshi, the 20th century sage and teacher of self-enquiry. A thought arises and subsides: notice where that thought subsides. Is there is an answer to this question? NO. We're noticing the space. Once you're in that space, there won't be anything. There will be nothing. Then another thought will arise called, "I don't know if I got it or not." Notice where that thought subsides to.

A student asked for a comment on images coming in because he found them to be the only thing that he was aware of. He thought perhaps he should be analyzing the images. Ramana Maharishi used to say, "When you're cleaning your house, you do not need to analyze the dirt." I told this student to slow the process down so that each image was like a movie frame. In the same way, if you slow down a film strip, what you have is the space between frames—which you could jump through. Thoughts and images appear like a stream of inter-connected consciousness, but actually there is a space from which each one arises and subsides back into.

Practice:
As thoughts come into your awareness, begin to notice, "Where does that thought subside to?" Follow the thought to the space where it subsides. There will be a space and then another thought will arise.WITNESS it. Where does that thought subside to?

THINKING DIMENSION EXERCISE #5

Focus:
Each time a thought arises, ask, "Whose thoughts are these?"

Practice:
Watch the thoughts that stream through your awareness. Ask yourself, "Whose thoughts are these?" Thoughts are always going by from the one mind. For some of them you're saying, "That's me," and for others, "That's not me." Ask, "Whose thoughts are these?"

You can't control the thoughts you're going to have five or ten minutes from now so why try to control them now?" Swami Prakashananda once said, "You can't even control very much the next time you're going to go to the bathroom. So let happen what happens. You WITNESS."

A Quantum Psychology principle is that in every thought there is an observer of the thought, a knower of the thought and a thinker of the thought. In other words, it is an illusion to imagine that there is a thought and a thinker of the thought. There is just thinking, *the observer and the knower and the thinker of the thought are contained within the thought itself.*

The basic principle of Kashmir Shaivism, which is the second aphorism of the Shiva Sutras, is Jnanam Bandhah: "Knowledge is bondage." It says that anything you know (about yourself or the world) will bind you. You think you're smart; you think you're strong; you think you're unlovable; you think you're spiritual; you think you're worthless. Whatever it is, what you know about yourself will limit your experience. Knowledge therefore is bondage.

EXERCISE #6

Step I: Notice a thought or feeling you are having.

Step II: Withdraw your attention from the thought or feeling prior to any knowledge or information about what the thought or feeling is.

Step III: View the thought or emotion from that space, like you are seeing the thought or feeling for the first time.

Step IV: Notice what happens.

CULTIVATING THE SECOND DIMENSIONAL AWARENESS

ASPECTS OF CONSCIOUSNESS[2]

Differentiated Consciousness involves the making of distinctions. It is that subtle something which makes distinctions.[3] It is that subtle something which makes distinctions.[4] For example, differentiated consciousness lets us know the difference between a table and a chair, your arm and my head. On a more subtle level, it lets us know the difference between a thought and a feeling, a sound and a vision, a memory and present time. Unfortunately, however, consciousness frequently muddles these distinctions, which causes chaos and confusion as to what is occurring in the present time, what occurred in the past of which we have a memory, and in an even more subtle way, which are "my" feelings and which are "your" feelings.

Before we can appreciate the **VOID OF UNDIFFERENTIATED CONSCIOUSNESS**, it might be helpful to distinguish the different aspects of consciousness and what they are. I discussed this approach in relation to trances in *Trances People Live* (1986) and *The Dark Side of the Inner Child*. As "I" mentioned earlier, Nisargadatta Maharaj once said, "You must first know what something is before you can give it up."

---

[2]This process was originally written about in *Trance People Live—Healing Approaches in Quantum Psychology* (1991).
[3]*The Shuranyama Sutra*, Buddhist Text Translation Society, Volume 3 (1980), California: The Sino-American Buddhist Association, p. 22.
[4]Please note that differentiated consciousness possesses a separate "I" which has all the psychological aspects of preferences, comparisons, etc. **UNDIFFERENTIATED CONSCIOUSNESS** does not have or know preferences or comparisons. **UNDIFFERENTIATED CONSCIOUSNESS** is **VOID**er than the **VOID** itself and has no separate "I." Hence, the Zen patriarch said "The great way is easy, except for those who have preferences."

Our first step in this process is to identify and define the aspects of consciousness, which often act as trances, so that we can begin to get clear about the meaning of the words and notice how they take us out of present-time reality.

THOUGHT is the single act of thinking; an idea or a notion.[5]

INTERNAL DIALOGUE: Also referred to in *Trances People Live* as a post-hypnotic suggestion. These are internal voices which suggest certain outcomes. For example, the internal voice: "It will never work out," or "I know you're going to break up with me so I'll detach and won't get involved."

INTUITION: A direct understanding independent of any reasoning process. An immediate cognition of an object not inferred or determined by a previous cognition.

Therapeutic Note

I want to give an example of intuition since it's often confused with training. Let's say someone comes to me for therapy and says, "I have a problem with relationships." If I say, "I wonder if this has something to do with your parents," this is not intuition, it's training. If I say to the client, "Did you have a dog named Fred who died when you were two?" that's intuition. To paraphrase Pir Vilayat, a Sufi teacher, intuition is when there is no way you could have known it Training is what you have been trained to know or do.

MEMORY: The mental capacity or faculty of retaining and reviving impressions, or of recalling or recognizing previous experiences.

---

[5]This definition and those which follow in this chapter are all drawn from *The American College Dictionary*, (Syracuse, NY: Random House, 1963).

BLOCKING OUT: The act of not seeing or remembering an event or situation.

REACTION: Action in response to some influence or event; the action caused by the resistance to another action.

DISSOCIATION: Dissociation is spacing-out, going on automatic pilot or disappearing.

CONFUSION: The act of creating a state of not knowing. Generally, this is caused by not knowing what to do or resisting a present-time occurrence.

FANTASY: A created dream, also called hypnotic dreaming, which is often used to buffer oneself against present-time pain. For example, feeling lonely and depressed and fantasizing someone will come and take you away from all of this.

HALLUCINATION: Existing in imagination or fancy, appearance of mental images. This is when old images like Mom or Dad pop into your awareness without your control.

BELIEF: A solidified thought which can become a value or evaluation of self or the world. It can be attitudinal if it determines a way of life or living.

OBSERVATION: The act of observing a thought, emotion, association, sensation, person, etc. It is part of the thought, association itself although it appears as separate It might appear to always be there or be prior to the thought, etc., when it actually arises with it, and some even believe the observer created it. It is important to note that oftentimes observation contains judgment (this is good or bad), evaluation (this means this or that), and significance (this is more important than that).

WITNESSING: The act of noticing or perceiving (without judgment, evaluation or significance). Beyond the observer-observed dyad.

Therapeutic Note

It is extremely important to note that, ultimately, the observer must fall away in order to stabilize in **ESSENCE I AM, NOT-I-I**, etc. *The observer is part of the personality and the mind* (to be discussed later). To explain further, Quantum Psychology states "Anything you know about cannot be you." Why? Because each knowing belongs to a separate know*er*, and you are beyond the know*er* or the known (see Volume III). Therefore, since you can be aware of the observer—you are not the observer. The observer can have a dissociative tendency. Often the observer can be used to reinforce defenses against unwanted feelings or other dimensions, especially emotional and biological (to be discussed later). As mentioned earlier in Quantum Consciousness, we must be free to merge with and either *be* something or *not be* something. If we are not free to BE it, and NOT BE it, we are not free. This is Quantum Observation, which is different from just observing.[6]

CONDENSATION: a condensed state or form, the act of condensing or shrinking down; the act of reducing a gas or vapor to a liquid or solid form. Condensations are everything. Since "Everything is made of emptiness and form is condensed emptiness," then all of the above are condensations of **THAT ONE CONSCIOUSNESS**.

---

[6]See Wolinsky, *Quantum Consciousness: the Guide to Experiencing Quantum Psychology* (Bramble Volumes 1993).

Therapeutic Note

This is extremely important to understand. Einstein has said that "Everything is emptiness and form is condensed emptiness." In this way, you can begin to see all manifestations as condensed **EMPTINESS**— including the observer-know*er* of thoughts, emotions, and objects. Then the observer and the object disappear. This is a step in moving from the observer-observed know*er*-known dyad into the **NOT-I-I** of pure awareness or **WITNESSING** (see Volume III).

WORKING WITH THE ASPECTS OF CONSCIOUSNESS

EXERCISE #7: USING THE MENU

Step I: During the day, either with eyes open or closed, notice what is happening inside your psycho-emotional processes.

Step II: Identify: Pick from the menu of the aspects of consciousness one or more of the terms that fit your experience. For example, if you have a troublesome thought, call it a thought; if you have a troublesome internal voice, call it an internal dialogue. In this way, you will be able to differentiate between the different aspects of consciousness.

Step III: Dialogue with the aspect. Ask the aspect, "What are you resisting knowing about yourself?" Write down your answers until nothing "pops up."

Step IV: Notice what the aspect is resisting as you continue to enquire.

Step V: Realizing what the aspect is ultimately resisting, allow the aspect to experience what it is resisting and then notice the

EMPTINESS surrounding it and "see/experience" the EMPTINESS and the aspect as the same substance.

Step VI: Stay in the nonverbal **I AM** level *prior* to the arising of thoughts and JUST BE (to be discussed later). This is the **I AM** which leads to the **NOT-I I** beyond observation (i.e. the observer-observed dyad.)

This exercise will hopefully help to open the doorway and help to stabilize beyond your identification with the thinking dimension.

SUMMARY SO FAR

The thinking dimension is how we (the nervous system) think and interpret the world. For this reason, it becomes important to notice how we interpret present time reality through the vehicle of this dimension. In this way, we can begin to discard these thoughts, which act as lenses through which we view ourself and the world. "In order to let go of something you must first know what it is."

One dimension is not higher or lower than another dimension. One dimension can be clear (not pull "your" awareness) while others pull your awareness. For example, I gave a talk in Germany. Collapsing the levels kept coming up for people. There was a woman who talked about some guru in India and he kept telling her to "focus (fixate) on me, look at me, focus on me, keep your mind on me. The only way to **THAT** is through me." So what you have here is a fusion of the **VOID** and his uncooked narcissism of the thinking and emotional dimension.

One Tibetan guru, died of sclerosis of the liver from alcoholism. His life and death were subsequently spiritualized as "crazy wisdom." He gave over his "lineage"—as if a person could give a lineage—to a person who had AIDS and spread AIDS through their community. When they went to him and said, "Why did you do this?" he said, "I thought I was the Dorje [an enlightened lineage holder]. I thought I couldn't transmit AIDS." Here you are talking about a thinking/emotional and biological dimension's collapsing with his understanding or experience of the **VOID**. *It's a collapsing of the levels.*

THE ASSOCIATIONAL TRANCE:
COLLAPSING THE LEVELS

"The concept of patterns only exist because of the Associational Trance"

The tendency of the mind, which is a by-product of the nervous system to scan-searching, seek and thus create generalizations and associations where there are none, is the mind's associational trance. When someone has had a trauma, for example, a past body image, a present body image and a future body image get associated together and fused with the external. For example, let's say someone has anorexia bulimia. They are hallucinating. They look in the mirror and do not see this skinny little person. Instead, they see a big-huge person. They are not in present time, they are in "past time" or in their imagination creating a body image. And so when someone has a trauma, not only do they have a thought process, an emotional process, and a biological process collapsing during the trauma, but they also have a past time body image confused with one in the present time. *Each identity or ego state has a body image associated with it.*

QUANTUM PSYCHOLOGY PRINCIPLE:
The image of your body is not your body.

For example, when someone is in a car accident and they are afraid to drive, it is because they are in their past time body image. Their body image is frozen and hence is unknowingly experienced as the same as when they were in the accident. In Quantum Psychology, you want to separate **WHO YOU ARE** from who you think you are. In this way, go beyond body images because you cannot experience present time if body images from the past are fused (associated with the present). At the thinking dimension, you not only have beliefs and thoughts, but you also have images. Clusters of images will justify and create a value system or philosophy. If I'm walking down the street and a picture of my mother pops up, the image exists in the thinking dimension and I might in my relationships associate the past with the present. When this occurs, we dissociate and lose awareness of our body and our biological level. That's why Alexander Lowen said that when he starts to work with clients bio-energetically, and they start loosening a lot of the emotional levels, they usually experience more and deeper levels of exhaustion because they have repressed exhaustion. This is why, when you see someone after a therapy session, they will often say, "I'm exhausted." They are fatigued because in order to keep this defensive tendency or image alive, they work hard and have to repress exhaustion which takes a lot of energy.

Often, the attempt to obsessively-compulsively understand is a defense against experiencing what is actually occurring. Chaos is defended against because of our belief structure of, "If I can understand what happened, then it will be okay." There are several basic beliefs in obsessive-compulsive tendencies. One is, if I can just understand it, the chaos will be organized. Two, if I find out what I did wrong, I can control it so that it will never happen again. Three, if I make or do it right this time, it won't happen again. In short, it is a resistance to what has occurred, and an associational tendency used as a survival mechanism. The tendency is if I could just understand this (*fill in the blank*), then somehow the chaos would disappear. In a short time the desire to understand becomes *a defense against experiencing and not knowing,* and is often the impetus and drive to type, characterize and diagnose people.

Unfortunately, in psychology, they are dealing with stories and trying to get people to understand their stories. Then, in psychology the work often becomes to create (new) stories about the stories. Accumulating information, reframing, creating new stories about the stories, future pacing (the trance of futurizing)—all of this keeps the associational trance alive with the belief that if I do (*fill in the blank*), this will or will not happen again. However, the associational trance is a defense against experiencing what is.

Your biology has the fight/flight scanning-searching and overgeneralizing mechanism. Unfortunately, these survival mechanisms are not in present time. They are a collapsing of the levels so that the fight/flight scanning-searching-seeking and overgeneralizing mechanism at a biological level is fused with past events. You get a fusion of earlier similar events with your survival mechanism. All you need to do to dismantle it is to *cut the associational network* and then you can *experience* what's truly a threat and what's not a threat in the present time. Your survival mechanism goes through your entire associational network, i.e., your psychology. Your biology runs your psychology, not the other way around. Therefore, you should trace your False Core back through your fight/flight scanning and overgeneralizing survival mechanisms (see Volume II).

THERAPY AND SPIRITUALITY COLLAPSE LEVELS

MEET THE PROBLEM AT THE LEVEL OF THE PROBLEM

You have to meet the problem at the level of the problem. If you have a psychological problem, then you had better meet it on the psychological level. You can get Feldenkrais sessions forever but they *probably* won't cure a financial problem. You might get Rolfed forever, it doesn't mean it is going to handle your relationship issues. Meet the problem at the level of the problem or refer them to someone who can work with them at that level. If someone has a bad back, yes, maybe we can cure it with prayer. But it might be wiser to see a chiropractor, a Feldenkrais practitioner or a Rolfer.

Quantum Psychology feels that there is a danger in giving someone a philosophy which they cannot take in. For example, if someone has their attention on their False Core and you tell them something like, "You are not the doer," that statement only gets superimposed onto their False Core. The philosophy cannot go in, it can only be used to reinforce their False Core (see Volume II).

Each dimension has a different function. It's the function of the thinking dimension to think. It's a function of the emotional dimension to have emotions. It's the function of the biological dimension to shit. It makes as much sense to say sexual abstinence will lead you to God as not going to the bathroom will lead you to God. They are biological functions and when you imagine that abstaining biologically will lead to the realization of the **VOID OF UNDIF-FERENTIATED CONSCIOUSNESS**, you are collapsing the levels. Each dimension has a function. It is important not to impose, overlap or try to overcome one dimension with another or oppose one dimension with another.

Multi-Dimensional awareness is developing a functional awareness which is the freedom to have all of the dimensions or none of them.

QUANTUM PSYCHOLOGY PRINCIPLE:

The greater the flexibility as to where "you" place your awareness, the greater the subjective experience of freedom.

CHAPTER VII
THE EMOTIONAL DIMENSION
OF MANIFESTATION

The emotional dimension comprises our emotional states such as anger, sadness, fear, joy, etc. All of these are emotional states. When a trauma occurs, the reason a trauma is so severe and causes such a frozen and painful experience and fixates our awareness so intensely is because the different dimensions of manifestation fuse together. They collapse, merge and become one rather than being differentiated. Let's say that somebody was molested by Uncle Bob. The intensity of the external experience creates a fusing together of all of the dimensions—the external dimension, the thinking dimension, the emotional dimension, the biological dimension and maybe even **ESSENCE**—all collapse and become fused, undifferentiated and solidified. When they collapse and become solidified, there is no longer any movement. The "present time" external world is seen as the "past time" external world through the lens of the past thinking, emotional and biological.

WORKING WITH THE EMOTIONAL DIMENSION[1]

THE TRANSMUTATION OF ENERGY

Transmutation can be defined as a change in condition or alteration, as in qualities or states of mind. In alchemy, transmutation

---

[1]For greater information and detail, see Wolinsky, Quantum Consciousness (1992) and Hearts on Fire (1995).

is the changing of base metal into gold or silver. In biology, it is the changing of one species into another, i.e., evolution. In chemistry, it is the conversion of one element into another. Transmutation: to change from one form into another form.

To the self-explorer, therapist, and spiritual aspirant, it is imperative to understand what freezes and holds emotions, events, or situations so that they are experienced the way they are. To illustrate, at the emotional dimension, anger without a label is energy in a form different from sadness. Sadness is energy in a form different from hate. Once experienced without labels and judgments, the steps of transmutation occur naturally. First, remove the label from the sensation, emotion, etc., and second, watch the experience with no judgment, evaluation or significance placed upon it. Just experience it as energy.

This is an effortless process. Energy and consciousness transmute themselves. In chaos theory, this can be compared to allowing the chaos to reorder itself (see *The Tao of Chaos*). This is a different process than changing one thing into another because you "imagine" this or that's better. This is precisely where the subtle judgment lies, which freezes, holds and locks an experience in space-time. Normally, psychology leaves us in the predicament of either expressing or repressing feelings that are judged, through prior learning, as bad or unwanted.

Transmutation affords the opportunity to add a third alternative to the expression-repression continuum. Taking the label off of the emotion and experiencing it simply as energy can lead to a transmutation. Simply stated, a transmutation takes place when you focus your attention on an emotion "as being made of energy."

It should be noted here that from 1960 to the present day, psychologists have believed that if you could re-experience the unfinished business, i.e., your non-experienced experiences, then healing would take place. But even though people might act out their feelings in psychodrama and "feel" better, relieved, more insightful, more powerful, still the work never got finished. Why? Because there was an error. *The error was imagining that expressing feelings was the same as feeling feelings.* In Quantum Psychology, we discovered that expressing feelings is not feeling feelings. Rather, expressing feelings is expressing feelings and feeling feelings is a different experience.

What is feeling feelings? *Feeling feelings is merging and being them and allowing them to do or not do what they do, without either expression or repression.* Without judgment, evaluation or significance placed upon them and without the intention of getting rid of them. This chapter focuses on the concept of feeling feelings without the intention of getting rid of them. Merely by watching and allowing emotions, thoughts, and feelings, etc. to be as they are, namely energy, the "experience" transmutes (reorganizes) itself.

QUANTUM PSYCHOLOGY PRINCIPLE:

If you are trying to get rid of feelings you place a judgment, evaluation and significance placed upon them and are resisting them.

It should be noted that the experience of "pure energy" is much closer to the quantum level because energy is an "earlier" manifestation of the condensation of the **VOID OF UNDIFFERENTIATED CONSCIOUSNESS** than are the labels anger, sadness, joy, etc. Descriptions, stories, beliefs about what experiences "mean" take us further away from the quantum level (to be discussed later).

The purpose of the following practices is to help you to allow for the transmutation of all your experiences so that thinking and emotional energies tied-up and collapsed can be experienced as energy. In this way you will free your awareness and become more aware of the quantum level or **VOID OF UNDIFFERENTIATED CONSCIOUSNESS**.

The basic idea of placing your attention on the emotion comes from the Vijnana Bhairava, which is one of the major texts in Kashmir Shaivism. It contains dharanas (how to affixate awareness), which are Tantric practices.[2] Dharana is defined as fixing your attention on a set point. Tantra means the expansion of knowledge. To sum up

---

[2]Dharanas are ways of fixating attention by choice rather than automatically. It is interesting to note that Quantum Psychology is using Erickson's idea that the symptom is the cure. In other words, the symptom, or the "problem," is that you have hypnotised yourself, i.e., you habitually shrink (fixate) your focus of attention. In Quantum Psychology, we ask the practitioner to knowingly, consciously and intentionally fixate on the emotion as a form of energy. In this way, we are using this fixating tendency, or better said, the early tantrics are using this fixating tendency to liberate you from its hold.

this practice, the Tantra Asana says, "One rises by that which one falls." Actually, the first set of exercises will focus on emotions as energy. The second set on the observer of the emotion and all objects as being made of the same consciousness. (This will be discussed in detail in Volume III.)

For example, when you feel afraid, your mind will give you about twenty reasons why you feel this way. Normally, people focus their attention on *why* they're afraid. Rather than doing that, I would like you to take your attention away from *why* you feel fear, and focus on the fear itself: Where is the fear in your body? Begin to focus your attention on the fear itself. This practice is about learning how energy transmutes and reorganizes itself once the label (which contains a subtle judgment, evaluation and significance) is taken off.

Sex or sexual energy can also be de-labeled. If you have a sexual fantasy and focus your attention on it, you get a bodily reaction of some sort. If you keep fantasizing, you begin to look outside yourself for this fantasy to be fulfilled. I started reading the Vijnana Bhairava more than twenty five years ago. To paraphrase one of the dharanas,

> From the mere memory of touching, pressing or kissing, there's a delightful feeling that arises, but since there's nobody there, then, obviously, the feeling comes from inside you.

This is very profound. Since there is no one in your room during a fantasy, then the feeling comes from inside you. If you take your attention off of the fantasy and focus on the feeling itself, then when you take the label off of the emotion and experience it as energy, it begins to transmute and reorganize itself.

TRANSMUTATION

Please note that *when the label is taken off it is done without a goal or intention.* If you try to change it into something else, then you have a goal and a subtle judgment, evaluation or significance, that this is *better* than—more *productive* than, more *virtuous* than, less *sinful* than, more *healthy* than, less *unhealthy* than, more healing than, more *godly* than, etc. Or, to say it another way, the emotion is already made of energy but how you experience it is transmuted. Take off the label called fear, and experience it as energy. If a tight chest is an indication to you that you are afraid, then focus your attention on your tight chest as contracted energy. In other words, your chest may be tight when you feel afraid. For somebody else, it might be in the pit of their stomach, in their heart, or in their hands. We're going to focus on emotion as energy rather than the story about what we're afraid of.

Hopefully, by doing these exercises, you will find out for yourself that fear, anger, joy, happiness—all of the emotions—are all made of energy in a different form.

GUILT

A person once asked me, "How do you deal with guilt?" I said, "First you have to know what guilt is." In Gestalt therapy, for instance, guilt is resentment turned against yourself. So first you have to straighten out the energy. In other words, if I resent somebody or something, and I don't express that resentment, it's retroflected back on me. That means that rather than expressing my resentment, I put it back on myself and what I get is guilt.

If I feel guilty, the first thing I need to do to straighten out the energy is to start off sentences with, "I resent *(fill in the blank)*. That will at least turn the energy around so that you'll start turning it toward the person or object that you are resenting. This is one way to do it. It can be that simple. If it's depression, it can be anger turned against yourself or a resisted experience. So either feel the anger (if there is any) or notice what experience you are resisting—then experience the resisted experience. Resentment (guilt) is a little bit lighter than (anger) depression. The deeper the depression, the more you have been putting anger back on yourself or the more you have resisted experiences. In Sanskrit, depression is defined as lack of shakti or lack of energy. "E" means outward, emotion is outward motion. When you have an emotion and don't express it or want to feel it, it takes a lot of energy to resist it, hence, depression.

EMOTIONAL DIMENSION EXERCISE #1[3]

FEAR

Focus:
Focus your attention on the emotion rather than on the story of why you feel the emotion; experience the emotion as made of energy.

Practice:
Begin by recalling a past event or a future something that you're imagining will happen that is associated with fear. It could have been last week, last month or last year. Let the memory come into your mind. Now, notice what you were wearing, the color of your clothes. Notice if there are any other people in this mind-movie. Experience any sounds you hear in the movie. I'd like you to notice the feeling of fear that you have. Where is it in your body?

Now, let your memory really develop. Notice the feeling of fear. When it's at a high point of intensity, I'd like you to take your attention away from the memory and focus on the fear itself (the emotion itself). Notice where in your body your feeling of fear is. I'd like you to focus your attention there. Where does it sit physically? Every time your mind wants to go back to the memory of why you're afraid, focus it gently back onto the feeling of the fear itself. Take the label off of the fear and view that fear as energy. See the fear as energy. See your emotion as energy and allow the energy to do what it does. Do not try to change it.

On emerging from this practice, a student once said that his head felt sensitive, with a sense of energy passing through it. "My head feels real different from the rest of me," he told me. I asked him if his head felt open at the top, and he replied that it did. "It feels as if there's so much energy in it, it's expanding."

I was in India in 1976 and one day in May I was sitting at 5:30 in the morning and chanting Sanskrit mantras. It was probably

---

[3]These exercises come from *Hearts on Fire* and *Quantum Consciousness*. If you have done them, then move on. If you want to explore them in greater depth, explore the earlier volumes.

about 110° and I was feeling incredibly angry. I stopped what I was doing (my mind was thinking up reasons why I was angry—it's hot, it's crowded, and so on). I put my chanting book down and focused my attention on my anger. To paraphrase a tantric text called the Spanda Karikas, when you're feeling extremely happy or joyful, or extremely sad or angry, or you are running for your life, if at that moment you could become introverted, you would experience Spanda, which is the divine pulsationor throb. Of course, what they leave out is, if at that moment you could remember to become introverted! I realized I needed to do that, to de-label my story and experience it as energy. I focused on the anger as energy and went into bliss.

This is what can happen with this exercise. It's critical, however, to *experience the emotion as energy without the intention of getting rid of it.* If you are trying to get rid of it, you are resisting it, which keeps it there. As you can see, it takes some practice to move your attention away from the story, to let it go and focus on the fear itself. But once you're able to do that, you'll see how emotions lose a lot of their power. So, rather than trying to get rid of our so-called negative feelings, as most kinds of therapy suggest, we can begin to experience them as energy.

You'll be amazed once you've done this a couple of times. When I first did it, I was feeling furious. But when I dropped the story—my mind was popping up reasons—when I really stopped and turned my attention inside, I was in ecstasy in about five seconds. From that point on, I understood experientially how to begin the work of transmuting the energy of emotions or transmuting my experience of them.

As you begin to turn your attention in—and it is a practice because you are turning habitual attention around—it will start happening on its own. It's like to learning to play some kind of sport. At first you feel very awkward, but after a while, things start falling into place. When get into a pool, you don't have to think about swimming, you just swim. You don't have to think about holding your breath underwater, you just do it. As you practice, it comes quite spontaneously.

EMOTIONAL DIMENSION EXERCISE #2

SADNESS

Focus:

Focus your attention on the emotion rather than on the story of why you feel the emotion; experience the emotion as made of energy.

We'll start off with our uncomfortable feelings and, as time goes on, move to more pleasurable ones. Let's recall some past situation in which you experienced sadness. Move your attention from that story of why you're sad to the sadness itself as energy. If you can't conjure up sadness, you can use any other emotion normally labeled unpleasant.

I know you have reasons why you should be sad, but I want you to move your attention away from the story and concentrate on the sadness itself. See what happens.

Practice:

Recall a time associated with sadness. Notice people who are involved in the story, notice where you are in the story. Notice if there are any sounds. Are you inside or outside? Are there any temperature differences? For a few minutes, allow the emotion to build as it arises in your awareness. Notice the feelings associated with the story. Notice the size and shape (the dimensions of the sadness), step into it and merge with it, and out of it and observe it a few times. Now, gently, move your attention from the story and all its details and focus on the emotion itself. See where the feeling or sensation is in your body. Notice its size, color and whether it has a sound. Continue to focus all of your attention on the emotion. As you watch it, take the label off and view it as energy.

EMOTIONAL DIMENSION EXERCISE #3

ANGER

Focus:
Focus your attention on the emotion rather than on the story of why you feel what you feel; experience the emotion as made of energy. We will also focus on the skin boundaries which appear mass like, or solidified as compacted or slow moving energy.

Practice:
Recall a time when you felt angry; it could have been last year, it could have been five or ten years ago. Let the emotion called anger come into your awareness. As you watch this scene in your memory, notice yourself in the memory and look around and notice the other people in the memory. Notice what the feeling is or what the sensations are in your body. Focus on the story. Allow the feelings or the sensations of anger to emerge, to begin to come to the surface as you watch the movie in your mind, and notice where this anger is in your body. Notice its shape and size. Begin to focus your awareness on this anger, rather than on the story and reasons why you're angry. Focus your attention on the anger itself. As you watch the anger, take the label off and see it as energy. Next take the label off of your skin boundaries and think of them as "slow moving or compacted energy." Notice what happens.

CONCLUSION

Please note:

1. This is not a cure all, it is just one piece in the very large puzzle of Quantum Psychology.
2. Once the label is off, things might shift quickly or not at all. Take the label off and have it as energy without the intention of getting rid of it, just to see what happens.
3. When there is no wanting to get rid of it there is no judgement, evaluation, or significance placed on the experience.

These exercises can be expanded and used in all Quantum work. Please refer back to *Quantum Consciousness* and *Hearts on Fire* for a much greater explanation and depth as reference sources.

W hat is
true at the
biological dimension
may not be
true at any
other dimension.

CHAPTER VIII
THE BIOLOGICAL DIMENSION OF MANIFESTATION

EMBODYING QUANTUM CONSCIOUSNESS

EMBODY:

1.   To invest with a body, as a spirit, to incarnate; make corporeal;
2.   To give concrete form to;
3.   To collect into or to include a body.[1]

"Embody" and "embodiment," as directly related to consciousness, are two misunderstood terms in psycho-spiritual communities today. For most of us, due to cultural indoctrination, the body, the mind, and the spirit have been viewed as split off from one another and taken to be separate. We are then made to believe that this is true.

Over the last 35 years, with the advent of the human potential movement, we have seen major attempts to correct this mis-perception. However, in order to do this we must look at and question many of the concepts we hold dear, such as the spirit or soul being separate from the body, or the body being separate from the underlying unity. Note that as we explore the underlying unity which is Quantum Consciousness, abstract assumptions, unquestioned ideas and spiritual concepts which are more subtle must be brought into the light of

---

[1]The American College Dictionary, Random House, New York, 1963.

awareness and questioned. As Nisargadatta Marahaj used to say: "Question everything don't believe anything."

In order to do this, we must take things one step further and look at the business of psychology and spirituality to notice how we have all been indoctrinated and hypnotized into this understanding, even in the light of quantum physics which states that everything is a unified whole.

EGO PSYCHOLOGY

I would like to begin by stating that I love the story and philosophy of psychology. It is a marvelous story. Ego psychology, and/or psychoanalytic developmental psychology have made important observations about early childhood development and its implications and applications to our psychological processes. I do not wish to throw the baby out with the bath water; however, I do wish to examine how psychoanalytic developmental psychology views, encourages and supports the mind being split-off from the body and how many of their philosophies and theories are taken as facts and remain unquestioned. This can be best described in the statement below:

> Lichtenberg's description of psychological structuring is as a process in which the child develops the capacity to live a little less in the body and a little more in the mind. Since here we are discussing problems which arise from subphase inadequacy, patients at such lesser levels of organization cannot be expected to have made as much progress toward structuralization as the neurotic; therefore, they (the neurotic) still live more in the immediacy of experience than in the mind. (Blanck, 1979, p. 136)

Notice how in the roots of modern-day psychology, the mind is seen as separate from the body. Furthermore, the movement from body awareness, from out of the present moment and into the mind, is called *structuring*. As seen above, this is supposed to be healthier than living in the body in the moment.

This whole idea of body/mind/spirit being split into separate components begins with our regulation of bodily functions during the socialization process. As mentioned in *Quantum Consciousness*, an Indian teacher of mine once said, "Your whole life is organized around eating, sleeping, shitting and fucking, or making more money so that you have a better place to do it in."

All of these regulations of body function by the external world (mom, dad, society, religions, etc.) cause a dissociation, a splitting off from the body which creates beliefs about "appropriate" actions at "appropriate" times, i.e., "There is a time and place for everything." This causes us to eat, not when we're hungry, but at about 12:00 p.m. Not to shit when we need to, but to hold it in. Not to sleep as much as we need, but to organize it around work. And not to have sex when it feels right but to wait until the evening. When a survey asked about when people mostly have sex, the overwhelming majority said after 9:30 p.m. on either Friday or Saturday night

In addition, bodily functions and impulses are seen as bad by many spiritual systems. The dissociation from the body is oftentimes labeled as good or as spiritual. Much of our early childhood training is about regulation of the body. In this way, there is an implication and message given to the child that there is something wrong with the body and its functions and certainly it is less than the mind, and of much less importance than the spirit.

It is interesting that the mind and spirit are mistakenly seen as somehow being in charge of the body, "as if" they came before it or are senior to the body—rather than their interpretation being reactions and creations of the nervous system. This dissociation further removes us from ourselves, organizes and justifies the painful regulation of bodily functions and as we dissociate from the body and create philosophies to justify it, we further separate ourselves from the rest of humanity. Soon we start to relate unsuccessfully from philosophy to philosophy.

It is for this reason and with this understanding that the body is placed as the centerpiece of "our" existence and the cornerstone of *The Way of the Human*.

QUANTUM APPROACHES TO BODY WORK

The Quantum approach to body work does not separate mind from body but sees that just as muscles and organs are connected to the head, so the mind is not separate from the body, but rather it is a by-product of the nervous system and the higher brain.[2] For example, when working with a client, one of my primary questions is, "Where do you feel that in your body?" Often clients respond, "I don't feel that in my body, I feel it in my head." I respond with, "When did you decide that your head was not your body?"

Often the viewpoint of separation and splitting are not questioned since it is assumed that the description of an experience is the experience itself. But as Alfred Korzybski stated, "The map is not the territory." The problem, therefore, not the solution, is *structuralization* when people think that the map (description) of their experience is the territory (or their experience). This is caused when the mind is seen as more important than the body. Even Freud disagreed with this when he said that "the ego is body centered" (i.e., it is a by-product of the body).

Quantum Psychology states that, not only is the map not the territory, but the story or description is not the state or experience. The description of a state or experience comes out of the body-mind and is the way the nervous system, later and after the experience has already taken place, creates a story to organize itself and to avoid the chaos of certain experiences.

Unlike psychologies which imagine a body-mind split, Korzybski in *Science and Sanity* refers to the organism as a whole:

> Experience and experiments show us that the natural order is sensation first, idea next; the sensation being an abstraction of some (lower) (earlier) order, and the idea clearly an abstraction of an abstraction, (sensation). . . . This reversal of order in its mild form is involved in the confusion of orders of abstractions; namely that we act as if an idea were an experience." (p. 76).

---

[2]In this case "higher" is called "higher" because it is physically higher; i.e., the cortex is physically higher than the reptilian brain. However, to be less confusing, from this point on, we will call it the "newer" brain since it evolved much later in time.

According to Korzybski, sensation, thought and emotion are all interconnected, they are all part of the whole organism although, *neurologically speaking, sensations come before ideas.*

From the ultimate point of view, using quantum physics, the entire body is made up of the same one substance, namely, different densities of solidness which serve different functions. In this way, thoughts, sensations, and emotions are made up ultimately of the same substance as the liver or bones, just with different densities and different functions.

This means that the body is not connected to the mind, but rather, the body *is* the mind, there is no separation, Hence, Nisargadatta Maharaj called it the *body-mind because at the biological level the biology (body) came first, and the "mind" (thoughts, interpretations, emotions, etc.) came later.* For this reason and to make it even clearer we will now refer to it as the body→mind.

As we go onto the thinking process we will further discuss beliefs, images, etc. which emerge from, and are a by-product of, the nervous system.

THE ORIGIN OF CONCEPTS

The purpose of this discussion is to see the organism as a whole, and yet not to go to the other extreme and make the body more important than the mind.

The origin of concepts and thoughts can be seen in the following way: I have an an experience and the nervous system, neurologically speaking, organizes that experience, much later in time. This organization of experience is what we call an interpretation of what the experience means; for example, something happens and I now have an interpretation called "I am bad." Later, that belief becomes the organizing principle which interprets what "subjective" and "outside" experiences mean. In this way the thinking dimensions and its accompanying beliefs are an intermediary between "inside non-verbal" experiences and the "outside external world."

A major question often arises from body-workers, such as Feldenkrais practitioners or Rolfers. They will maintain (since both Dr. Moshe Feldenkrais and Dr. Ida Rolf, the founder of Rolfing, implied that all you need to handle is the body) that if the body is the central aspect of the organism as a whole, you don't need psychotherapy—body work will take care of it all. According to Quantum Psychology this is incorrect. Why?

QUANTUM PSYCHOLOGY PRINCIPLE:

The problem must be met at the level of the problem. In Quantum Physics we are dealing with probabilities; it is possible for a chair to float up into the sky—but what is the probability of that occuring

To appreciate this, let us suppose someone has a phobia or low self-esteem. Can Rolfing or Feldenkrais handle the phobia by itself? The *probability* is low. If someone has low self-esteem, can Feldenkrais or Rolfing handle this psychological issue by itself? The probability is low.

To illustrate the interconnection of body→mind, obviously if you have a phobia, there must be a change in your breathing pattern and the way your body is standing (posture) in order to heal the phobia (or bad self-esteem, etc.). Maybe your feet lose their connection to the ground and you're not properly supported when you're feeling phobic.

This interconnection must be appreciated and understood so that the *body, mind and spirit are seen as the same and equal.* Therefore, not only is "psychological" work *alone* not enough, but "body-work" or somatic re-education *alone* is not enough either. Neither is "spiritual" work *alone* enough to discover *WHO YOU ARE.* Why not? Because each dimension, i.e., thinking, body-work, etc., uses different (although interconnected) parts of the brain as in holistic medicine. If the liver is not used or orchestrated well with the digestive tract, then the stomach must work harder. The results may be that your food will not be metabolized as well. In the same way, if your cortex (thinking center) is overused, your sense of the body will be underused (to be be discussed later).

To illustrate further, let us take the example of incest survivors. Incest survivors can receive psychotherapy and yet, when their bodies go into the same or a similar position as when they were molested, their psychological issues come back again. Why? Because the body and psyche are holographic; that is, they have different functions but yet are totally interconnected and not separable. For this reason, the "unprocessed" body memory forces the psychological fears around the molestation to re-emerge.

In the same way, if body work is done without psychological therapy, although the body will be clear, the mind will continue to associate past emotions with certain bodily positions or sensations which occurred when the incest occurred (i.e., numbness in the genitals, holding of the breath, etc.). This is not to say psychological work will not help or impact the body, or that body work will not help or impact the psychology. Rather, they will impact each other, but the work cannot be completed unless it is met at the *level of the problem.* This old saying, "When the only tool you have is a hammer, every problem is a nail." This illustrates the problem with therapists, body workers, health care professionals spiritual teachers, etc. Just note, we are one interconnected holographic whole, and the easiest way to realize this is to utilize appropriate tools for appropriate problems.

QUANTUM PSYCHOLOGY PRINCIPLE:
The problem must be met at the level of the problem.

QUANTUM PSYCHOLOGY PRINCIPLE:
No one system can do it all.

THE HOLOGRAPHIC HUMAN: THE CONTINUUM
To understand the continuum, compare the most solid thing in the body—our bones—to the less solid muscles, the less solid organs, the less solid emotions and thoughts. When we understand the holographic human continuum, Korzybski's organism-as-a-whole gives us a different view of the body/mind and its structure.

This holographic continuum could be illustrated thus: Bones→muscles→organs→blood→sensations→emotions→thoughts (or vice-versa), all in one interconnected holographic whole.

THE SPIRIT/SOUL IS THE BODY

One of the most controversial—and, probably, one of the most crucial concepts to discuss is the assumption that there is a spirit or soul which is separate from the body. This idea is at the core of almost all religions. Hindus, for example, think of a soul, which incarnates again and again. Christians, although they do not think in terms of past lives, do talk of a future life for this soul or spirit in Heaven, if you're good, and Hell if you're bad. Gautama, the Buddha and founder of Buddhism, has as his most basic tenet, *that there is no individual soul or self which transmigrates (incarnates) from lifetime to lifetime.* However, throughout the world, this basic tenet of Buddhism has been ignored, lost and forgotten, and instead, we are offered a soul which incarnates again and again. This incarnation theory, said not to exist by Buddha, is still professed by popular teachers, that we are not the body, but rather a spirit which inhabits the body.

THE QUANTUM APPROACH

The Quantum approach says something much different. Quantum physics demonstrates to us that there is only **ONE INDIVISIBLE SUBSTANCE**. With this understanding, then, there is no separate spirit or soul which incarnates, but rather different orders of densities of substances, all of which are made of **THAT** same **ONE SUBSTANCE**. In other words, your arm is as much your mind as your head. Your feet are as much your mind as your thoughts. To take this one step further, your legs are as much spirit as your thoughts are your soul. Your stomach is as much your spirit as is the WITNESS of all experiences. Why? Because since everything is made of the same substance, then the body, mind, and spirit are not merely connected. Rather the *body is the mind, the body is the spirit, the mind is the body, the mind is the spirit, the body is the witnessing presence; there are no distinctions.*

This can be illustrated by a story from the Buddhist tradition. One day a student of Buddhism asked the Buddha about the WITNESS. The Buddha replied by holding up his sandal and saying, "This [the sandal] is the WITNESS." Buddha was demonstrating that everything--not only mind, but body, spirit, the witness, even his sandal—is made of **THAT ONE SUBSTANCE**.

With this understanding, let us look at the solidness of bone through the lesser solidness of muscle, moving through the less solid organs to the less solid emotions, through the less solid sensations, the less solid thoughts, the less solid space inside the body, through the less solid EMPTINESS. This continuum is ONE SUBSTANCE, differing only in density yet totally interconnected and holographic, separated only by definitions and labels, and containing the entire universe within each.

In other words, since everything from bone to EMPTINESS is made of the **THAT ONE SUBSTANCE**, then everything is the same substance as the entire universe. The old metaphysical statement that the macrocosm is in the microcosm and the microcosm is in the macrocosm can be changed in the light of quantum physics to the macrocosm *is* the microcosm and the microcosm *is* the macrocosm.

QUANTUM BODY WORK

What then is Quantum body work? The Quantum approach to the body is not one of exclusion but of inclusion. Muscles are not seen as separate from thoughts any more than waves are seen as separate from the ocean. For example, when I had some somatic work done recently, I experienced major changes in my shoulder blades after having work done on my cranium. Recently, my lower back pain disappeared after my feet received awareness and redirection. This was the true holistic vision of both Ida Rolf and Moshe Feldenkrais. Each part affects the whole and they are all tied together. The first step is to understand a sense of groundedness within the body. Then, to include the body as being made of the same substance as everything else.[3]

---

[3]See, Appendix, *On Compassion*, *Tao of Chaos*: *Quantum Consciousness Volume II* (Bramble Books 1994).

To repeat, the biological world consists of our physical body. Our physical body contains four major biological functions or *have to's*, on which our time is focused—eating, sleeping, shitting, and fucking (and how to make more money to have a better place to do it in). In order to survive, the physical body has to eat, it has to sleep, it has to shit and it has to have sex.[4] Those are the four major functions which the body must do.

Quantum Psychology (to be discussed later) believes that there are two other functions in addition—a *merging response* and a *learning response*. Any repression through socialization, internally or externally, of any biological function causes a splitting off and a dissociation from one dimension or another and a substitution response. In other words, if your biology is put into a state of deprivation, there is a shock to the body. To handle the shock, the nervous system dissociates and there is an accompanying loss of awareness of your body. This often yields a philosophy (newer brain and, after the fact, neurologically) which not only organizes the chaos of the deprivation but also moves us further away from bodily experience and hence the underlying unity. When this occurs, a substitution also occurs. For example, if my mother only touches me and is affectionate (biological merging) when I get good grades in school, then the only way to become merged with her is to achieve (see Volume II).

In Quantum Psychology when you *substitute* an action (like good grades) as a way to receive a biological *"have-to"* (merging), this is called *substitution*. In other words, if during the socialization process a biological need is substituted, as in the above example, soon "good grades" or "achievements" equal merging. However, notice that no matter how much is achieved there is *no satisfaction*.

Quantum Psychology separates needs from wants. Needs originate from biological deprivation; obsessive-compulsive wants which never feel like enough occur are when you substitute a biological need with a psychological want, which later becomes a "desire for" with an obsessive-compulsive action. For example, *Biological Need*: I want to merge (this is not met)→psychological want (I have to get approval).

---

[4]Recently a guru wannabe said to me that "sex is a trance." It should be noted that sexuality is wired into the nervous system as a survival of the species.

This is substituting a psychological want (approval) for the biological need (merging). This imagined *way* to merger by substituting (the biological need) for a psychological wants (approval) gets ingrained and even though it yields no satisfaction, the tendency becomes engraved on the brain like a groove on a record. The biological need comes before the psychological want. This substitution process is a survival technique by the body (nervous system) to survive and get biological needs met.

In Buddhism, Buddha says, "All pain arises from desire." In Quantum Psychology this means that when biological *"have to's* are not met, the substituted biological need becomes an aberrant psychological want (obsessive-compulsive desire) and, hence, is exaggerated and distorted. If this occurs, you chase an image of gratification (achievement) which is different from the biological need in an attempt to satisfy the merger response. In this example, wanting to have others say you are great could be an attempt to get the biological need of merging met. This yields no satisfaction because the real biological need has not been met. This substituting of dimensions (external and thinking in this case) for another (biological) yields pain. The need which is natural and biological must be met first. This is why, when the Zen master was asked, "What is enlightenment?" he replied, "When you are hungry, you eat. When you are tired, you sleep." (There is no longer any issue or internal considering about it.)

QUANTUM PSYCHOLOGY PRINCIPLE:

You must meet the biological at the biological level. And do not substitute one biological need for another biological need (i.e., food for merger).

QUANTUM PSYCHOLOGY PRINCIPLE:

Substituting a "psychological want" for a biological need yields an obsessive-compulsive action, desire and reaction *and no satisfaction.*

Quantum Psychology says that there are two other major biological *have-to's*: (1) the merger response, i.e., the biological desire to merge at one of the dimensions; and (2) the learning response, i.e., at a biological level, a drive to learn at greater and greater levels of differentiation and complexity.

As with the other four biological drives, any thwarting of the merger or learning response yields a biological deprivation and shock.

The fourth dimension of manifestation is the body. Our body comprises our animal nature eating, sleeping, shitting, sexuality, libido (the desire to merge)—and learning at greater levels of complexity. Often we lose awareness of our physical body. For example, in a workshop, I once met a woman who was not in her body. She was not around her body. She was not even aware of what she was saying. You could say to her "I hate you," or "I'd like to kill you," and she would say, "Oh, thanks very much, I hope it is nice day for you." She had no real awareness of her thinking, emotional, biological or external dimensions. She was split off and dissociated from those dimensions.

QUANTUM PSYCHOLOGY PRINCIPLE:

With the splitting-off and dissociation from any dimension, there is a corresponding loss of the present time body and of the potential for stabilization in the underlying unity.

QUANTUM PSYCHOLOGY PRINCIPLE:

If you lose awareness of your body, you lose the external dimension.

QUANTUM PSYCHOLOGY PRINCIPLE:

Psychology is caused by a dissociation from the biology (to be discussed later in the section on the BIOLOGICAL CORE).

The biological dimension is pivotal because it is the cornerstone of all eight dimensions. If there is no body, there is no external world, no thinking world, no emotional world, no biological world, no **ESSENCE**, no **I AM**, No Awareness of the Archetypes of the **COLLECTIVE**, and no "**Not-I-I**".

THE BASICS

At this juncture, let us review several basic Quantum principles:

1. The body and the nervous system are a quantum event, i.e., the body is condensed **VOID OR UNDIFFERENTIATED CONSCIOUSNESS**. This basic principle is both Einstein's and Buddha's foundation. "Everything is made of **EMPTINESS** and form is condensed **EMPTINESS**." Or Buddha's "Form is none other than **EMPTINESS, EMPTINESS** none other than form.

2. When we "see" the body as a quantum event, we mean that the **EMPTINESS** condenses down forming a body with a nervous system and that the body and the nervous system cannot see the Quantum event.

3. Given that the body and the nervous system are also a condensation of **EMPTINESS**, they therefore select certain experiences and reject others. The latter part of the statement comes from the work of Alfred Korzybski. *What was "left out" or omitted from Korzybski is that the perceiving mechanism and the nervous system itself are an abstraction of that Emptiness or Quantum level.* This is a major error in Korzybski's general semantics. Its omission explains why Korzybski's students face frustrating problems in getting the "changes" they want through what Korsybski called Neuro-Linguistic Feedback.

4. That the nervous system of the body is a trance-former,[5] trancelating (after the fact) the Quantum level **OR VOID OF UNDIFFERENTIATED CONSCIOUSNESS**→electrons, etc.— into experiences. The nervous system "takes" Quantum expe-

---

[5]Please note that trance is defined as the shrinking of the focus of attention. During this shrinking process many stimuli and facts are omitted. Thus you (the nervous system) Trancelate the stimuli *later* after the facts and stimuli are omitted.

riences which cannot be known to the nervous system and organizes them into the "knower's" experience.

5. The nervous system is the producer of the "I thought" and, hence, the I thought and our psychology come out of the body, not the other way around. In Quantum Psychology we understand that different dimensions have an impact. We also realize that thoughts (maps) come from the body and the nervous system, which comes from a condensation in the Quantum Field **OR VOID OF UNDIFFERENTIATED CONSCIOUSNESS**. To "think" you can make changes in the external by changing words, beliefs, or mental pictures is to believe in the "magic of words," which is a term used to denote how "primitive people" believe words are things. This can be demonstrated by a child who cries for food and is given food by mom. Soon the word "food" means the food (milk) itself. Though you obviously can't eat the word, still there is an understanding that the word *food* is *food*. Words are further from the sensation level and the non-verbal experience of **I Am** and occur in a different dimension and use a different part of the brain. Furthemore they are "further away" from the Quantum level.

6. The nervous system and the "I" thought cannot know the Quantum level of **NOTHING/EVERYTHING**. The *I* which is produced by the body/ nervous system which is a condensation of the Quantum level cannot know the **VOID** from which it came. However, *"YOU"* can know *that* Quantum level when the I thought begins to disappear or no longer arises. This is called period deicity, a neurological process whereby the nervous system wipes itself clean for an instant. This can be likened to the attempt during meditation to notice the space between two breaths or the space between two thoughts.[6] In this way **NO-I** can be "seen" as a neurological process.

---

[6]This was discussed in the *Tao of Chaos*. It should also be noted that at the present time (1997) Quantum Psychology, with Alfred Schatz, is doing research on the functions within the brain which uses and is beyond space-time and its four-dimensional reality. These relate directly to Superstrings and the Biological Brain function of other forces; gravity, electromagnetics, strong nuclear force, and weak nuclear force (to be discussed in Volume III). As of 1997, further research into dark matter, partial reality, light waves and sound are underway.

QUANTUM PSYCHOLOGY PRINCIPLE:

The "I" which tries to change words and inferences (reframing) is further from the Quantum level than the words themselves and hence more "disconnected." Stated another way, the changer of works and influences is further from the preceding level or words and hence further from the Quantum Event level.

QUANTUM PSYCHOLOGY PRINCIPLE:

Changing inferences and maps only impacts the thinking dimension. The "I" trying to make the changes is part of the nervous system and thought itself. This is why change is so hard. Within each thought or belief (since it is a by-product of the nervous system) is the survival mechanism (fight/flight) of the nervous system itself. *So each thought and changer of thought is part of the thought itself which is a by-product of the nervous system.*

QUANTUM PSYCHOLOGY PRINCIPLE

To experience the Quantum level, one must go into the Non-verbal **I AM,** the silence and Beyond.

With all of this in mind, in the Appendix of *The Tao of Chaos*, "I" wrote an article called "On Compassion" where I spoke about possible "stages" within the biological dimension. The first stage is the "grounding" in one's body, the second stage, the realization of the body being made of **THAT ONE SUBSTANCE** as everything else. It should be noted that *the body is ultimately not a vehicle of the soul.* As will be discussed later, the body-soul are one and are made of **THAT ONE SUBSTANCE.**

THE BIOPSYCHOLOGICAL:
THE BIOLOGICAL→THE PSYCHOLOGICAL

For nearly 25 years, I have been a consistent receiver of body work. "I" have received Reichian therapy as well as hundreds of Rolfings and Feldenkrais sessions. "I" did Tai Chi for several years and have been doing Hatha Yoga everyday for almost 12 years. It has become apparent that it is the body which links together all of the dimensions, i.e., the External dimension, the Thinking dimension, the Feeling dimension, the Biological dimension, **ESSENCE**, the **I AM**, the **COLLECTIVE** and the "**Not-I-I**."

Quantum psychology defines the mind as consisting of a person's thoughts, memories, emotions, associations, perceptions and a scanning-searching device which scans the "external" and tends to create overgeneralizations, using past associations. It is important to know that the mind comes from the body. In other words, the nervous system and the biological fight/flight system, which are part of the physical body's nature, are also the governing and ruling principles behind a person's psychology (i.e., the thinking and emotional dimensions along with their memories and associations). The fight/flight body response becomes distorted because of the fusions and associations between thoughts, feelings, and the external, devised and perpetrated by the scanning-searching device and the organizing survival tendency, which is part of the neurological system of the body.

In the world of psychology, however, it is somehow believed that a person's psychology is senior to, and hence more important than, the body. This is also true with schools of spirituality that have not understood that the body is senior (prior to) the mind and not the other way around.

QUANTUM PSYCHOLOGY PRINCIPLE:

The "mind," which is kept alive by the scanning-searching-seeking device and the overgeneralizing tendency, is a by-product of the nervous system and is part of the fight/flight survival system of the body.

BIOLOGY'S TENDENCIES→PSYCHOLOGY'S RESULTS

To illustrate, the biological nervous system has several basic tendencies which are based on fight-flight, survival, and merger:

1. To illustrate, notice a "random" pleasant fantasy. Notice that it could be the body's attempt to fulfill the biological need through the "newer brain's" creation of fantasy.
2. Notice an unpleasant fantasy such as "Someone doesn't like me." Notice how the other person is seen as not-me, and with no merger possibility your basic nervous system reaction of fear, anger, rage, envy, etc.
3. Notice how many thoughts or fantasies are what Fritz Perls called *rehearsed*. Notice how the nervous system attempts to rehearse events and plan explanations; in a word to *BE PRE- PARED* for any **NOT-ME** incoming survival events which could be viewed as "threatening," even in an imaginary way. This could be seen as an obsessive-compulsive tendency to over-plan, over-work, over-achieve, over-do, over-give, over-perfect etc., etc.

In short if you study your psychological make-up with this biological understanding it is easy to see psychology's roots within the biology. Rather than keeping them separate, Quantum Psychology calls them Biopsychological, since first comes the biological then the psychological with its logical explanations, reasons, and justifications.

QUANTUM PSYCHOLOGY PRINCIPLE:

The "I" or "I" thought which claims ownershp or doership arises after the experience has already occured.

QUANTUM PSYCHOLOGY PRINCIPLE:

Explanations only explain. They come "after the experience" to explain what and/or why something, which has already occurred, occurred.

QUANTUM PSYCHOLOGY PRINCIPLE:

Reasons and their accompanying beliefs are just that. They occur at the thinking dimension but are a by-product of the nervous system and can only give reasons and justifications much later for what has already occurred in the past. Furthermore, the reasons and justifications are further away from reality (the experience itself) and hence, more disconnected from what is.

Still, even though these are Quantum Psychological Principles, we will have to meet the problem at the level of the problem in order to understand the BIOLOGICAL CORE and what Quantum Psychology calls BIOLOGICAL REALIZATION.

THE BIOLOGICAL CORE:
THE PHYSICAL MANIFESTATION OF ESSENCE

The development of awareness of the BIOLOGICAL CORE seems to be one of the "slowest" for two reasons: First, because it is in physical matter (as opposed to a thought or a feeling), it is denser. Second, the present time demands of our industrial society force us to lose awareness of our biology and push us beyond what a body can do. In short, "our" psychology and the external world try to get us to overcome the body with the thinking and emotional dimensions. For example, overworking, poor air and water—not to mention the socialization process which thwarts our biology and creates greater dissociation. Simply put, modern day time pressures put more of an emphasis on psychology and force a loss of awareness of the body.

However, years of body focus can yield BIOLOGICAL REALIZATION. What is BIOLOGICAL REALIZATION? *It is the realization that "your" body is made of the same substance as everything else and there is no separate individual body.*

In order for *THAT* explosion of awareness—that your body is made of the same substance as everything else—to be stabilized, and not just be an experience that comes and goes, it *might* be helpful if the BIOLOGICAL CORE were also stabilized.

But what is the BIOLOGICAL CORE? It's the core of your physical being which extends from your cranium to your pelvic floor and which holds the body up. The BIOLOGICAL CORE is a biological awareness and a felt sense. It is the alignment between the gravitational pull of the sun and the earth. In other words, the gravitational pull of the sun and earth meet through your BIOLOGICAL CORE and combine to hold the biological "you" (your body) up. Your BIOLOGICAL CORE is the physical and biological manifestation of **ESSENCE**. It should be noted that Quantum Psychology is presently doing research on the possibility that the dimension ruling the BIOLOGICAL CORE is not gravitational but electro-magnetic.[7]

Your False Core (to be discussed in Volume II) is the *idea* you have about yourself, which surrounds your BIOLOGICAL CORE. It is the underpinning and collapse within the body which are mirrored in your muscles. However, the False Core is an *image* you hold of yourself and try to overcome psychologically and biologically—it is not you. It is an "I" thought the nervous system produces after the fact. Why is it not you—*because "you" were "there" before the "I" thought arose.*

Ida Rolf, the founder of Rolfing, used the metaphor of "sleeve and core." She called the exterior muscles "the sleeve." They can be likened to the psychological compensating identities which *try* to over-compensate for your False Core (Volume II) and which *you* try to hold yourself up with rather than allowing yourself to be held up by the gravitational pull between the sun and the earth through the BIOLOGICAL CORE. Quantum Psychology calls this psychological compensating structure the False Self Compensator. The False Core is a psycho-emotional concept which acts like a covering over the Biological-Core.

What Rolf calls the sleeve (compensating identities) is foreground, which can be biologically experienced as sore muscles. The BIOLOGICAL CORE remains an unexperienced background. However, when aligned with gravity, the BIOLOGICAL CORE becomes foreground and the sleeve background. What does this mean experientially? It is the experience of living out of your true BIOLOGI-

---

[7]At present the majority opinion in physics is that gravity is the major force coming out of the BIG BANG. There is, however, a minority opinion that the major force is Electromagnetic (Kaku, *Hyperspace*, 1992). (This will be discussed in greater depth in Volume III).

CAL CORE and biological **ESSENCE**. It is experiencing, at a biological level, everyone's **ESSENCE** and your **ESSENCE** as the same. In short, it is an effortless process whereby you are being *held up* by gravity. However, like a fish who does not notice the water, gravity (once aligned) goes unnoticed and is effortless.

I met with Jack Donnelly, a Rolfer of some 29 years, and asked him what Rolf meant when she talked about the BIOLOGICAL CORE. According to Jack,

> You are dealing with gravity. When you are dealing with gravity, you are dealing with what Ida called, the primal core, which goes from the pelvic floor up to about the solar plexus, and the high core which goes from the cranium down to about the solar plexus. That is where they meet. . . .

Rolf felt, according to Donnelly, *"that psychology was formed by a breakage in the core."* She said that

> the primal core and gravity are related to the earth, and that the high core is related to the gravitational pull of the sun, and that line between the sun and earth on a gravitational level is the Rolf line. According to Donnelly, It is the alignment around the BIOLOGICAL CORE (and it is a physical core not only energetic, like Yogis would say) that aligns the biology with earth and the sun on a gravitational level through the vehicle of the body.

Rolf's statement has enormous ramifications in regard to what Quantum Psychology calls the realization of **BIOLOGICAL ESSENCE**. This experiential realization leads us to an understanding that the body is made of the same substance as everything else, and we begin to see the BIOLOGICAL CORE's relationship to other spiritual disciplines. For example, Taoist literature says something like, "When heaven and earth are aligned, the Tao is realized. When heaven and earth are aligned balance will occur," or "when heaven and earth are balanced, the true nature of the Tao [the way] will be revealed." I realized if we substitute the word *Sun* for the word *heaven* we have the true biological meaning of BIOLOGICAL CORE.

In other words, "when we realize and experience the effort-lessness of the gravitational pull on a biological level between the Sun (heaven) and the earth, then we will experience alignment with *The Way* (The Tao). And when the BIOLOGICAL CORE (high core and primal core) are aligned, the gravitational pull between the sun and earth occurs, hence, there are no interruptions, and the Tao is *naturally* realized.

In this way, when your biological connection is aligned be-tween the sun and the earth, *you just are*. This is the Tao (way). There is no psychology because there are no breakages or interruptions[8] in the BIOLOGICAL CORE. There are no past, present, or projected future body images. There is not even a present time body image. Rather, *you just are* on a biological level. To appreciate this, accord-ing to Rolf, we must understand that the interruptions (breakages) in this "gravitational" connection and alignment between sun and earth create psychology.

This breakage creates a subjective biological experience of separation-merger, which is ultimately imaginary. This separation-merger response is noticed by psychology's idea (thinking dimen-sion) and underlies many psychological processes. Psychology is then formed as an abstraction, a resistance, a way to explain pain, stress, shock or, in a word, *chaos*, to explain this natural separation-merger experience. In this way, psychology is a manifestation of the biology that occurs in to order deal with the chaos which occurs when trauma breaks (interrupts) the BIOLOGICAL CORE. *Psychology arises af-ter the fact.*

---

[8]In Quantum Consciousness the summary of the human potential movement was "all neu-rosis is caused by an *interruption* in the outward motion. (E-motion, E meaning outward, motion).

T he purpose of
the Nervous
System is to
organize chaos.
Moshe Feldenkrais

In this way, images are formed to distract and explain to you the pain of the present time experience. Misalignments of the BIO-LOGICAL CORE create thoughts which occur because of the lack of this realization.

The ideas you have about your body create your biological→psychological, or your ideas about a separate biological self. The way you experience this idea about who you are at a bio-logical level is not the BIOLOGICAL CORE, which has no ideas. During trauma, ideas and body images are formed because the BIO-LOGICAL CORE is shocked; hence, there is a breakage in aware-ness, a psychological interruption, in the awareness of the BIOLOGI-CAL CORE. This breakage causes a subjective interruption, in this essential biological experience of beingness which Wilhelm Reich (the father of body therapy) termed "vegetative."[9] What gets formed out of this trauma, and to organize the chaos of this trauma, then, is a separate self or "I". In short, at a biological-psychological level, what you call "you" is caused by interruptions in biology due to the regu-lation of socialization.

In this way, a trauma is a memory, a picture or an image of a past time event which emerged during shocks which caused inter-ruptions in the BIOLOGICAL CORE. In this way, you identify or fuse with past body images. This occurs as an aspect of the nervous system. In other words, the nervous system (brain) holds memories and creates associations as a survival mechanism.[10] Using its search-ing-scanning-seeking overgeneralizing mechanism *IT* sees the present as the past in an attempt to insure that (something undesirable) will not happen again. Because of the natural survival mechanism of memory and creating associations, you lose awareness of your present time body and your BIOLOGICAL CORE. In short, you get further away from your body *as it is* and this prevents you from experienc-ing your BIOLOGICAL CORE which is the physical manifestation of your **ESSENCE**.

---

[9]I particularly like Reich's term "vegetative" because vegetables don't have a self or psy-chology, they just are.

[10]Note how the idea is reframed in psycho-spiritual work where "learning lessons," mirrors the nervous systems's survival mechanism of organizing associations.

Dr. Carl Ginsberg says it this way:

For potent, erect action, the extensor system must bring the skeletal structures to a center core around which action can be organized. I am convinced that the sensing of this skeletal security equates with the ability to be present in the moment, and to act without self interference or overt over-conscious control. A very young child can hold the head in near perfect balance with clear support from the central structural core of spine and pelvis.

Fear, however, produces the flexor responses which contract the system away from this core of support, and require that muscular action be produced to counteract this contraction in order for the person to continue to be able to act in gravity. In the ideal state all action is produced with an even distribution of tonus throughout the musculature. In the more typical situation this clarity of organization is lost through the overlay of responses including emotions, feelings and thoughts impressed by parents and social conditioning. The person, sensing the inner collapse, produces a masked state of the musculature to control the appearance to the outside world, and to provide some sense of control and security given the loss of the inner core. Thus a False Self is created.

In my practice of the Feldenkrais work I often find that the central issue behind a person's complaints is the lack of awareness of their BIOLOGICAL CORE in the sense in which I have described it above. My clients, however, do not usually come to find a new center. They complain of holding tension in their shoulders and neck, or between the shoulder blades, or in the lower back. What I observe is that the tension in question is the consequence of necessity. Without it, and given the state of the spine, they would fall over. Thus in restoring the sense of natural strength and stability through the spine, the tensions disappear. That is, the person experiences a new state in which they no longer feel a necessity to hold themselves up. The notion of holding tension was an illusion. I find in this a profound possibility. And that is the opening to **ESSENCE**.

QUANTUM PSYCHOLOGY PRINCIPLE:

The BIOLOGICAL CORE is the physical manifestation of **ESSENCE** and is the physical bridge between the **spaciousness** of **ESSENCE** and the physical manifestation of the biology held together by gravity.

"GETTING THERE"

When past time body images are dropped and the CORE is realized, you are not only in your BIOLOGICAL CORE and biological **ESSENCE**, you realize that "your" BIOLOGICAL CORE is the *same* as—and made of the same substance as—everyone else's biological **ESSENCE**. This is the biological realization of the interconnection and oneness of everything. It is truly a physical experience. To illustrate, several years ago I was giving a workshop in Kansas City. There was a woman there who was deeply age regressed and even began singing. *When I lost awareness of "my" BIOLOGICAL CORE*, I felt really separate from her." I noticed, however, that when I dropped into my own BIOLOGICAL CORE, I felt one with her BIOLOGICAL CORE. I could see the pain in her eyes and felt the *essential biological* experience of compassion.

It should be noted again that body workers should not fall into the trap that "if we handle the body, the images *too* will get handled." *Not so*. This has been a major flaw of understanding in many of the most popular systems and subsystems of today, i.e., Feldenkrais and Rolfing. The images of the body, as well as the body itself, are holographic. However, you need to follow the Quantum

Psychology Principle: *Meet the problem at the level of the problem.* If there is an image problem, handle it at the thinking dimension. If there is an emotional problem, handle it at the emotional dimension. What Quantum Psychology has noticed is that when images are dismantled the BIOLOGICAL CORE, like **ESSENCE** becomes more available. Why? Because the interference patterns, or habitually fixated awareness, is unfixated and free. This allows body awareness and its re-education to be greatly enhanced and speeded-up.

QUANTUM PSYCHOLOGY PRINCIPLE:

The realization of this spinal connection up and through the spine to the cerebral cortex and beyond ignites the realization of biological spirituality (i.e., the grounded experience that the body too is made of **THAT ONE SUBSTANCE**).

INTEGRATING THE OLDER WITH THE NEWER BRAIN

To integrate this awareness:

Step I: Notice a thought you are having.

Step II: Follow or trace it down to the non-verbal sensation level in the lower brain (spine).

Step III: Take a deep breath and take it down into the lower spine (lower brain); the no-state silent level.

Step IV: Notice what happens.

PSYCHOLOGY'S CREATION

Ida Rolf saw the core as bipolar, with poles at the lower and upper cores, and that breakages in the balance create "psychology." It should be noted that after conception the first part of the body formed is the bi-polar (i.e., electromagnetic) spine or core. Let us look at this statement from both a Quantum Psychology and also from a Reichian therapy perspective. Ida Rolf was saying that alignment on a biological level takes place when this core is aligned with the gravitational pull of the earth and sun. Quantum Psychology would say that breakages in the gravitational alignment in the core causes psychological structures to emerge (thoughts, beliefs, etc.) to compensate or explain for this breakage or interruption. In short, *"your" individual separate "I" is a creation of the nervous system.*

Moshe Feldenkrais once said that "the purpose of the nervous system is to organize chaos." In this way, it can be said that this natural neurological process creates psychology to order the chaos. Korzybski's structural differential is a pictorial representation of what he calls the nervous system's abstracting process. This is a process whereby the nervous system, as part of this natural neurological order, describes, labels, and makes inferences from the non-verbal. It can be said that Korsybski's structural differential is a diagram which represents how *the nervous system selects out to create its own reality and organize what it views as chaos.*[11]

What needs to be stressed again is that the "I" and the "observer" (to be discussed later) are also part of this natural neurological and sometimes dissociative process whereby the body (nervous system) creates a psychology as an attempt to continue its own survival. This helps us to answer the often asked question, "Why *don't* identities (psychology) change rapidly?" Because the psychology is the body's survival mechanism. In other words, the "I" (psychology) is a defense against the over or under stimulation of the body. Psychology's (the I's) emergence is an attempt to order and explain that deprivation or over-stimulation.

Furthermore, *the "I" (psychology) which tries to change the unwanted "I" (psychology) is also part of the same nervous system,* hence "you" are trying to get rid of "yourself." This goes against the natural fight/fight survival mechanism of the nervous system and it will not let that happen. Why? Because the one that wants to get rid of *(fill in the blank)*, the one to be gotten rid of and the "observer" of both are all by-products of the nervous system and contain the same fight/flight survival mechanism.

---

[11]It should be noted that "you" do not create or select out your own reality. The idea of "you" is a by-product of the nervous system which has formed this idea of a "you." The idea of creating or selecting out and the "you" which follows have already done ALL of that choosing, creating, deciding etc., long before the "you" (which comes later) claims "you" did chose or created this or that. Thus, the ego, or what you call "you," comes after the fact, event, etc., and creates explanations of choice, claims ownership of actions, justifications, motivations, preferences, volition and will—when, in fact, it has none.

T he I or ME is the name the body gives to and calls itself.

Stephen H. Wolinsky

THE SHOCK

It is the shock of the Realization of Separation and deprivation which causes the break in your awareness of the BIOLOGICAL CORE. Please note that this separation story is a story, a theory to explain what or why. However, it is a *symbolic representation* of what is—*not* what is. This, in turn, creates your False Core and your psychology (see Volume II). This is also sometimes mirrored in the images we have of our biology. And that an infant's learning to stand up and face the world is inhibited at a psychological level by the False Core (psychology). The False Core as a representation mirrors the loss of awareness of the BIOLOGICAL CORE rather than the biology mirroring the psychology.

In Reichian therapy, it is said that all neurosis is caused by an *interruption* in the body's ability to discharge excess energy. Reich said that this inability forces the energy upward into thoughts, and then forces those thoughts even "higher" upward toward the head (cortex) and above. The greater the trauma (breakages and interruptions), the greater the *inability* to release energy, and the more the cortex will create stories and reasons—an "I" and a "you"—to explain and justify what you call "your psychology," etc. If this upward process continues, according to Reich, it perpetuates the mystification of the world (making it into a world of Gods and Goddesses (see the Trance of Spiritualization, Chaper14, *The Dark Side of the Inner Child*).

Quantum Psychology suggests as a story: 1) That the shock to your BIOLOGICAL CORE is mirrored at a psychological level and is solidified by the narcissistic injury (to be detailed in Volume II). 2) On an energetic level (a bioenergetic level), it is the uninterrupted flow of energy which occurs when the BIOLOGICAL CORE is aligned with the gravitational pull of the sun and the earth that helps to *eliminate* beliefs, thoughts, and mystifying the world (trance of spiritualization). This is why you feel so quiet "inside" after a "body session—your psychology disappears! However, shortly afterwards, your psychology comes back because we still have to *meet the problem at the level of the problem*. For Quantum Psychology, this is not a world of Gods and Goddesses, but of ONE INDIVISIBLE SUBSTANCE. 3) The breakages in the BIOLOGICAL CORE

(Quantum Psychology would say breaks in awareness of your BIO-LOGICAL CORE) create the illusion of a separate "I" and "you" which, when identified with, prevents realization of THAT ONE SUBSTANCE.

QUANTUM PSYCHOLOGY PRINCIPLE:

THAT ONE SUBSTANCE cannot be divided or separated. Rather, the images of separation and division (which are your psychology) are created by the body (nervous system) as a survival mechanism (i.e., a learning device so that it can "never happen again").

Simply stated being in the world is what the biological function and BIOLOGICAL CORE are about. This occurs naturally and spontaneously without psychological considerations when the core is realized and the False Core dismantled.

When you lose awareness of your BIOLOGICAL CORE, the "I" gets fixated in the thinking or emotional dimension and feels disconnected from the body and from the world, and hence, the Underlying Unity. When you are aware of your BIOLOGICAL CORE, a natural *body bliss* is experienced. It is an effortless and pure energy pouring out of the body's tissues by which "I" feel a oneness with the "external." It is the loss of the awareness of, and disconnection from, the BIOLOGICAL CORE which causes a disconnection from the external world. In other words, the muscles of the body are disorganized and fight one another. This is mirrored in the psychology where parts of "yourself" are fighting one another. The energy is drained and there is a defense of the trauma of separation and loss of the BIOLOGICAL CORE. To illustrate this, I use the metaphor of Alfred Schatz, founder of the Institute for Applied Physiology in Germany:

Imagine a symphony orchestra where the instruments are all out-of-tune, not playing together, and on different beats. There is a conflict going on. But if the conductor can get all the instruments organized so that they're playing the same music and are *orchestrated*

at the same time—rhyme, rhythm and beat, etc.—there
is no fighting and it's a beautiful experience.

The same is true with the brain (the conductor). The muscles are
orchestrated not to resist and fight the BIOLOGICAL CORE, but to
let go and be led by the BIOLOGICAL CORE. Then, there is a connection, and a symphony in pure orchestration and organization.

When you are in touch with your BIOLOGICAL CORE, suddenly there are no thoughts, there are no fantasies. And I *do and
know* what to do without any of what Gurdjieff called *inner considering*. I just am, I just do. Everything just is. I am instantly connected
not only to my body but to the external world as well. When that
occurs, I more than know **I AM**. "I" am on the way to the realization
that my body is made of the same substance as everything else.

In order for this realization to be stabilized, being grounded
at the biological level through the BIOLOGICAL CORE seems important. Otherwise "your" experience of unity is limited to only certain contexts. For example, I've met many gurus whose experience
of the underlying unity is limited to an Ashram, a cave, a monastery,
a retreat, or someplace where they are taken care of. They limit actions, trying to control thoughts, and relationships with people. This
form of "keeping the state" or having to do or perform certain rituals
in order to maintain a certain state is not enlightenment—it is an
enlightenment prison. It demonstrates that there is not a full integration at all dimension and that the so-called "state" is context dependent. Gurus and teachers who try to *maintain a state* are not integrated at a biological level—and maybe other levels, too. Take them
out of their context and place them in a relationship or working in the
world and unity consciousness eludes their awareness.

Maharaj was once asked, "Are you in Samadhi?" He said,
"No, Samadhi is a state. I am not in a state."

NO DOER—NO SUBJECTIVITY

When biological realization occurs, doing with NO-I occurs
at a non-verbal level; there is no thinking and, paradoxically, no subjective experience of doing. There is *no doer* because there is no

interruption in the gravitational biological flow to create a psychology of separation or an "I"-Thou dualistic relationship. The brain is organized to handle gravity, and awareness is further liberated—even the energy it takes the brain to manage it is freed. There is no interruption of the bipolar connection between the earth and the sun, no breakages in awareness and *no psychology*. There is just pure biological being and that is realization at a biological level.

THE BIOLOGICAL CORE: ANOTHER PERSPECTIVE

Recently, I met with Ron McCombs, a Rolfer of some 25-30 years and I asked him, "What exactly did Ida Rolf mean when she talked about the BIOLOGICAL CORE?" Ron said there was one sentence he remembered that was important to him. "The core is what you cannot live fully without." The two words that are important to me are *live* and *fully*. How can I live fully if I am not aware of and connected to my BIOLOGICAL CORE? Without this connection, I'm going to experience breakages in myself due to breakages in the awareness of the gravitational force. With breakages, and interruptions in my psychology there are automatic thoughts and feelings. I become indecisive and unable to see or "experience" the non-verbal **I AM** at a biological level, not to mention **THAT ONE SUBSTANCE**. In short, Rolf suggested, *if you are not connected to your BIOLOGICAL CORE, then you cannot live fully*. I can be breathing and walking but remain disconnected from the world, without the awareness of biological oneness[12] in the experience of biological separation or in a fantasy land of Gods, Goddesses and spiritualized trances. But according to Rolf, you cannot live fully and completely until you are in touch with your BIOLOGICAL CORE.

---

[12]Once again, it is not total merger in the development of multi-dimensional awareness, it is realizing separation at an external thinking, emotional and biological level while simultaneously realizing the inter-connection of **THAT ONE SUBSTANCE.** The excess pain continues after the realization of separation (Volume II) because the "separate" experience remains frozen, due to trauma (i.e., there is a fusion-association merger, pain or shock, so that to not let it happen again, as a survival mechanism, the nervous system freezes on separation). Hence, the natural biological merger which should occur like a pulsating merger-separation is frozen on separation, or resisting separation.

QUANTUM PSYCHOLOGY PRINCIPLE:

The more you are in touch with, coming from, and aware of your BIOLOGICAL CORE, the greater you will experience personal aliveness.

QUANTUM PSYCHOLOGY PRINCIPLE:

The greater your connection to your BIOLOGICAL CORE, and the natural alignment of the gravitational pull of the sun and the earth, the greater your connection to the external world as one solid unity.

QUANTUM PSYCHOLOGY PRINCIPLE:

The greater your connection to the BIOLOGICAL CORE, the greater will be the probability that "you" might experience unity or experience the body as made of the same substance as everything else.

QUANTUM PSYCHOLOGY PRINCIPLE:

The more you are aware of the BIOLOGICAL CORE, the more making decisions becomes a nonissue, life becomes a nonissue and your psychology becomes a non-issue, you just are, things just occur.

QUANTUM PSYCHOLOGY PRINCIPLE:

The BIOLOGICAL CORE is the vehicle for the thinking and feeling dimensions. When they are aligned, there is pure being at a biological level: The **NON-VERBAL I AM**.

Simply put, doing, or walking in your being occur. The being naturally becomes functional in its movement. That is the Tao, and what it means to be in your BIOLOGICAL CORE. In this way, the BIOLOGICAL CORE is what you cannot live fully without. Quantum Psychology says that the degree to which you cannot be in your BIOLOGICAL CORE is the degree you get more into random thoughts, more into breakages, more imbalances, more energetic interruptions, more trancing-out, more into spiritualization and more disconnected from the other dimensions of your humanity.

For this reason, from a Quantum Psychology perspective, the BIOLOGICAL CORE is a core dimension that needs to be worked with, acknowledged, and explored so that wherever your awareness is, i.e., **ESSENCE**, thinking level, etc., you can *stay connected with the underlying unity which moves through the BIOLOGICAL CORE.* Without this, your connection becomes disjointed, there are breakages and your realization of **THAT** becomes an idea, a concept rather than pure IS-NESS.

ARCHETYPES AND THE BIOLOGICAL CORE

When Quantum Psychology suggests that the BIOLOGICAL CORE is the meeting place between heaven (the sun) and earth, this can also be seen archetypically. The sun (metaphorically and archetypically) represent the father or God and the earth (metaphorically and archetypically) represent the mother. People's awareness must rest between the two in order to be permanently established in the awareness of unity or **NOT-I-I** (see Volume III). This is the true meaning of "Honor your father (sun), the gravitational force, and your mother (earth), the gravitational force. This is biological spirituality.

THE BIOLOGICAL CORE AND YOGA SYSTEMS

Yoga systems often times require that in meditation you sit upright with your back totally straight. This posture should naturally be done from the core, not from the sleeve. When you are in your core, then there is a natural balancing between the gravitational pulls of the sun and the earth. There are no breakages, hence, no thoughts—or, as Ida Rolf said, no breakages no psychology. In this way, on a biological level there is the non-verbal **I AM** or pure BEINGNESS which is a no-state state and is a natural meditation (see Volume III).

Actually by being in your core, meditation as an act or action is unnecessary. With this understanding, the *"act of meditation"* can be seen at best as a preparation for the no-state state; and at worst as medication or a spiritualized defense and compensation for the break in the BIOLOGICAL CORE→the False Core.

Unfortunately, the technique of sitting straight is seen as a spiritual *should*, something to be done by an "I". For this reason, Yogis often use their outer muscles (their sleeve, i.e., compensating identities) to create and hold themselves up, with effort straightening the spinal column. Because it is done from the "sleeve" *with effort* rather than the BIOLOGICAL CORE *which is effortless*, it becomes counterproductive thus creating more thoughts and reinforcing the False Core and the compensating False Self Identities, and bringing forth yet more thoughts and more psychological breakages in a vicious circle. Moreover this "forcing" of the back and spinal column to be straight reinforces the psychological breakages since it reinforces the "sleeve" (external muscles) or False Self (psychological sleeve).

Biological and psychological breakages can be seen as a metaphor for the term *splitting off* in object relations therapy. In other words, there is a splitting off from your real core when you "hold yourself up" and split off and dissociate from other dimensions of awareness. This dissociation creates "spiritual experiences," which can sometimes be "Spiritual" trances. They are dissociated from the whole (i.e., other dimensions of awareness), and hence, they are distortions created by breakages in the BIOLOGICAL CORE. It should be noted from Chapter One that Spirituality in Quantum Psychology is defined as the realization that everything is made of **THAT ONE SUBSTANCE.**

All experiences—be they a thought called "I hate myself" or "I love myself," anger or a vision of "God"—should be acknowledged, *not interpreted*, at a <u>biological level</u> as having been created by breakages in the BIOLOGICAL CORE and let go of.*

---

*Please note that <u>biological level</u> is underscored, in Volume III, we see all *I*'s and experiences as arising and subsiding with the **VOID OF UNDIFFERENTIATED CONSCIOUSNESS.**

QUANTUM PSYCHOLOGY PRINCIPLE:

The only real "spiritual" experience is the no-experience experience, the non-verbal "**I AM**" or the pure awareness of the **NOT-I-I** of **THAT ONE SUBSTANCE** .

QUANTUM PSYCHOLOGY PRINCIPLE:

Any experience that is dissociated from the other dimensions of awareness is not grounded in the whole. Therefore, it can lead to a distortion of reality and not **THAT ONE SUBSTANCE.**

This is why so many mediators have "spiritual" ideas about spirituality. In Quantum Psychology, *your idea of spirituality is not spirituality.* Spirituality is a no-experience experience. It has neither meaning nor purpose. not appreciating this is why the changeless background of "spirituality" goes unnoticed.

QUANTUM PSYCHOLOGY PRINCIPLE:

Any idea you have about spirituality is not spirituality. *Spirituality has no ideas.* It is not even the idea of **THAT ONE SUBSTANCE.**

BIOLOGICAL CORE YOGA

A body yoga or a core yoga is a natural yoga. Once the breakages in Awareness and splitting off end, there is a no more trancing-out (see *Trances People Live* or *The Dark Side of the Inner Child*). Because of the awareness of the BIOLOGICAL CORE, there is a natural walking around, daily awareness a free no state-state, which means that there is *No-I.* Actually there is no meditation because there is No-I meditating. There is no longer any internal considering, no voices or internal dialogue and no more interruptions in emotions, i.e., the outward motion. That is core yoga. It is Taoist yoga. It is Buddhist yoga and with it, the *you* you call yourself ends. There are no more trances or, better said, **TRANCE-ENDING** occurs naturally. In other words, *when you are ready to meditate, meditation is not necessary.*

Unfortunately, sometimes people practice yoga from outside of themselves so that their bodies can look a certain way, appear a certain way, or act a certain way. This is not core yoga. Core yoga is about moving from the BIOLOGICAL CORE which is from inside out. If you have Yoga teachers who are trying to get you in particular positions or postures so that you "look" a certain way, you are doing yoga from your sleeve and the postures are dissociative postures. In other words, you are doing yoga from the outside—how do I look?—in. In this way, you are doing it from your compensating identities as a way to resist, or hide your False Core. This reinforces thoughts and breakages in your biology—and your psychology. This is the reason why people who have mastered Hatha Yoga rarely, if ever, have quiet minds, or they have a very large ego about postures they can get into. Although their health might improve, because certainly Hatha Yoga is a health practice, at the same time, the purpose of Hatha Yoga is much deeper. One of its purposes is to realign your physical body so that you can realize that it is made of **THAT ONE SUBSTANCE**. The purpose of Hatha Yoga is not to "look" better and reinforce your compensating identities which reinforce your False Core. It is through Core Yoga that your biology and your BIOLOGICAL CORE meet your **ESSENTIAL CORE** (Volume III). This is Biological **I AM THAT**.

YOUR IMAGE OF THE BODY IS NOT THE BODY

Korzbyski said that, "The idea is not the thing it is referring to." In the same way the "image" of you, you have, and even the "you" that is having it, are not you.

Einstein said, "Everything changes except the way people think about it." And so the problem is, I'm holding onto an old image of my body in a present time situation that does not exist any more. In other words, in the context of 1955, the image of myself might have been appropriate but the problem is, I'm still holding it, still seeing the world through the past-time body image which acts like a lens rather than the no lens of present time.

This is what occurs in trauma. Not only do you carry the psychological scars but the past time body image as well, seeing the world and yourself through this past time image. At this dimension you see yourself, and imagine the world sees you, in past time or as your parents did. For example, let's imagine a car accident. What accounts for there being paranoia around cars or a driving phobia afterwards? Because the person holds a "past time body image." Upon entering a car (specific external [context] dimension), the person then enters the past time body image of the accident which has been frozen. As another example, let's imagine a five-year old is molested. Later during sex (specific eternal [context] dimension), they enter into the same past-time body image and hence experiences the same bodily experience in present time through the vehicle of the past-time image of being five years old.

QUANTUM PSYCHOLOGY PRINCIPLE:

In order to experience your present time body, past time body images must be dissolved. In this way, you can have your present time biology without being fixated on the past or your past time body image.

On a biological level, just as at a psychological level, there is a tendency to fuse with another, usually a parent, as a survival mechanism. In biology, there is a survival strategy for merging, which is the survival of the species. At a biological level, human beings have a merger response—a natural biological tendency to merge. For example, if I get involved with a woman, there's going to be a biological interest in merging and that's fine as long as I simultaneously know she is a human being, has her own life and a whole universe that is separate from mine. In other words I do not collapse the levels and think she is or has to be the same as me (see Volume II).

In this way, I can have a biological merging or unity experience at one level while simultaneously maintaining other levels of separation (i.e., thinking and emotional, biological, external). Problems in relationship occur because people do not distinguish levels. If you have a past time body image of yourself, you have to hold a past time body image of her/him. This might make her/him into my mother or father. This means I have frozen and collapsed the external biological, thinking, and emotional levels. Then, you go through rages, fear, depression, etc. when she/he says "I can't make it Friday night." Why? Because you are in your past time body image, and hence you are collapsing the levels.

The images of your body are not you. If all of the images of the body are gone, then you just are, you are *prior to* having taken on these images. As Jesus said, "To enter the kingdom of heaven (the **VOID OF UNDIFFERENTIATED CONSCIOUSNESS**), you must be like a child (prior to all images).

THE BODY AS AN ANIMAL

On a basic level, the body is an animal with animal tendencies. This must be clear otherwise you will always have a problem. It's biological. The animal underlies biology and it is a survival mode. All of the externals—mom, dad, society—try to control this animal nature, whether by toilet training, getting you to eat at a certain time, or to go to bed when you aren't tired. Society/Mom/Dad, etc., are totally trying to organize the animal. When our basic animal nature becomes socialized the repression is very painful. It is because of this pain that much of our psychology develops. Simply put, in reality, parents or society are trying to regulate the animal.

QUANTUM PSYCHOLOGY PRINCIPLE:

The greater the repression of your animal nature, the greater the False Core and the False Self substitutions.

Furthermore, when repression continues, the external (Mom and Dad) can become spiritualized (made into Gods and Goddesses) and/or anthropomorphized. These Gods, Goddesses or Gurus are created by the trance of spiritualization, a state which sees the body as a source of "pain." If I didn't have a body and all of these urges, then I wouldn't get spanked, hit, yelled at, punished (sent to hell). Rather I would be loved and merged (heaven). If you look at almost any spiritual system other than Tantric, most of them label the body and all of its urges as bad, as something to be overcome. Christianity sees the body's urges as being against goodness, holiness and thus as sinful. Many systems suggest an infantile understanding that to find "enlightenment" requires overcoming our animal nature in some way. This is a clear transpersonal trance-ference whereby enlightenment is gotten, through overcoming bodily functions. In this way the socialization process and the *spiritual system has now become the super-ego with all its shoulds*. The bodily functions once repressed, however, comes out in "less appropriate," out-of-context ways (like priests molesting children). Parents often say to children, "What inside of you makes you act this way?" Quantum Psychology says "It is the repressed animal."

QUANTUM PSYCHOLOGY PRINCIPLE:
You can never overcome your animal nature.

You cannot overcome your animal nature, it is not possible, and why should you even want to? As an exercise, Quantum Psychology suggests viewing life through the animal dimension. If you look at your relationships with people, you can view them through several lenses. For example, if I view people situations, people and my relationship to them, etc., through the lens of my thinking dimension, I will get one understanding. If I view this through the emotional level, I will get another. If I view my relationships through the animal dimension, however, I will get a yet another different understanding.

Let's say I get into an argument in a business arrangement and feel that they want me to sign a contract so they'll own me. If I look at this through the thinking dimension, I might think, "They've got stuff about ownership." But at the animal level, it is the same as a dog peeing around a person. In other words, it becomes much clearer and easier to understand what's going on. Obviously in this particular business situation, they want me to sign an exclusive contract so that I won't work with anyone else. At the *external* business dimension that makes total sense; but at a deeper level governed by biology, they're acting like *territorial animals* and their "business explanation" is a justification coming after the fact to justify something governed by the nervous system. In other words, the animal rules and the explanation take place after the fact, as a kind of story line, a psychology/philosphy to explain and justify everything. Viewing from this animal level helps to make things more understandable.

QUANTUM PSYCHOLOGY PRINCIPLE:

You have to unleash your animal energy. Acknowledge it, allow it to be there. It's very powerful, otherwise, the repression of it makes you crazy.

IT IS NOT HUMAN TO REPRESS

The nervous system is biological, there are survival instincts. No matter how enlightened you are, there are certain things that are hard-wired into the nervous system.

Look at all of the body functions such as eating, sleeping, shitting and fucking. They are all biological. How would you feel if you didn't get enough sleep? Probably irritable and cranky. No matter how much psychotherapy you have done, sleep's a basic biological function. Sexuality is the survival of the species. Spiritual systems often suggest that you can become enlightened (spiritualized, purified) through biological deprivation such as giving up food or sex. This makes as much sense as saying, you have a better chance of "attaining" enlightenment if you don't go the bathroom anymore. *This spiritualization by repression of biological urges fueled by the spiritualization process of making Dad and Mom into Gods and Goddesses creates a massive distortion, whereby the spiritualized Dad/Mom are Gods, Goddesses, a path, etc., which is really a spiritualized super-ego.*

Society attempts to repress our animal nature; and thus we have society's rules vis-a-vis the church placed on our biology. Naturally the biological-energy goes crazy and produces a "crazy" psychology. In Quantum Psychology we are not talking about "acting it out" as if imagining expressing sexuality equals liberation—as some gurus suggest. We are not talking about the repression-expression continuum. We are talking about taking the label off and being with the energy of it.

Many forms of therapy consider substitution a "good" thing. For Quantum Psychology, substitution can be repressing some basic animal drive and substituting it for some socially acceptable behavior. For example, let's say when you expressed sexuality as a child, you were rebuked by your parents but when you expressed interests in achievement and success, you were rewarded. You then substitute sexual impulse for achievement. Some say this is "good."

Quantum Psychology suggests two major pitfalls:

1. That the achievement never reaches a state of satisfaction or completion (climax).

2. The repressed-substituted sexual impulse comes out in other ways.

First of all, substitution yields no satisfaction, it only yields more escalating substitution (i.e., driving for more and more success). Secondly, as homeopathic medicine suggests, sexual and other impulses do not go away with substitution but create a supression and sometimes a perversion of symptoms, since the energy must come out in some way. For example, the high number of priests caught in sexual scandals with children shows a clear age-regression of the priest who then "acts out" this sexual repression, or the high occurrences of uterian cancer among nuns..

Substitution occurs *because* of the *repression of the animal*, i.e., we are forced to find a socially acceptable way to express our underlying biological needs. To illustrate further, we substitute having money to bolster our "self" worth," because the more money we have, the more love (merger) we imagine we will get. This too is a substitution of the merger response. It is no wonder it never works or is never enough.

FORGETTING THE CONTEXT

Psychology's and spirituality's *biggest mistake* is that they *forget or misunderstand* the context of our *animal nature*. There is no getting around that. They forget where our psychology is fueled from and want us to deal with our thoughts and emotional processes "as if" we didn't have a larger biological context from which these thoughts and feelings were being fueled, and were a by-product of.

Psychology oftentimes splits the person off, taking them out of the animal context of their biology and creating a false context "as if" psychology were not a part of biology, thus causing their thinking process to become dissociated from their biology. In this way social rules (external) become the context rather than the animal and biological nature which we are all organized around, i.e., I have to hold in my shit until a certain time, and even if I'm hungry I can only eat at dinnertime. Psychology tries to gain control over the animal but it can't be done, and this makes us feel even more chaotic and split-off from "ourselves" and "others."

This is why Nisargadatta Maharaj did not say "mind and body" or "mind body," but rather "body-mind."

BIOLOGICAL SPIRITUALITY

Through biological deprivation, trauma and the dissociation or splitting off that occurs from the pain story of that narcissistic injury (see Volume II), you get psychology. When *psychology* is *aberrated and dissociated*, you get a high percentage of what people call "*spirituality*." Biological spirituality is experiencing the body as grounded and being made of **THAT ONE SUBSTANCE**. Biological spirituality is getting that your body-mind spirit is one whole piece. There is no separate body, separate mind, and separate spirit. It is all a unity.

FEAR

I was recently doing a workshop and a participant told me that a famous Buddhist Vipassana teacher said, "All fear is psychological. It doesn't exist." Quantum Psychology disagrees. The nervous system has a fight/ flight reaction and a sense of biological fear. For example, I'm walking down the street and a car nearly hits me. He slams on his brakes, my body freezes and I go numb all over. That's biological fear (fight/flight) and it is hard-wired into the nervous system.

However, if not in that moment, probably within a few minutes, I will label that bodily experience as fear. *The labeling is psychological, but the rest is biological.* In recent studies, they found that when people were in an accident and part of their brain was removed, they did things like walk in the middle of the street in dangerous places and had to be taught what was safe and what wasn't. There *is* biological fear.

Psychological fear, on the other hand can be the associational trance at work. For example, in the emotional dimension "I got hit by a car when I was 5 and now 25 years later when I see a car, I go into terror." That is psychological overlapping, collapsing memories and associations from the thinking dimension with the emotional dimension. This occurs when a thinking image and an emotional experience are replayed through the biology.

LIBIDO: THE BIOLOGICAL MERGER RESPONSE

Libido is the natural biological merging response. It is the natural biological drive to merge, either physically or at an external thinking, emotional or essential level. It has been greatly misunderstood. Libido does not mean sex. If someone says their libido is down, this is interpreted as meaning that their sex drive is low. But this is not what it really means. As the natural biological drive to merger response, the primal energy of the libido is actually a natural merging energy.

Society has confused this, and made libido into sex. Think what it would be like *if we accepted the fact there was a natural merging energy and a natural unmerging energy.* That means we could meet somebody and if we were on the same wavelength, we could feel that energy with them in whatever dimension, whether it be thinking, feeling, sexual, essential, or external, without any associations of, this means this means this. We could then unmerge without any guilt or frustration and be free to naturally merge or unmerge at any level—whether playing tennis or having an incredible conversation or just "vibrating" with someone, without all of the, "I can't do this, I'm married," or "If I have lunch and enjoy myself, then it means *(fill in the blank)*, "or" my partner might get jealous, therefore, I have to close down (the *natural merging/unmerging energy which is natural libido*).

A CONTAINER

Unfortunately because of personal history, trauma, etc. many people cannot contain (have) sensation. They cannot contain it inside their skin boundary. This can be an inability to contain any sensation, idea, or emotion, which means they have to express it. This occurs because sensation (often sexuality) is fused with trauma making it difficult for people to contain or have it. Why? Because sensation is not experienced as sensation. Rather, the thinking and/or the emotional dimension get collapsed with the biological sensation level. When this occurs, interpretations of past emotions are placed on top of sensations themselves. Hence, people judge sensations as "bad" or something to be gotten rid of in some way rather than just having sensations as sensations themselves, without judgment, evaluation or significance placed on them.

Unlike psychologies which imagine a body-mind split, to repeat again Korzybski in *Science and Sanity* refers to the organism as a whole:

> Experience and experiments show us that the natural order is sensation first, idea next; the sensation being an abstraction of some (lower) (earlier) order, and the idea clearly an abstraction of an abstraction, (sensation). . . . This reversal of order in its mild form is involved in . . . or the confusion of orders of abstractions; namely that we act as if an idea were an experience." (p. 76).

"Sexual" sensations are often repressed or labeled as bad by society and spiritual systems reinforce this process. When you label sexual sensations as bad, not only do you reinforce the fusion that *they are bad* but you also drive this natural biological response metaphorically upward, further away from experience, creating thoughts and philosophies which only reinforce and justify repression.

Dissociating from sensation can occur as sensations intensify and *you* yourself disappear or dissociate. For this reason, first become grounded in your body, developing the ability to have and be a container for sensation. Once that occurs, you will naturally realize your body is made up of the same substance as everything else. If you are unwilling to have the body as it is, you will never stabilize in this awareness. If this step does not occur, dimensions and boundaries collapse leaving a person without the ability to be aware of separation, while simultaneously being aware of the underlying unity.

TANTRIC YOGA

The ability to have and contain sensation first is paramount in the practice of Tantric yoga. This yogic practice utilizes sensation to expand awareness. Its aim is to develop the ability to contain an intense amount of sensation and then be able to turn the attention around and see that the sensation is made of the same substance as everything else. But you cannot do that if you don't have a container, i.e., the body. If you don't have a container to contain your sensation, you cannot build enough charge to explode and go beyond. In other words, if you dissociate from sensation or dribble it out through mushy boundaries whenever the energetic charge increases, you automatically lose it or it dissipates. When this happens, there is no container from which to explode out. You need to be able to have a container (body) and contain and hold sensation without labeling it.

QUANTUM PSYCHOLOGY PRINCIPLE:

Stories and explanations come out of the resistance to having sensations within a container (the body) and accepting them as they are.

The nervous system has an automatic abstracting process. It immediately labels and goes into thoughts and justifications during which you move further and further away from the non-verbal experience.

If I am not willing to contain and have my sensations, then I cannot be grounded in the biological dimension and it would be difficult to walk around in life and experience **ESSENCE** or **I AM**. A person can meditate and have an experience but you still have to be able to contain the biological level and be willing to have it. *The biology is your grounding wire, the point where ESSENCE and I AM meet the world.*

THE BIOLOGICAL FALSE CORES

The biological False Cores are different from and yet similar to the psycho-emotional False Cores (see Volume II). The psycho-emotional False Cores are conclusions drawn from the realization of separation and can be processed by tracing back and staying in the False Core, removing the later traumas which re-enforced it and, ultimately, dismantling this False Core conclusion.

The biological False Cores are also part of the nervous system yet they somehow seem more basic. They are interpretations of the nervous system which have been passed down through evolution and hard-wired into it. This means they are *earlier*, biologically rooted, pre-verbal, and difficult to process.[13]

---

[13] It should be noted that Alfred Schatz, is doing research into processing these neurological Nervous System hard-wires.

What you can do however is:

1. Unfuse the later chains of associations which trigger the biology.
2. Acknowledge with awareness the difference in dimensions. For example, I have a biological fear when I have the flu, or I break my arm, as opposed to, I have a psychological fear that the world will destroy me which is an association of the thinking dimension collapsed into the emotional dimension. The former is hard-wired into the nervous system. The latter is an abstraction and distortion and a catastrophic projected future.

THE REMEDY

1. Acknowledge the dimensions.
2. Cut the chain of associations by processing associations (going beyond) which are fused to the biological False Cores.
3. Go into the non-verbal levels of the biological False Cores prior to the associational networks.
4. Breath into and "have" the experience.

Often times, I notice (with #4 above) that "my breath" seems to move from upper to lower spine. The lower spine is "older" evolutionary-wise (i.e., before the cortical brain took over spinal function in directing neurological impulses). Thus, this integrates the most basic "reflex" and earliest functions.

Quantum Psychology sees not only False Cores at a thinking and an emotional dimension (see Volume II), but it also sees that there are biological False Cores which are hard wired into the nervous system.

FALSE CORE AND BIOLOGICAL DEPRIVATION

Any deprivation of the biological functions will tend to trigger your biological and psychological False Core. If you haven't had enough sleep, then you are more irritable, more vulnerable to the triggering of your biological-psychological False Core. If you haven't had sex for a long time, either you are going to try to deaden it or substitute something else because it can trigger your biological False Core. If eating is deprived, you will notice how hyper you might become. It triggers your biological False Core. And certainly constipation or diarrhea doesn't help. Biological deprivation makes you vulnerable to the triggering of your False Core.

WHO AM I

The drive to "know who you are" is an inborn function and a biological drive, i.e., learning response. In this way, **WHO AM I** is viewed as a primary biological learning function.

QUANTUM PSYCHOLOGY PRINCIPLE:

The greater the biological deprivation, the greater the "**WHO AM I**?" learning reaction. If it is totally denied or forced to NOT MANIFEST, substituting will occur and continue to exaggerate itself yielding no satisfaction.

(I can't get no satisfaction—Rolling Stones)

THE BODY MIND

The mind emerges out of the body as it moves to different levels of complexity and attempts to order chaos. Korzbyski said, "You can always say (think) more about what you said." In other words, systems too have a neurological component to delve into deeper and deeper levels of explanation.

The fight/flight response of the nervous system ultimately rules the psychological process. So, to *meet the problem at the level of the problem* you have to dismantle the fight/flight fusion with *past associations.*

"Your" identity, "your" psychology, and "your" False Core are formed as a survival mechanism. Quantum Psychology suggests that a shock occurs when both the fight and flight systems of the body are simultaneously ignited (this is also the feeling of a nervous system breakdown). Such a shock causes the body's electrical systems to clash and crash into one another. When this occurs, the body itself cannot "handle" this stimulation and begins to dissociate, to split and/or separate from itself. The chaos (energy) which the dissociation attempts to order are unlabeled electrical responses in the nervous system which later become fear, anger, etc.

With the shock (over-stimulation) of the emotional area, for example, comes the next dissociative attempt (to order the chaos), namely, the creation of thoughts, images, beliefs, values, etc. This could also explain the experience of opposing thoughts, i.e., the nervous system is in shock and electrically is opposing itself.

QUANTUM PSYCHOLOGY PRINCIPLE:

Trances are the Nervous System's attempt to order the chaos caused by a shock.

When trances do not work, in order to handle the level of chaos, we create mystical realms inhabited by Gods and Goddesses, etc., which are the next dissociative move after thoughts and labels. All of these biological attempts to preserve itself are intrinsic to the body's survival mechanism.

QUANTUM PSYCHOLOGY PRINCIPLE:

The greater the shock, the greater the dissociation and separation from the biology. In this way, the body has a fight/flight response and a dissociative trance response—in short, a way to battle shock using an emotional, thought or spiritual buffering trance process to organize chaos.

Why then is it so important to separate out the dimensions? Because the experiences which are run through the nervous system lose their survival accuracy, and the body neurons use the same pathways to recreate the same patterns of emotional response regardless of the present time external. It sees the past as the present and the future. It is as if the nervous system were playing the same record by placing the "needle" into the same groove each time and producing the same song, regardless of the external present time context. In other words, *the body carries an internal memory and goes into a trance.*

For example, imagine someone in a car accident who now has a phobia response to driving. Is the person experiencing present time driving? *No.* The body's nervous system is reacting "as if" it were in danger. The body's shock→abstractions→fear→images of death, etc. This is why the biological→psychological trance must be broken.

PROCESSING THE BIOLOGICAL FALSE CORE
1. Tracing it back to the fight/flight response.

To be done by yourself or with a partner:

Step I: Notice a tension, pressure, pain, etc., you have in the body.
Step II: Ask yourself or another, "Tell me an idea you have about the pain, pressure, tension, etc. ((*fill in the blank*)."
Step III: Continue this until nothing pops-up.

This simple process can help dismantle the collapsing of the biological with the thinking and/or emotional dimensions. Incidentally, boredom is a reaction to the unmet biological need of learning. Learning must continue to deeper and deeper levels of complexity.

BIOLOGICAL FALSE CORE #1
FALSE CORE CONCLUSION: "I have no control," "There is no control in the world" "I am out of control,"

FALSE SELF COMPENSATION: "I must control myself, others or the environment."

As with all False Cores, this biological-False Conclusion is an attempt to handle the chaos the nervous system experiences by using the newer brain. This conclusion by the newer brain is not true, it is further away from the experience itself as are all conclusions or interpretations about experiences.

This inaccurate solution to this False Conclusion represents the newer brain's never-ending although unsuccessful attempt to handle the False Conclusion. Why is it unsuccessful? Because it is a solution to a False Conclusion, it does not address the problem. In other words, the conclusion or the basic premise is false, so the solution must be false too.

QUANTUM PSYCHOLOGY PRINCIPLE:

A False Conclusion about what or why something is occurring can only yield a solution which cannot solve the problem because the solution is based on a false conclusion.

The above is paramount to understanding the dilemma of the psychological and spiritual world. Both fields work with pain and both claim to know why people suffer. If, for example, the False Conclusion to why I am stuttering is, "My mother never loved me," this is the conclusion and if we somehow handle this, the pain will go away. In the spiritual world, False Conclusions can range from karma theory to lessons we need to learn. But these too are False Conclusions. If I attempt through therapy or spiritual practice to solve my pain and its false "cause," I can only get a solution based on a False Conclusion because the cause or reason for the problem is False. This is why psychology and spirituality continue to fail in the "world" (see Volume II) False Conclusions→False Solutions→no satisfaction.

A predominant biological False Core is "no control." It is expressed because the nervous system is overstimulated. This forces the newer brain to come up with a reason for this experience and it comes up with the idea, "I am out of control." The animal appears to have *no control* because the externals (mom, dad, society) are trying to control it (i.e., eating, sleeping, excretion, sexuality, etc.) during the "socialization" process. The externals (mom/dad society) get internalized to form the superego which you fuse with and think *is you*. These internalizations try to control these animal instincts.

As mentioned earlier, age regressed philosophies, stories, spirituality, and psychology, are going to justify the controlling of the animal. For example, "If I can control this (animal), God (mom/ dad) will reward me (maybe with enlightenment, or a new bike)." If I control emotions and create new beliefs I can get what I want from the external. In short, I'll be able to merge (i.e., with the unity, Mom/ Dad). If I can control this animal, then I will get love and acceptance which means I will be able to merge (be one and not separate from Mom/Dad etc.). This is an underlying belief from infancy. "If I can control my biological urges, I can control another," or "If I can control my biological urges," I can control what the external world gives me (Mom/Dad later spiritualized as God or guru giving enlightenment for being good) and how the world responds to me. But notice how much pain you go through because you can't control the situation or another by controlling yourself (the animal). This is the collapsing of the levels.

"I am in control" or "I have to be in control" is a solution based on a false conclusion which covers and hides this and/or does not let it (the animal) show itself. In this situation, you project the animal out onto another and try to control them, or I'm going to *be* the animal and I *imagine* (project) they are going to try to control me and hence resist them.

CHAOS

Chaos occurs when we try to control basic animal urges that have been defined by society or religion as inappropriate. In this way, unwanted chaos and conflict get fused with our Animal Nature.

BIOLOGICAL FALSE CORE #2

The next biological False Conclusion formed by the newer brain.

FALSE CORE CONCLUSION #2: "I am Crazy."

FALSE SELF COMPENSATOR: I Have to Prove I
am not Crazy and be Sane, Clear, Healthy, Virtuous,
etc.

False Core Conclusion #2 is, "I am crazy" because I have
these sensations, urges, drives, etc. The False Self Compensator tries
to prove you are not crazy and attempts to "act sane," rational, and
"healthy," "virtuous", etc. This can collapse the thinking dimension
with the biology. Identities can prove others crazy because this justifies and gives reasons for you wanting to be separate (sour grapes)
(see Volume II). This structure makes for a therapist.

We feel crazy and out of control because we deny our natural
animal tendencies, labeling them as bad, as something to be controlled. Thus, we cut ourselves off from the biological context of our
animal nature. From a Quantum Psychology perspective, the ego (the
mediator) between the id (animal) and the superego (society/parents,
etc.) must feel crazy. Why? Because the ego is a coping device that
sells out the animal for some societally substituted rewards which
can never satisfy the biological urges. It would be like your wanting
food and someone giving you a photograph of a barbecued chicken,
or your wanting sex and someone give you a photograph of a naked
man or woman, or your wanting food or sex and someone handing
you a dollar bill or a diploma as an attempt to satisfy you. It won't
work. That's why money, diplomas, achievement, etc., when substituted for biological needs escalate, ending up with a psychological
want which is dissociated from the original biological need.

BIOLOGICAL FALSE CONCLUSION #3

FALSE CORE: I am not safe.

FALSE SELF: I have to make myself safe or create safety for others to feel safe.

Another Biological False Core is "I'm not safe"; hence you have a False Self Compensator which tries to create safety. Adjuncts to this, "I feel safe when others don't feel safe, or "I am not safe" and "They will make me safe." *There are many therapists who feel it is their job to make others feel safe.* This too is hard-wired into the nervous system and is part of the Biological False Core of survival.

QUANTUM PSYCHOLOGY PRINCIPLE:
Personal psychology is formed to defend against Biological Deprivation order chaos and restore biological equilibrium.

THE REPRESSED ANIMAL AND THE FALSE CORE CONCLUSION-FALSE SELF SOLUTION

A DEMONSTRATION

Wolinsky: When you feel these urges called "no control," what do you do so you don't have to feel them to gain control?

Denise: I develop body tension immediately.

Therapeutic Note
Notice how the exterior muscles of the "sleeve" organize to defend against animal urges.

Wolinsky: So you feel a tightening down?

Denise: I feel a tightening and a pulling in of my energy. A tightening throughout the center of my body, tightening of the thighs. A quickening in my brain so I start to go into my head to try to figure it out.

Wolinsky: So you get body tension and then you try to figure it out. So it moves up.

Denise: Away from my pelvis.

Therapeutic Note

Here we see Wilhelm Reich's basic premise. As the animal energy is repressed, that energy moves upward into thoughts, etc.

Wolinsky: (*To group*) So we are going to look at it in terms of an energetic process as well as a psychological process. (*To client*) So this no control thing, I want to call it almost like a roaring, energy—it's an energy moving underneath.

Denise: Something coming at me or coming up in me, rising. Yes, I know that one.

Wolinsky: Where do you feel that?

Denise: I would have to back up before my tightening. I feel it in my thighs. I feel it in my legs.

Wolinsky: Take a look and see how far up.

Denise: There's two levels. First, there is like a front first. It's in the inner thighs like a wash of energy coming up and then afterwards it's like there is a following, something on the backside of the calves. Like a little gentle, pulling, tugging thing.

Wolinsky: Recall a time when somebody else was doing something in your external environment and you felt no control.

Therapeutic Note

Here we are bringing up the biological False Core Conclusion by exploring the relationship between the external environment and the False Core.

Denise: There was more of a fear response. A terrible fear of a person who was being manic and their eyes were glazing and moving quickly toward me.

Wolinsky: What did you create in response to his manic response to you?

Denise: I clamped down and got cooler instantly. I could feel the energy in me but what I do with it was, phew.

Therapeutic Note

The clamp-down on the repressed animal is part of the False Core Conclusion—False Self Solution cycle.

Wolinsky: Trace the event, notice your clamp down and notice where in your body you intentionally push that energy down that might have responded to in another way.

Denise: Yeah, it was like stepping into a cold shower. It was in my pelvis. I would lock it in my pelvis. Not in my feet, not in my knees, not in my thighs, but in my pelvis.

Wolinsky: So this basic, root, core, I don't know what word to use. Energy. What would you call it that is in your pelvis?

Denise: Yeah, it's a burst of fire, energy.

Wolinsky: So this primal energy that you feel there.

Denise: As I'm talking about it. It's warming up.

Wolinsky: Now you have this other thing that is going to hose it down. Where do you feel that closing down?

Denise: It's almost like pulling a hood over myself. It's very quick and it's very cold and it's very nonfeeling.

Therapeutic Note

The False Core Conclusion is the repressed animal of "No control," the False Solution—clamping down the pelvis, "I must gain control"

Wolinsky: Who modeled if for you?

Denise: Huh, I almost want to say nobody modeled it for me. I figured it out by myself.

Wolinsky: And the out-of-control primal energy?

Therapeutic Note

The "I am out of control" is fused with primal energy.

Denise: There's no modeling there, it was a response to my mother. My mother was manic.

Wolinsky: Now, as a little girl, what did you call this wild, manic, *crazy* energy that your mother had? Or did you have a word?

Therapeutic Note

Here again we see the primal repressed energy fused with mom and labeled as the False Core Conclusion, "I am crazy"→A False Self

Solution, "I must be sane," and prove I am not *crazy*. Notice also that Denise is a psychotherapist.

Denise:	Busy, hyper, tireless, crazy.

Wolinsky: If you are separate, primal energy equals crazy, what doesn't occur?

Denise: Containment around that energy.

Wolinsky: How are you doing now?

Denise: I feel very peaceful for some reason.

Wolinsky: Now, if you fuse together this primal energy equals, "I will be alone" (her thinking-emotional False Core), what occurs?

Therapeutic Note

Another False Conclusion and association. The primal energy = "I am alone" thus→False healing solution "I have to connect."

Denise: A quickening in my body. Quickening to put a hood on and clamp down.

Wolinsky: What did you assume, decide or believe that got you to develop that quickening to put the hood on and clamp down?

Denise: Well, the first words were, "I can't be alone." It was very fleeting. There wasn't much energy or emotion with it.

Wolinsky: If you fuse together this energy equals alone, what does not occur?

Therapeutic Note

Her False Core of "Alone" gets fused with that primal energy which is also fused with "I am crazy."

Denise:	Well…permission to claim the energy as mine or a right to have it.
Wolinsky:	What was assumed, decided or believed that got you to not having this energy as mine?
Denise:	I didn't want it because it looked like it was too much.

Therapeutic Note

People fuse their False Core Conclusion with the primal animal energy. This primal energy (in this situation) equals "Alone." For example, if I have this primal energy, associated with "There's something wrong with me," would yield the False Healing Solution: I must be perfect.

Wolinsky:	If you separate primal energy and alone, what occurs?
Denise:	Nothing.
Wolinsky:	How does primal energy feel in your pelvis now?
Denise:	It's just kind of warm in there. It's just right there. I feel wonderful. I feel very peaceful. It's very simple. Where I feel the energy is up here in my shoulders, especially this one.
Wolinsky:	Notice where, if anywhere, the hood and clamping down is right now. Now, have the hood over there (another place in the room) and the primal energy over there (another place in the room). See them as an archetypical battle between two forces.

Denise:	I see that. It's almost like sane versus crazy.
Wolinsky:	Take the label off of primal energy as crazy and the hood as sane. Take the label off of both of them and allow them both to be energy and an archetypical struggle. Now notice the EMPTINESS they are floating in. See the energy and trace the energy back to the EMPTINESS. Where does it trace to?
Denise:	It's like fire itself. Like a log burning, fire, almost like lightning.
Wolinsky:	Now trace it back to the EMPTINESS. How are you doing now?
Denise:	Just fine It's a different feeling of energy in my body. There is a peacefulness with it. I moved to if I feel that energy, I will alienate my mother and then I will die. I think that I stuffed upon that realization, I stuffed that energy.
Wolinsky:	How are you doing now?
Denise:	Great. Peaceful.

DEMONSTRATION

PSYCHOLOGICAL SUPPRESSION OF THE BIOLOGICAL SPARK

Nancy:	It feels like if I experience this primal energy then I will alienate my mother and I won't have anyone to take care of me, then I won't survive and I will die.

Wolinsky:	So if you fuse together this primal energy equals alienation of mom, what occurs?

Therapeutic Note

This fusion/unfusion process is demonstrated in the *Tao of Chaos,* Part #8.

Nancy:	Terrible, I feel like it is dangerous to alienate mom.
Wolinsky:	It was dangerous because if you alienate mom, then you won't survive. If you fuse together primal energy equals alienation of mom, what gets resisted?
Nancy:	The energy itself.
Wolinsky:	What was assumed, decided or believed that got you to resisting the energy itself?
Nancy:	Same thing.
Wolinsky:	Now if primal energy is separate from alienation of mom, they are separate issues, what occurs?
Nancy:	A sense of the expansion and then immediate contraction. Because my inner defenses are acting so quickly that I will get a sense of something like a spark and then it will be like a box going over me.
Wolinsky:	To harness and contain the primal energy.
Nancy:	Right and it is faster than what I can verbalize or feel, the first part, before it gets contained.
Wolinsky:	Let me make sure I understand. So there is a spark but instantaneously there is a containment of the spark.

Nancy: Correct.

Wolinsky: If we assume your mother contains your spark,
                where in your body do you feel the inner con-
                tainer? In other words, the external mother who
                has now been internalized and contains your spark.
                Where do you feel it in your body?.

Therapeutic Note:
Here I assumed that an internalized mother was the container for her
spark.

Nancy: It happened real fast. The containment feels like a
                box, like a coffin almost. I feel numb. And yet, in
                my genital area, there is a little bit of energy that
                the coffin didn't get.

Wolinsky: So when you had energy as a kid, it was like your
                mother tried to bury it, and tried to put you in a
                coffin and bury you.

Nancy: Yes.

Wolinsky: What I would like for you to do is to have an im-
                age of mom over there (another physical location)
                as an undertaker. And I would like for you to have
                this coffin next to mom, the undertaker. Have the
                numbness almost as a protector of your light or
                spark, if you will.

Nancy: Okay.

Wolinsky: How does that feel or seem to you as you look at
                mom the undertaker and then your energy, spark,
                along with your numbness to act as a buffer be-
                tween you and mom?

Nancy: At first when the coffin was over there, I felt some fear. A lot of fear right here (Solar plexis). Then when I realized that there was a little buffer around that, then I felt safer then I could feel way inside a little bit of light, or energy.

Wolinsky: Now, I used the word buffer, in terms of the numbness being a buffer that you created. Now, is that fear, your fear of this initial light/energy or is it that your mother was afraid of your light and energy?

Nancy: My mother was afraid of her light and energy and if my light and energy got too close to her she repressed my light and my energy.

Therapeutic Note

This demonstrates Reich's *emotional plague*. Briefly stated, we feel threatened by another's aliveness and try to damp it down or destroy it as ours was dampened down or destroyed. "Do onto others that which was done onto you."

Wolinsky: So she got scared of yours because she was scared of her own.

Nancy: Uh-huh.

Wolinsky: So this fear is actually your mother's. Can you delabel that fear and allow that energy of fear to go back to your undertaker mother?

Nancy: No, that's dangerous to do.

Wolinsky: Why would that be dangerous?

Nancy: Because I help her. Because if she feels fearful, then she acts that fear out towards me in hurtful ways. So I help her contain that fear and protect myself.

Therapeutic Note:
Here we see how in family therapy they say a child *imagines* she is helping mom. In this situation she is able to have a relationship with mom by dampening her own fire

Wolinsky: What I would like for you to have over there is an image of a little girl, and what I would like for you to do, is notice the fear. Have the light inside the little girl and then the numbness to protect the light and the little girl taking on the fear of the mother so as to help the mother. Does it seem accurate to you?

Nancy: Yeah.

Wolinsky: How do you feel here looking at that over there?

Nancy: That I'm a little split off from it but I can see that energy happening between the two of them.

Wolinsky: You are observing these two?

Nancy: Right.

Wolinsky: Is that what you mean, split-off?

Nancy: Yeah.

Wolinsky: How do you feel in your body?

Nancy: There's a heat, and at the same time, a pull to contain that heat too.

Wolinsky:	Now, a few minutes ago, you said you had some energy that your mother was not able to get to which was in your genitals. Is that correct?
Nancy:	Yeah.
Wolinsky:	Can you feel that in your genitals now?
Nancy:	Uh-huh. It feels sparkly. Like sparkly cider, energy.
Wolinsky:	Now experience your skin boundaries as being made of condensed or contracted energy and look at this little girl and notice the energy inside the buffer of the numbness. Would it be possible for you right now to take the label off of the energy that's inside the container, the buffer/numbness, and for you right here and now to absorb that energy from her (the little girl image) for now. Let this little girl have this "dance" with your mother and for you to absorb the energy that she had to hold and repress.
Nancy:	Yes.
Wolinsky:	How do you feel?
Nancy:	Contained again a little bit but it's more diffused.
Wolinsky:	Do you feel the energy in your body?
Nancy:	The containment around my energy is more diffused but it feels good, it feels safe. And there's a feeling of concern for the little girl who doesn't have that.
Wolinsky:	Who does not have the container?

Nancy: She doesn't have the container because I have the container.

Wolinsky: How would it be if you gave her the container and let her have the container and you take the energy?

Nancy: Do you suppose we could share it?

Wolinsky: The container, the energy or both?

Nancy: Both.

Wolinsky: Okay. Have like an energetic link between you in present time and over there at three or four. So have an energetic link between you both. I would like for the present time you to say to the undertaker mom, "You were able to bury her energy (this little girl's energy), but you are not able to bury my energy any more."

Therapeutic Note

Internalized mom and little girl. The only way this little girl identity could stay connected to her mother and be taken care of was to bury her energy the way her mom had buried her own energy when she was a little girl.

This is also representative again of what Reich called an *emotional plague* (see *The Murder of Christ*) whereby we squash another's life force the way ours was squashed. In other words, Dad squashed your life force, then you internalize Dad and when you see another person you see them through the eyes of the internalized dad and so you feel like you have to squash their life force.

Nancy: Well, I feel sadness about seeing that life. I mean that's life energy. That's been squashed and repressed. That's really sad. I think I still do that.

Wolinsky: You (pointing to the present-time body) do that or the little girl identity (pointing to the image on the other side of the room) did that?

Nancy: I think that in order to stay connected with people that I do that still. That I monitor my energy to not offend or to not overwhelm or not be rejected or humiliated.

Wolinsky: Could you make the statement to the undertaker mother that the little girl had to monitor her energy so that you (mom) would not reject her or humiliate her?

Nancy: (To mom) The little girl had to contain her energy so that you wouldn't abuse her, so that you wouldn't humiliate her, so that you wouldn't reject her. It's like the little girl killed her energy for her mom.

Wolinsky: Now tell me a difference between you (pointing to her), this present-time body, and this little girl's three year old body (pointing to little girl image across the room)?

Therapeutic Note
I want to separate her present time self from her past time self.

Nancy: The difference between my present-time body and her. I'm bigger, I'm stronger.

Wolinsky: If this little girl fuses together mom and all people, what is that little girl creating?

Therapeutic Note

Here we are working with the "little girl's" trance-ference and fusion of mom onto everyone and the world, thus separating it again from her present time body!

Nancy: Carefulness and cautiousness.

Wolinsky: Okay, if this little girl identity over there fuses together mom and everybody, what experiences of energy is this little girl repressing or not allowing?

Nancy: Love and openness of expressing her love and caring and affection, tenderness, vulnerability and kind of like a joy, a real openingness to life, playfulness, joy, the lord.

Wolinsky: Where in your present-time body do you feel the love, the playfulness, the vulnerability, the affection, the sensualness, the joy, the loud?

Nancy: I feel it like if I were to take that zipper down and open that up, it would be right there.

Wolinsky: And as you take a zipper down (pointing to the middle of her body) just for a second, how do you feel?

Nancy: Kind of vulnerable.

Wolinsky: If you took the label off of vulnerable and had it as just energy.

Nancy: Yes. Great!

Wolinsky: Now, if this little girl identity fuses together mom and everybody else in the world, what is she resisting?

Nancy: Resisting all of those things.

Wolinsky: What did she assume, decide or believe that got her to resisting all of those things?

Nancy: That's dangerous.

Wolinsky: Yes, it *was* dangerous to the little girl identity. Right now, if you look at me from your present-time body does it feel dangerous?

Nancy: No

Therapeutic Note

Here we want to get a difference when she looks at me in present time or through the past-time lens of the little girl.

Wolinsky: Now, if this little girl identity over there separates everybody else from the mother, what is she creating?

Nancy: A diving into life, into the unknown, an unwillingness to splash into the unknown.

Wolinsky: Where in your body do you feel the unwillingness to splash into the unknown?

Nancy: In my legs.

Wolinsky: Good, notice where in this present time body you experience the unwillingness to splash into the uknown and take the label off and give it back to the little girl identity. And if this little girl identity

186

there separates everybody else in the world from mom, what is that little girl identity not creating?

Nancy: She's not creating contraction.

Wolinsky: Good. And if this little girl identity over there, if she separates mom and everybody else in the world, what's this little girl identity resisting?

Nancy: Nothing.

Wolinsky: How are you feeling now?

Nancy: There's more space. There's more spaciousness inside. And energy too.

Wolinsky: That kind of energy that you are feeling, where does it originate from? If you were to trace it, where does the root of it come from?

Nancy: It's way back, way back there. I don't have a name for that. It's way back there.

Wolinsky: So go way back there into EMPTINESS and **ESSENCE** and notice that the energy emerges from there and allow that essential energy to come through your biology. How are you doing?

Nancy: I feel like the Star Spangled Banner.

Wolinsky: How does your body feel?

Nancy: Tingling.

Wolinsky: Do you have a tingling all over?

Nancy: Uh-huh and I still have my zipper. It's open but if I have to I can zip it back up again.

Wolinsky: Anything else you want to say?

Nancy: No, it doesn't have words to it…just peaceful and energetic

Therapeutic Note (To Group)

The numbness was a buffer to protect the light. The major track is to try to get her to give this stuff back to mom (i.e., externalize the internalized Mom, who she had thought was her). We have the external mom who is going to try to quelch the fire, which is now internalized. We need to externalize both acquired identities which are frozen in time so they can be given up. In this way, she can have her light and primal energy in present time.

You don't have any issues. Identities have issues. You can never work on yourself, *you can only work on the identity which you took on and fused with and think you are*. What I did was to keep differentiating her present time body and person from the three year old body image of a little girl which she was identified with and operating out of unknowing.

The question always is, Is she experiencing her body image in present time or through a past time body image which she is unknowingly acting out of in present time? If someone were overweight as a child, are they seeing themselves in present time or through the past-time body image?

When you chip away at the False Core (see also Volume II), you are going to get somatic reactions. This happens because your past time body images and stresses are going to move to the foreground and be given up so that you can live out of a present time body image or, better yet, no body image.

DESIRES AND SUBSTITUTIONS

When Nisargadatta Marahaj got up in the morning I'm sure he had the biological desire to shit, the biological desire to eat, etc. It's all part of what desires are. Desires become a problem when you are in substitution. In other words, I have a desire for eating, shitting, fucking, and sleeping and all of a sudden, the only way I get food from my parents is by having to sing a song (metaphorically speaking). So I become a professional singer in order to get fed or let's say, in order for me to get my parents' love and attention, I have to get good grades in school so I become an over-achiever.

But no matter how much I achieve, it still is not going to fill the basic desire for merger, which has a biological function. So where biological desires become a problem is when they become substituted for psychological wants. One of Buddha's Four Noble Truths is that all pain comes from desire. Quantum Psychology suggests that *pain arises from substituting biological desires for psychological wants.*

Quantum Psychology attempts to dismantle substituted psychological wants which come out of biological desires. It's the old Zen question, What is enlightenment? When you are hungry, you eat. When you are tired, you sleep. There is no resistance or substitution. Pain arises when, "I'm tired but I can't go to sleep now, it's too early" or "I have to get up to go to work but I'm tired. I force myself to get up." Substitution acts as an obsessive compulsive neurotic (self-defeating) drive and this is where the problem is. But when you root it back to biology and body sensation, then you just do what comes next. And if there is no resistance, then there is no issue, and no suffering.

WORKING WITH BIOLOGICAL NEEDS

The purpose of these exercises is to bring you back to biological sensation and away from the newer brain's image producing. Or better said, back to biological sensation as a vehicle for realization and away from substituting the psychological for the biological.

SEXUALITY

Focus:
Focus your attention on the sexual sensations rather than on the story as to why you feel sexual. (Singh)

If you have sexual fantasies and you focus your attention on the sexual fantasy, or on the memory of a person, what happens is that you are always looking outside yourself trying to fulfill the sexual fantasy. Your mind is always popping up pictures of a sexual fantasy in some form or another. More than likely, you won't get too much satisfaction because you'll always be fantasizing about somebody else outside of yourself.

During the years I was celibate I noticed that I had incredible fantasies. Since the fantasies were still there, so were the bodily reactions and I had a difficult time for two years. It was a 180° shift from my sexual behavior in the 1960's and 1970's where free sexuality was the rule and everybody slept with everybody.

When I started this exercise, it shifted my habitual pattern of the way I focused my awareness on the fantasy of sexuality by placing my attention on the energy itself. Where did I feel it? The process is similar to the emotional one except that now we're going to look at what is normally labeled as one that's more pleasant.

Shift your attention away from the fantasy, or away from the movie in your mind, and place your attention on the energy itself. Notice what happens as you start focusing your attention on the sexual feelings as energy. To paraphrase the *Vijnana Bhairava*, from the mere remembrance of what it's like to be touching, pressing, kissing and holding, certain delightful sensations arise *inside* of you; since there's nobody there they come from you. This seemed very profound to me at the time, that the sensations are coming from inside of me because there's no one there. In other words, if you're fantasizing, and you have the remembrance of those types of things, it brings about such feelings in your body. Since there's nobody there these feelings are coming from inside of you. Therefore, rather than focusing on the fantasy and trying to fulfill it by looking outside of yourself, begin to shift your attention. This simply means moving your attention off of the fantasy and into the experience itself as energy, rather than seeing it as sexual energy and something to work with. It's energy, it's not good or bad, wrong right, high or low—it's simply energy.

I remember saying to Baba Prakashananda that I was having problems with my second chakra. Babaji said, "Only one chakra: energy." So it's all energy, only the mind compartmentalizes it into higher and lower chakras, placing judgments, evaluations and giving significance to the labels. The difference and beauty of Tantric meditation is that it is for people who live in the world. Rather than trying to put your mind someplace else, in Tantric meditation you're always focusing on what *is*. In this way feelings and thoughts are used as fuel to bring you into a deeper connection with yourself and your humanness.

Practice:
Close your eyes and get yourself comfortable. Develop a sexual fantasy. You can start by picking someone that you'd like to be with. Notice what they look like, whether there are any sounds. Watch the sexual fantasy. Notice the temperature, notice if there are any smells or any tastes, any sensations. Let the movie in your mind run for a moment.

Gently, shift your attention from the sexual fantasy to the energy in your body itself. Begin by noticing where in your body you feel that energy, where those sensations and feelings are. Take off the label of sexual feelings or sensations and have it as energy. Focus your attention on the energy itself. If your attention goes toward the fantasy, bring it down again, and focus your attention and watch the energy. Continue to watch, with no label called "sexual energy."

The purpose of this practice is the same as the others in this series, namely, to shift the habitual focus of our attention on the story, and learn to see our thoughts and feelings as being made of energy. I ask you to take your attention, which is focused on the fantasy, and move it into the feelings themselves and to begin to view feelings that you have inside yourself as energy. In this way, there is no reason to resist, deny or judge yourself for your experience.

As I mentioned earlier, when I lived in an ashram many of us were celibate. I was a very horny celibate for the first two years. I had a lot of fantasies, and whenever I put my attention on them, I would have bodily reactions. But when I shifted my attention from the fantasy toward the feelings themselves, the energy suddenly started to shift.

Tantric scriptures say that, "if at the moment of orgasm, you could become introverted, you would experience Spanda (the divine throb)." What they did not mention was that if, at the at moment you could remember to become introverted, your energy would go *in* rather than out, and you would go into a deep "no-state." That's the purpose of this meditation.

BIOLOGICAL DIMENSION EXERCISE #2

FOOD

Focus:
Focus your attention on the delightful sensations around food, rather than on the food itself. (Singh)

Working with food is a very big issue, probably the most difficult thing to process, but this meditation will plant seeds for you. As we go on, you'll be focusing on your ideas about food and about hunger as hunger—but not with the associations about hunger.

The method for this meditation is the same as the others. For example, let's imagine that you're working at your desk and you have a thought that says, "I want chocolate," or whatever your fantasy is. Your mind takes off on that and you react to it. If you want to lose weight, you can use this meditation when you're hungry, i.e., focus your attention on hunger as energy rather than on a food fantasy and notice what happens. That's a whole meditation but you can't do it if you're not hungry.

You can use the sensations and joy of a chocolate chip cookie or an ice-cream soda or whatever. Take your awareness away from it and meditate on the sensations. To paraphrase the Vijnana Bhairava, Focus your attention on the delight (as energy) rather than on the object of delight (chocolate, etc.). If it's sexuality, meditate on the delight, rather than on the object. If you're having sex with somebody, you're more than likely focusing on the person. Turn your attention away from the person toward the delight itself and see what the experience is.

With food, it's the same. There's really only one teaching that Swami Muktananada ever had and that was to meditate on yourself. This can be seen at the *biological dimension* as meditating on the delight as energy rather than on the object of delight as food (or a sexual object).

For fun, choose something you love to eat, something that you want to take a bite out of. In class, I ask studentss to bring their favorite treats. What I want you to do is to take a taste and put it in your mouth. Let your eyes close. You can chew it, but do everything slowly. In other words, don't just swallow it and reach for another bite.

Practice:

I'd like you to notice something. Now that your eyes are closed, I'd like you to focus your attention on the delightful feelings as if they were made of energy rather than a picture you might have in your mind of the object of delight. As you experience the sensations—the delightful feelings, thoughts or whatever are associated with the food you have in your mouth—I'd like you to focus your attention on these sensations. See if you can keep your attention on the delight, rather than on the object of delight. Experience the delight as energy. Gently, bring your awareness back to the room and let your eyes open.

DESIRE

Desire:
To long for; to wish for earnestly; to hope for.

Desire can be described in several ways. Desire can occur at any point in a child's development. For example, notice that with an infant or a young child, most of their wanting is to relieve biological pain such as hunger or cold. Or it is the need to fill a lack, like wanting a hug or wanting to feel safe. Later in life, the child uses what is called transitional objects like blankets, teddies, pillows, which they carry around as "substitute friends" so they don't have to feel separate. Another perspective equates desire with resistance and says that if I desire X it's because I'm resisting Y. For example, if I desire to have money, it's because I am simultaneously resisting my *subjective experience*, (be it real or unreal of no money).

In this way, desiring and resisting are two sides of the same coin.

Unmet biological desires are painful (see Volume II on the False Core). When pain is resisted it is often substituted, replacing psychological wants (i.e., for food, sex, etc). Since many wants exist to relieve biological and/or emotional pain, problems arise when we try to substitute one pain reliever for another. For example, when we feel a lack of love (merger), rather than experiencing that, we eat or have sex. Often, status symbols like big houses or cars are attempts to relieve pain for feeling a lack of self-worth. This is how desires escalate and get distorted

Understanding that desires are often a way to resist unfelt experiences gives Buddha's Noble Truth, "Be desireless," a new meaning: Instead of trying to be desireless, don't resist, allow yourself to experience what is driving the desire rather than the substituted idea or image of what will satisfy the desire.

As the practice begins to deepen, people often develop a non-judgmental approach toward exploring their desires as opposed to trying to get rid of them, overcome them, deny them, or transform them. Instead, they see them as made of energy.

BIOLOGICAL DIMENSION EXERCISE #3

Focus:
Focus your attention on the energy of desire rather than on the object being desired. (Singh)

Practice:
Let your eyes close. Allow an object of extreme desire to come into your mind. Imagine it is out in front of you. It could be a person, a situation, or anything that you want. Notice what the object or situation or experience looks and sounds like. Feel or notice sensations and feelings, the sensations inside your body associated with that particular desire. Notice its size and shape. Take the label off and see it as energy. Focus your awareness on the desire inside you, the energy or sensations called "desire" inside, rather than on the desired object. Pull your attention inside to the desire itself, delabel it, and experience it as energy, allowing it (the energy) to do whatever it does. Simply watch the desire as energy inside you.

A student asked if he should see desire as something negative. I replied that desire is desire. There is no bad or good about it, it's just energy.

I would suggest that as you go through your life in the next few days, you work with any desire coming into your awareness. Suppose you are driving your car and you notice a new Porsche, or you might see a Porsche in your mind's eye. For that moment, your desire is called, "I want a Porsche." When they focus on the Porsche or anything else they want, some people will do everything possible in the universe to make that desire come true. It could be a relationship, it could be new clothes, it could be a job, it could be any one of a thousand things. But instead of focusing on the Porsche, I would like you to pull your attention away from the desired object and turn it toward the desire itself as energy.

Most people have desires—it doesn't matter what they are—and they spend most of their lives reacting to that desire, trying to fulfill it externally. If you're always thinking about having a relationship, you're always out there looking for someone. But if you focus your attention on the energy itself, my experience has been that you can either have the relationship or not, but that either way is okay. This is what I mean by focusing on the energy of the desire, rather that on the desired object. Turn your attention inward and focus on the desire as energy.

SUMMARY

Dissociating from our body and animal nature not only dissociates us from the world and from people, but ultimately from the underlying unity as well. It is no wonder that spiritual and psychological philosophies which diminish the body as "not you," or "unimportant," act as impairments to "spiritual" and psychological understanding. They ask us to deny the "body," and in the case of psychology, our "human-animal nature," in favor of our "mind." Once you can appreciate the thinking and emotional world and external world, let your attention be split four ways: 1/4 external, 1/4 thinking, 1/4 emotional and 1/4 biological.

Psychological and archetypical explanations are created by the newer brain; hence, they're further from experience and only exist as a way to order the chaos of a shock or of a biological deprivation. Mystification, a creation of the new brain, occurs when the biological animal is repressed. This repression takes us out of biological and into psychological and interpretations which lead to False Conclusions that yield unresolvable False Solutions.

We are all going to die. All we know and think we are will die. But we as individuals and as a society are totally dissociated from this reality In fact, death is the most dissociated reality the biological-psychology faces. That could be why the concept of souls reincarnating came about to defend against this: if I have a soul, I will keep on going, I won't have to face death. Many religions are based on this as well (see *The Tao of Chaos*). The "I" wants to go on, it does not want to die and to defend against death, it makes up stories.

EXERCISE #4

Let your eyes close and divide your awareness in four directions:

1/4 to your animal dimension,
1/4 to your thinking dimension,
1/4 to your emotional dimension,
1/4 to the external dimension.

This is a practice that helps to develop the skill to allow you to stay simultaneously in touch with the outer world, the inner psycho-emotional world and your animal nature.

In conclusion, we must bear in mind that all life problems and solutions are viewed through your limited lens or the limited lens of the person you go to see for help. For example, if I had a marriage problem and went to a priest, he might say the problem was spiritual; an accountant would say economic; a body worker, "It's in your structure"; a psychotherapist, "It has to do with Mom and Dad"; a family therapist, "It's in the context," etc. For this reason, we must learn to become more open to the fact that no one system handles it all. See the level the client needs to work on and be willing to refer them to an appropriate person. This is part of the art of a therapist or spiritual teacher.

In the ancient Sufi tradition, a Sufi master would send individuals to different teachers so that the student could get the help they needed. This demonstrates that not only does one system not work for everybody or everything but one master's teaching does not work for everybody either. These Sufi masters made the student's "progress" the center of their approach and work, not their own personal desire to teach.

This is client- or student-centered work. Unfortunately, nowadays when people go to a teacher or guru, *they all get the same techniques*. This "one size fits all" is a guru- or technique-centered approach.

QUANTUM PSYCHOLOGY PRINCIPLE:

A therapist or "teacher" should not be there to get their needs met in a workshop training room or therapy room.

To summarize, the body-mind-spirit are one and yet all holographic; all the same but with different functions. Meet the problem at the level of the problem. This is the Way of the Human.

The Quantum approach asks of us to BE just that, a human, which is already the Quantum whole. One who practices the Way of the Human is asked to not compartmentalize body, mind and spirit, but to see them as different densities of **THAT ONE SAME SUBSTANCE**.

With this in mind, let us look at the following demonstration:

DEMONSTRATION

In this demonstration we go through the dimensions, noticing the impact of the thinking dimension. This is an extremely important exercise because your thoughts about what is happening give it meaning which is not what is happening. When you let go of your thoughts, ideas, and meaning placed upon experiences, resistance leaves and you can have what is as it is.

Wolinsky:	I am going to go through the dimensions with you. So, tell me an idea that you have about the external world.
Mark:	The external is concrete. The external is something we do. The external is something I need like money, a job, work, house, all of those things that give me security.
Wolinsky:	Those are *interesting* ideas—what just happened?

Therapeutic Note
Once ideas are pointed out as ideas, they disappear.

Mark: Kind of a flash of humor.

Wolinsky: Tell me another idea you have about the external.

Mark: That it is a necessary evil. That I'd rather not do it. I would like someone to do it for me.

Wolinsky: That's an interesting idea. Tell me another idea you have with the external.

Mark: See what happens when I start doing this, it is hard for me to think.

Wolinsky: Tell me an idea you have about thinking.

Mark: That thinking is something that keeps me grounded or here. That if I didn't think I would float away.

Wolinsky: Tell me another interesting idea you have about thinking.

Mark: Thinking is necessary. Thinking is fun. It gives me something to do. If I didn't think, I wouldn't exist.

Wolinsky: That's an interesting idea. How are you doing now?

Mark: Good.

Wolinsky: Are there any other ideas about thinking?

Mark: No.

Wolinsky: Tell me an idea you have about emotions.

Mark: Emotions help me to know that I am alive. Emotions are like sensations or making me feel alive.

Wolinsky: That's an interesting idea too. Tell me another idea you have about emotions.

Mark: Emotions are scary.

Wolinsky: That's an interesting idea.

Mark: Some emotions are good and some emotions are bad.

Wolinsky: (With obvious humor) Obviously. Tell me an idea you have about being alive.

Mark: That it requires work. That being alive requires a constant tracking of keeping it together.

Wolinsky: Tell me another idea you have about being alive.

Mark: It's fun. There is a fun part to it.

Wolinsky: What's fun?

Mark: This is fun.

Wolinsky: Tell me an idea you have about sensations.

Mark: Sensations are uncomfortable.

Wolinsky: That's an interesting idea.

Mark: Sensations tell me that something is going on with me. Sensations are scary. Sensations are like they hold the range of feeling for me. Sometimes they feel good, sometimes they don't.

Wolinsky:	That's an interesting idea. How do you feel?
Mark:	Good.

Therapeutic Note

Next we explore ideas about the biological dimension, which are not the Biological Dimension.

Wolinsky:	Tell me an idea you have about eating.
Mark:	I like to do it. Eating is necessary. Eating is social. Eating keeps me alive.
Wolinsky:	What's alive again?
Mark:	Alive is being here on this earth.
Wolinsky:	That's an interesting idea. Now, tell me an idea you have about sleeping.
Mark:	Sleeping is rest. Sleeping is time out. Sleeping is not being here. Sleeping is comforting.
Wolinsky:	Tell me idea you have about shitting.
Mark:	It feels good sometimes. It is necessary. Sometimes it is an inconvenience. It has a lot of bad connotations.
Wolinsky:	That's an interesting idea. Tell me another idea you have about shitting.
Mark:	Oh, that it is dirty or that it is part of the body. I can hear my mother saying, wishing I didn't do that. Sort of like it is something wrong.
Wolinsky:	Tell me an idea you have about fucking?

Mark: That it is fun. That it is exciting. That it is connection. That it is not connection. That fucking is sometimes a way to be hurt or to hurt someone. Sometimes fucking can feel that way. Sometimes it is just sensation.

Wolinsky: Tell me an idea you have about learning.

Mark: Learning sometimes is hard. Sometimes it is anxiety producing. Sometimes it is exciting and fun and interesting, all of those things, but sometimes it is pressure.

Wolinsky: That's an interesting idea. Any more interesting ideas about learning?

Mark: That it has nothing to do with being smart.

Wolinsky: That's interesting. Tell me another idea you have about learning.

Mark: (no response)

Wolinsky: Tell me an interesting idea you have about merging.

Mark: Merging is feeling really connected and close. Merging is losing yourself.

Wolinsky: That's an interesting idea.

Mark: Merging is scary. Merging is seductive. Merging is something I do. Merging is part of our biology, like babies and moms. It's terrifying.

Wolinsky: What do you feel like now?

Mark: Just here. There is this feeling that I just am— feeling sort of diffuse.

Wolinsky: When you say diffuse, you mean?

Mark: Spacious, less solid.

Wolinsky: Tell me an idea you have about this experience called less solid or diffuse.

Mark: That if I kept going, I would disappear.

Wolinsky: That's an interesting idea. Tell me another idea you have about this diffuse.

Mark: That it means I'm not really here.

Wolinsky: That's an interesting idea. Tell me another idea you have about the idea called diffuse.

Mark: That diffuse is bad. That when someone is dif- fuse, they are not doing what they are supposed to be doing.

Wolinsky: Any other ideas about the idea or concept called diffuse?

Mark: That you are not supposed to be diffuse because you are merging or meshing, all those kind of bad terms.

Wolinsky: Tell me another idea about the idea called diffuse.

Mark: That diffuse is a defense.

Wolinsky: That's an interesting idea. Tell me another idea you have about the idea called diffuse.

Mark: You can't function when you are diffuse.

Wolinsky: How does diffuse seem to you now?

Mark: It seems just like a word.

Wolinsky: How does your experience seem to you right now?

Mark: Clear. There is a starting to become clear but still that diffuse feeling.

Wolinsky: Is diffuse okay with you or is there a problem?

Mark: Sensation is a little bit of a problem.

Wolinsky: Tell me an idea you have about the sensation.

Mark: That it is fuzzy.

Wolinsky: That's an interesting idea. Is fuzzy bad?

Mark: No, fuzzy is an idea.

Wolinsky: Tell me another idea you have about sensation.

Mark: It is unclear.

Wolinsky: That's an interesting idea. From what, where or who did you get this idea?

Mark: My mother.

Wolinsky: Take the label off and give it back to your mother.

Mark: It's just a belief and energy.

Wolinsky: How you doing now?

Mark: Clear—great.

Therapeutic Note

We went all the way down through the biology. Now whenever you are working with yourself or another person, and someone comes to you and says, "I feel sad but I don't want to feel sad," you can say, "Tell me an idea about sad. Tell me another idea about sad. Tell me another idea." You want to blow out the idea. Sadness is not a problem. It's your *ideas* about sadness that *make it a problem*. Take away the ideas and have sensation without the label, then you can begin to have experiences as they are without judgment, evaluation, or placing significance on them. Since all it is, is simply a sensation.

SPECIAL SECTION
Part I
TRANCES PEOPLE LIVE
REVISITED

Looking through the Lens of the
Trances of Developmental Psychology

TRANCE-FERENCE: THE ULTIMATE TRANCE

> Living is easy with eyes closed—
> Misunderstanding all you see—
> It's getting hard to be someone, but it all works out—
> It doesn't matter much to me.
> > John Lennon, "Strawberry Fields"

Let us begin by illustrating one of the most profound *collapsing of the levels*. In other words, the major trances and pitfalls which prevent us from discovering and experiencing our human nature. Arguably it is the trance of trance-ference/counter trance-ference which are the least questioned, most powerful, most frequent, and least acknowledged of all trances. How they get in the way of our human nature and interrupt us "psychologically" as well as "spiritually" and in our relationships, are the focuses of this section. As you know (and it will be explained more fully later), the spelling of transference has been changed to "trance-ference." This has been done to emphasize that, in order to unknowingly imagine, create and treat someone as your mother or father, or unknowingly imagine and treat another like you are their mother or father and they are your child, or to be a child and treat another as your parent, you must go into an age regressed trance.

Trance-ference should not be seen in the classic sense of an analyst analyzing a patient lying on a couch. In fact, let us put ourselves on the couch so we can see how we distort our perceptions of ourselves, the world, and our present-time relationships, and in the process lose our human nature. We lose our human nature when we lose the awareness of our present-time body, and the degree to which we lose awareness of our present-time body is the degree to which we trance-out and consequently lose our humanness. It is not that people "leave their body," but rather they lose awareness of their present-time body or leave their awareness of their present-time body, and with that they lose their humanity. We must understand that our body is necessary to have a relationship to our humanity and the underlying unity. To lose body awareness is to lose that relationship. Quantum Psychology says that when everything is seen as the same substance, nobody is an individual—rather, everything is seen as the same substance, including the body. This is the realization of, **I AM THAT ONE SUBSTANCE**.

It is through trance-ference that we lose our present-time body experience, we lose the present time external world (seeing the past time external world) and we imagine and, hence, see, think and feel the other person as a significant other from the past. In short, we collapse the dimensions of manifestation. It is our pre-verbal and pre-conscious cognitive understanding which acts as a lens and which distorts, affects, impacts, and removes us from our human nature (this will be discussed throughout this section).

It is with this in mind that the most powerful trance of trance-ference must be understood and dismantled so that the present can be experienced as the present, thus freeing our human nature and leading us to stabilize our Quantum nature. How do these distortions prevent us from experiencing present time? In the words of the Arica master Oscar Ichazo:

> The accumulation of experiences in my paracon-
> sciousness results in the formation of abstract con-

cepts called structure patterns which my psyche uses to explain reality.. Since my explanation of external reality is rooted in structure patterns which originate in accumulated . . . [past] experiences, my psyche cannot explain the present except in terms of the past. (The Fourteen Pillars of the Perfect Recognition).

Notice how Ichazo understands that the present time is experienced as the past, as long as past-time structures, such as trance-ference, are still operating. Let us define transference:

Transference is the displacement or projection of the patient's feelings, attitudes, reactions, or thoughts that properly belong to significant figures of the past onto the analyst. (Marshall and Marshall, 1988).

This rather traditional definition of the trance of transference was considered by many to be Freud's greatest contribution to the understanding of the therapist-client relationship. To further appreciate the implications of trance-ference, let us first look at the major components stressed in two earlier books, *Trances People Live* and *The Dark Side of the Inner Child*. Quantum Psychology sees seven major effects of collapsing of the levels which help to create trance-ference.

First, the trance of trance-ference requires that the individual age-regress, acting younger than they are. For example, recall a time in your relationships when you felt powerless, helpless or trapped. These are all red flags that you are age-regressing and collapsing the levels.

Second, the individual who is age-regressing will generally not be aware of what is occurring. For example, recall a time you felt powerless or trapped in a relationship and you could not find your way out of the situation. Unfortunately, more often than not, we remain unaware of our age-regressions while they are occurring, not realizing that we are collapsing the levels.

Third, the individual who is age-regressing is not in present time, but rather moves from a present-time experience of self-to-other, to a past-time experience of self-to-other. For example, recall a time in your relationship when you felt angry that your partner was not available to fill your needs, or where you expected your partner to want to do what you wanted to do and then felt angry when they did not. These common experiences are characteristic re-enactments of very early childhood experiences, particularly in relationship to your mother and father. Simply stated, you act as a child and expect your spouse to act as your mother or father. This is collapsing the levels.

Fourth, the past-time "self" is relating to the internalized (past-time) other (usually mom or dad), and hence, trance-fers the past-time other onto the present-time relationship. You treat the present-time other as the past-time other. For example, recall a time you felt *abandoned* by your partner for not being there when you wanted them to be there for you. This is a sure sign of collapsing the levels and an age-regression. Abandonment as an issue should be another red flag that a collapsing of the levels and an age-regression has taken place. The adult trance-fers mom/dad onto the other in their relationship and becomes the past-time self and then feels abandoned.

Fifth, the past-time "self" actually hypnotizes the present-time "self," making them believe present time is past time. For example, notice in your life when you age-regress that later on, you cannot believe your own behavior. This is because you lose your present-time self when you age-regress. This is why the solvent for the glue of the trance of trance-ference is the development of uninterrupted awareness and a differentiation of the dimensions of manifestation.

QUANTUM PSYCHOLOGY PRINCIPLE:

The greater the ability to differentiate the dimensions of manifestation, the greater the subjective experience of freedom.

Sixth, the past-time self relating to the internalized past-time other (mom/dad) carries with it all the stories, associations, emotions and memories of the past-time self. Once this trance-ference occurs, the present-time other is treated like, and often feels like, the past-time other. When this occurs, the "awareness" of the dimensions goes to sleep and the past-time self unknowinlgy conducts an interaction internally with the past-time other, thus again losing the present-time other. For example, many women I know have said about their relationships, "He treats me like his mother." Unfortunately, we *imagine* the present-time self and the present-time other are relating when they are not.

Seventh, the past-time self can trance-fer the past-time other not only onto a person but also onto a religion, guru, teacher, therapist, political leader or political system. For example, during a 1992 TV interview Alec Baldwin said, "I could not believe people were asking presidential candidates about family values. I was waiting for Bill Clinton to say, 'Hey, I am not your father, decide what values you want for your family, it's not up to me'." This astute statement by Baldwin was describing how "family values" voters look to politicians, the church or gurus to tell them how to live. Thus the age-regressed voter wants mommy/daddy, i.e., the church or politicians, to tell them the "right" family values.

Another example is the recent landslide election in the 1994 Congress. Here again, as the Republicans go back to tax breaks for the wealthy so that it will trickle down to us, we see voters in an age-regression. *The basic principle of trance-ference is that the greater the survival needs, the greater the tendency to age-regress.* In this case, survival needs being high, the lower middle-class voters age-regressed with the philosophy, Let's give tax breaks to the wealthy (Mom and Dad who controlled the money for them as children) and they will "take care of us" (give us our allowance) by creating jobs (errands).

THE TRANCE OF SURVIVAL

The need to survive ignites this age-regression and the collapsing of the levels. Survival is the trigger and represents the most powerful trance of all. Survival can be defined as the fight/flight mechanism which contains a survival scanning-searching-seeking and overgeneralizing device which is the physical, psychological and emotional survival of an individual. For example, let's look at the physical body. As the physical body develops, a psychology and an individuality develop. As children move from thinking that they are merged with the mother and they are their mother (to be discussed later) in the early phases of childhood, they develop an individual self, a personality, and they begin to differentiate. They notice that they are separate from their mother, and separate from the world. In this developmental sequence, the survival trance begins when children realize that they are separate and independent from their mother or father. This creation of an individual self is a crucial period. It is also a time for the development of a dissociative observer which is formed to defend against the loss of self in relationship to the world or to defend against the body's biological needs not being met.

Identities begin to emerge to interact with the world and other people, hiding our deep feelings of total separateness. This dissociative observer might be a major reason for feeling apart from humanity. Since the trance of survival is so powerful, the dissociative observer feels both separate and special, often feeling more spiritual or more grandiose (since they are not connected to their bodies, hence losing the world [the trance of spiritualization will be discussed in greater detail later]). For example, I spoke to a woman in New York who wanted to be a guru and whose heart was broken in a relationship several years ago. She said to me that she no longer felt sexual, that she was so spiritual now she had "gone beyond" sexual desire, not realizing sexuality is hard wired into the nervous system's survival of the species.

From a Quantum Psychology perspective, a dissociative observer had emerged to defend against the pain and thus she lost her present-time body and her sexuality. She then labeled this process as spiritual. Also she had become grandiose by beginning to promote herself as a spiritual teacher/guru. This is the trance of the dissociative observer, who spiritualizes the dissociation which in this situation was created to defend against the pain of her relationship breaking up. Quantum Psychology has set aside several principles relating to the dissociative observer. (How to dismantle the observer will be discussed in Volume III, "Beyond Quantum Psychology.")

QUANTUM PSYCHOLOGY PRINCIPLE:

The greater the fear of loss of self, the greater the power of the dissociative observer.

QUANTUM PSYCHOLOGY PRINCIPLE:

The greater the trauma or the unmet biological needs of the child, the greater the tendency for a dissociative observer to emerge.

QUANTUM PSYCHOLOGY PRINCIPLE:

The more dissociative the observer becomes, the more there is a loss of the body and, consequently, a loss of humanness and connection to humanity.

QUANTUM PSYCHOLOGY PRINCIPLE:

The stronger the dissociative observer, the greater the personal grandiosity.

In order to survive, an observer, as well as a personality with many identities is formed, such as, "I like this," "I don't like this," "I like you," "I don't like you." These particular observers and identities contain trance states with emotions, associations and memories. Each observer-identity has many trances and ways to fixate attention. For the observer who wishes to keep and defend the individual self, these trance states must be kept alive. Inherent in all of this is the understanding that if energy is not continually put into them by the observer and these identities, then they will die or disappear. When two people argue, it is an argument of two trance-positioned observer-identities. In this way, observer identities get more and more energy put into them because people imagine and, hence, feel their survival is dependent upon them. This is a survival trance.

Survival trances come in many different forms. For example, when you are growing up, if your parents say you're wrong and they're right, then being wrong is something that is bad and generally a child is punished for it. A child may be punished by being spanked or sent to their room (which is labeled as a devastating experience, something to avoid at all costs). It's like a mini-death, which becomes fused with the idea of being wrong, and must be avoided in order to survive. This is part of the trance process. Children fixate on this mini-death of being wrong, and thus fuse together the idea that being wrong = punishment = death. Being wrong becomes a trauma. Thus, to resist the trauma, an observer and an identity are formed to defend against the experience of that mini- death.

Another survival trance occurs when the child fuses with and becomes the parent, and takes on the parent's identity. For example, many people vow when they grow up they will never be like mom or dad. Notice, however, that under stress when you are dealing with your own children, you sound just like your parents. Living so close to Santa Fe, New Mexico, I often jokingly say in workshops that if this is your experience, you are channeling your parents.

To explain further, inherent within parents is the idea that if they want the child to agree with them, they should intensify their stance to get the child to succumb. In this way, the child will go along with them and play their game. Around 1975, "I" as a client had a particularly powerful therapy session. I was working with a woman who did a combination of Gestalt and Reichian therapy. Her sessions lasted several hours and in one, I got to the emotional place where I realized that, in order to survive, I had to play my father's game. The pain of this recognition was so overwhelming that I felt *shattered*.

As time passed, however, the integration of this work freed me deeply at the level of individuality and broke open a major identity with my father out of which I had been unknowingly living. In this way, the child fuses with the parents' game and becomes like their parents because to be separate means punishment. Punishment can be anything from being spanked, to being sent to their room, to the withdrawal of love. In this way, the child develops a survival trance.

Here are three characteristics of this type of survival trance: 1) the child becomes the parent and fuses with them in order to survive; 2) the child resists being like the parent in order to survive as an individual; and 3) the child pretends to be like the parent when actually inside themselves they are resisting the parent. How do these survival trances manifest themselves in relationship to the rest of the world?

RACISM AND SEXISM

Racism exists as does sexism. But what exists at a much deeper level is the predominant trance of what I call "differentism." What causes racism? The survival trance of differentism which triggers the early re-enactment of the shock of the Realization of Separation (see Volume II).

Unfortunately, the chaos which one feels when facing differences is oftentimes turned automatically into anger as a survival defense. Rather than the Ku Klux Klan acknowledging the chaos they feel around African-Americans (which would require feeling vulnerable), they express defensive displaced anger. Truly, groups like the KKK are cowards. Why? Because they hide behind sheets and travel in groups. To paraphrase Malcolm X, you never see one unsheeted member of the KKK trying to fight one black man—they need many. This is because they feel vulnerable and chaotic and they are afraid and unwilling to take responsibility for their own experience of that, hence, a deep survival trance of resisting the experience of differences→vulnerability→anger.

It is crucial to understand and identify the collapsing of the levels which keeps trance-ference alive. This helps us out of our automatic behavior and into present-time reality. Furthermore, without the knowledge of trance-ference, the process of spiritualization, whereby we trance-fer our divinity and power onto others, cannot be ended.

Therefore, in order to follow *The Way of the Human*, we must first know our trances and identities and examine them and take them apart before we can move into and stabilize in multi-dimensional awareness. In order to do this, we will look at developmental psychology and its possible parameters and combinations of spiritual trances so that we can become aware of and dispel our trances, thus becoming more human.

DIFFERENT TYPES OF TRANCE-FERENCE

MERGER TRANCE-FERENCE

Merger trance-ference can best be described as the event during which someone merges and fuses with another. This is an early childhood boundary issue, wherein the infant believes she/he is still merged with mommy. In other words, the child believes they are their mother. Furthermore, although this is a normal developmental process, the child sees Mom as omniscient. People who are stuck at this level of development demonstrate particular types of behaviors and trances as they grow older.

For example, in present time, we might call this type of person an "empath." This merger trance-ference can make the appearance of great contact and even psychic abilities. Actually, the adult is very age-regressed and infantile, transfering mom onto others and then merging with them. The empaths who cannot stop automatically merging with others, lose themselves and what they feel. Instead, they take on the other person's feelings. Developmentally, this is the earliest form of trance-ference. The adult has collapsed the levels and is age-regressed and not in present time, trance-ferring mommy onto another. These are the types of people who tend to take on other people's stuff and lose themselves. Often people stuck at this level of development (because they see Mom and themselves as omniscient) believe they are psychic, intuitive or are spiritual teachers. In relationships, these people are often great to be around because they always know what you want to do. For example, I remember a woman I once had a brief relationship with. If I said, "I want Chinese food," she would say, "That's exactly what I want." If I said, "I like purple shirts with pink polka- dots," she'd say, "So do I."

TWINSHIP TRANCE-FERENCE

Twinship is the feeling that some people have with others that somehow we are their twin. Actually, this is trance-ference. Psychologist Stephen Johnson says it this way, describing noted Self Psychologist Heinz Kohut's position on the twinship transference:

Kohut (1971) posits that the "twinship" transference is somewhat more evolved developmentally than the merger transference just outlined. Here, separateness is acknowledged but the individual assumes that he and the object (mother) have more or less identical psychologies with similar likes, dislikes, and philosophies, etc. The maintenance of this illusion is necessary for the maintenance of significant relationships. The discovery that another is not "just like me" even in some insignificant respect is enough to threaten the relationship. The twinship attachment, together with its fragility, is often seen in early teenage romances, where part of the function of the attachment is the discovery of self. The currently popular literature on "soulmates" seems to me, at times at least, to perpetuate this transferential relationship based upon the search for the perfect alter ego (Johnson, 1987).

This twinship trance-ference negates separation. For that reason, the individual sees their partner as a twin, and goes into the spiritualized trance, calling the relationship partner a *soul mate*. This also can be linked to the honeymoon period in a relationship, where the two people are merged as one and everything is agreed upon. However, at some point you realize there is another person out there separate from you. At that point, people often become angry—and the honeymoon is over.

THE MIRROR TRANCE-FERENCE

In the ideal situation, the mother is able to mirror back to the child, reinforcing the child's growth and differentiation while frustrating the child's grandiosity and omnipotence. The "good-enough mother" (to use the words of D.W. Winnicott, father of developmental psychology) must frustrate the child's grandiosity. This means that, since the child is fused with and sees mom as magical, omniscient, and always able to fill their needs, the mother must gently frustrate the child's feelings while, simultaneously, allowing their uniqueness and differentiation to emerge. This allows the child to develop a self which is separate from the imagined magical, omniscient, grandiose mom, a self with a realistic understanding of who they are and who they are not, at the level of personality. For example, many women whom I have worked with and know, have said that their husbands expect them to give them everything they want, whenever they want it without their having to ask. These age-regressed men are trance-ferring magical mommy onto their wife or partner.

The "good enough" mother is a little different in Quantum Psychology. Here, the "good enough" mother can mirror **ESSENCE** and essential qualities, not just personality. In order to do this, the mother must be able to acknowledge her own **ESSENCE** and being. This allows her to acknowledge the **ESSENCE** and being of her child, while simultaneously differentiating the child's **ESSENCE** from the child's identities while simultaneously realizing their underlying connection at the level of the underlying unity. For example, rather than the mother fusing together **ESSENCE** and personality when the child misbehaves by saying, "You are bad," the mother can let the child know, overtly or covertly, that what they are doing is not okay, even while their **ESSENCE** and who they really are is untouched and perfect. Moreover, the "good enough" mother, to avoid the trap of identity creation, must be able to do this in order for identities to be weakened and the awareness of **ESSENCE** strengthened.

Unfortunately, this rarely occurs. The "good enough" mother in Quantum Psychology is, of course extremely rare. However, the idea would be to acknowledge **ESSENCE** and/or the underlying unity so that you and the infant "know" that connection while simultaneously allowing the child to differentiate at the external, thinking, emotional and biological levels.

The mirror trance-ference becomes spiritualized (as will be discussed later) and is trance-ferred onto teachers and gurus. For example, spiritual seekers often call their guru the "perfect mirror." This is the trance-ference wherein an age-regressed adult is unknowingly relating to an internalized mom. It should be noted, however, that most gurus re-enforce these early pre-verbal developmental patterns. Some teachers and gurus I have spent time with allow their disciples to age-regress and imagine that they (the guru) are both magical and omniscient. This reinforces these patterns rather than ending them, which is trance-ending.

When this is not done for the child in a "good enough way," a false grandiose self is developed which thinks it can do, create, have whatever it wants, that it is *source* and that it can create and control the subjective experience of another. Unfortunately, when this occurs, adults don't see themselves clearly; they believe they're special, magical or chosen. This feeling of specialness, magicalness, or being chosen, denies human limitations and removes them from humanity, separating them further from other people and from the underlying quantum unity. It must be understood that feelings of being special or different from another are red flags that identities are operating. Why?

To really experience and stabilize in the Essential experience of compassion, we must give up our feelings of differentness and specialness and see ourselves as part of the same human family. Magicalness and specialness develop because the infant sees mom as magical and stays merged with this magical mom fantasy and begins to believe the fantasy and, hence, see themselves as magical. Many workshop leaders, teachers and gurus *hook* their participants with claims that "you can have it all." These *hooks* appeal to the unprocessed infant within an adult who is grandiose and fused with magical mom. Why? Because you cannot have it all, unless you have the talent, training, ability, a context and luck. This, therefore, denies personal limitations and society's restrictions (the external context) placing you in a magical grandiose identity. Again, how do you know if you are in an identity? When you feel special or different from another, you are in an identity. Johnson (1987) on Kohut:

> Kohut's most evolved form of narcissistic transference is the "mirror transference." In this form of relationship, the other is used primarily for the purpose of acknowledging or aggrandizing the false self. Here, the need for attention, "prizing," respect, and echoing is the focus of the relationship. This form of transference is more mature, in that it is directed more at the development of the separate self In this transference,

the false self has been somewhat more developed and others are narcissistically cathected to help support it. The tragedy, of course, is that others are used to aggrandize the false self. . . . The internal experience of this need for mirroring reduces to a more or less constant need for others to notice, confirm, and bolster the insecure self presented to the world. Narcissists with this level of development often have some insight into their narcissistic character, even though they may not know this pejorative and unfortunate label. (pp. 51-52)

I have seen this form of narcissism quite frequently with people who organize their entire external world to support their false self.

Here we also see the guru trance and the False Core of "Worthless" seeking flattery (see Volume II). For now, it can be said that gurus often allow their personality to be worshiped more than their real **SELF (THAT ONE SUBSTANCE)**. They do this by allowing disciples to "take on" the guru's personality, rather than frustrating the disciples' infantile attempts to realize the truth through mimicry, fusion or modeling. This is like a child mirroring the parents' behavior. This demonstrates both the disciples' age regression and misunderstanding of the guru's teachings about the **SELF AS THAT ONE SUBSTANCE**, and the guru's unwillingness to give up the narcissistic sense of being the center of attention.

I once met a very well-known body therapist who took on the identity of her teacher. People always commented on how awful she was as a person—but always claimed what a great teacher she was, and when she taught she was just like her teacher. The problem was, in doing her somatic work she was fabulous, but she had never integrated the work into her life. Rather, she had an identity which was taken on from her teacher, which was a compensated age regression while in her life she remained a decompensated age-regressed child.

Regarding the mirror trance-ference, I know several married couples where the wife continually tells me of her husband's ability to succeed financially, even though he owes money or has nothing.

In the second type, the wife not only tells herself and others of her husband's ability to succeed and make money, but continually over-works supporting him financially. Stephen Johnson (1987) says it this way:

> In defense of that state, the narcissistic personality will go to extreme lengths to find mirroring objects or to coerce those he has into the desired response. The idealization of others which narcissists exhibit may be usefully conceptualized along the developmental continuum—merger, twinship, mirroring. In the merger transference, the individual will seek out and then mispercieve the other as the perfect object with whom to merge. In ordinary life this perfection is most often sought in the potential mate—potential because it is nearly impossible to maintain idealization at close quarters. The individual is still looking for the symbiosis which was either insufficient or prematurely lost.
>
> (This is one phase of the guru/disciple trance which is the spiritualization of the mother). The perfect twinship is the idealization of the alter-ego transference, as seen in many adolescent love affairs. The perfect role model is the idealization of the mirroring transference. In this later developmental arrest, the individual needs someone to look up to, believe in, and emulate. (p. 52)

LOOKING FOR A MODEL

Throughout my life, I have found both friends and trainees of mine who were looking for a role model. Simply put, they have collapsed the levels and are age-regressed, trying to find a model of how to be. For example, recently a former trainee of mine said to me, "You are my model of how to do therapy." Another trainee watching me do a Quantum process in a workshop said that I "modeled the state."

221

I said to both trainees, "I am not a model for how to do therapy, nor do I model a state of consciousness. I do therapy as I do therapy, and the state I'm in is not a modeling but rather just who I am and where I am at the moment." But people age-regress and look for models or formulas of how to be or do, imagining that when they model in this way, they can get the same or similar results, rather than discovering who they are in life and doing therapy from who they are.

Therapists often imply that they are, or they should be, a model. This desire to model another, to look for a model, or to want to be a model, is an age-regressed reenactment of that early childhood state. Think about who's good at modeling behaviors, matching words and positions to gain rapport, and who is good at fusing with a person. Children do that all the time with their parents. But therapies and spiritual groups often encourage and support this trance-ference and the creation of a brand new shiny identity. This attracts, seduces and is easy for the client or trainee because it reinforces the unprocessed age-regression, or better said, it reinforces a false grandiose self. For example, in India I saw many people beginning to walk like, talk like, and have the same mannerisms as their gurus. These early age-regressions or spiritualizations are misunderstood as a person being spiritual.

I often meet therapists who look, act, and think that they are their false selves by acting out of an unconditionally positive regard identity. Very often they have so integrated this false self therapist's identity, that they have placed it on top of a neurotic self. In other words, rather than examining and dismantling their self-defeating tendencies, they create and take on an image of what a good therapist should do. For example, one Ericksonian trainer I knew had on his training brochure, "Emphasis will be placed upon developing a professional persona." Many therapists and therapies are more interested in their image and persona than in being human. Recently, I have seen many different forms of therapy whose focus is on *developing new strategies* to handle relationships (with their mother, for example), rather than on dismantling their childlike identity which has a problem with Mom, because they are seeing her not as a human being and a person, but rather through the eyes of a child.

These are the trappings of the age-regression trance-ference which is looking for a model. As Johnson (1987) says:

> Though I think there are many valuable ideas and strategies provided by the transformational psychology movement, I think that it is particularly prone to this form of error. Its ideology and claims for instant success are often characterized by grandiosity, and its participants sometimes appear to be great exemplars of "transference" cures based upon an unintegrated identification with an idealized charismatic leader. Here there is a collusion of the narcissistic idealization transference of the client with the narcissistic need for mirroring transference in the leader or therapist. Since both are thereby bolstered in their false, grandiose compensatory selves, there is nowhere to push for resolution of the transference. (p. 79.)

Unfortunately, in our society until we "wake up" to our own trance-ference and deal with our personal talents, abilities, and limitations, we will continue to be hooked by so-called charismatic workshop leaders, teachers and gurus. But to be human first requires we know where we are stuck so that we can become freer and appreciate with compassion the plight of our brothers and sisters.

To paraphrase from the Sanskrit: One must first realize he is in bondage so that he can get free. Then and only then can he have compassion for others and be able to help free them.

Part II

THE TRANCE OF
COUNTER-TRANCE-FERENCE

Watch out now,
take care, beware of greedy leaders
who take you where you should not go,
while each unconscious sufferer
wanders aimlessly.
Beware of Maya.

"Beware of Darkness," George Harrison

THE TRANCE OF COUNTER-TRANCE-FERENCE

Counter-trance-ference is a common everyday experience. In trance-ference, the adult age-regresses and becomes a child and makes the other into mommy, daddy or a significant person from the past. In trance-ference, the identification is more with the child identity. In the process of counter-trance-ference you identify more with the mommy/daddy or significant person from the past. This can be best illustrated in relationships. Notice how one partner might act like a child in the relationship while the other might act like the parent. The age-regressed adult is in trance-ference, acting like a child, while the one acting like a parent is also age-regressed and in counter-trance-ference, unknowingly seeing their partner as a child through the eyes of their parent, or you might say seeing their partner as their parents saw them as a child, and then projecting it on their partner.

Quantum Psychology sees counter-trance-ference occurring when the person has an internalized other (mom/dad) and an internalized child. In this process, the person trance-fers the child onto another, and acts like a parent. It should be noted that therapists and teachers can go into trance-ference—making their client into dad or mom—or counter-trance-ference—becoming a parent and making the client into a child. This usually occurs in forms of psychotherapy which teach therapists that they should be the "good-enough" mom or dad to their clients, guiding them through the developmental phases and giving them the "corrective experience" (to be discussed later). I have also seen this happen with family therapists who, when the couple approaches divorce, age-regress and become the child trying to save the marriage, or become a parent telling them or imagining that they know what to do. This re-enforces the client's dependency, age-regression, and trance-ference issues as well as the therapist's trance-ference and counter-trance-ference issues.

Imagine you're in a relationship. Your partner has a problem. You begin to treat them the way your parents or idealized parents (the wish) treated you. You no longer are in present time; rather your partner has become the child and you are acting as your parents did to you as a child—this is counter-trance-ference. This is different from and expands the traditional definition which says that

"Counter-transference is in large measure a counter reaction to the transference of the patient" (Marshall and Marshall, 1988, p. 59).

Quantum Psychology deeply disagrees with this above statement because it *implies* that the patient, client or student is responsible for the therapist's or teacher's counter-trance-ference, when it might be the other way around. For example, many clients and friends tell me that when they decided they wanted to leave (separate) from a therapist or a teacher, they (the therapists or teachers) began to lecture them, scold them, and put them down for asserting their independence. This is also what parents do when teenagers want to leave home and become independent. In ego psychology, there is a belief that by using trance-ference, the therapist can re-parent the client into health or provide the corrective experience

Quantum Psychology says, "Any therapist or teacher who believes that you can be the 'good enough' parent in present time and re-parent or provide the corrective experience for a client or student by guiding them through developmental phases into health has counter-trance-ference issues." Why? For two reasons: One, the therapist or teacher is being the "good enough" parent for a price. Secondly, what happened happened, and to imagine that a 1995 therapist can be a parent and "put in" in 1995 what was left out in 1955 is both magical and grandiose thinking on the part of the therapist or teacher. Noted family therapist Carl Whitaker once gave a workshop to about 300 therapists at which he said, "You are all prostitutes." The therapists got angry and asked him why. "Because you act unconditionally loving and supportive for a price," he said. "When your client doesn't pay his bill, you are no longer unconditionally loving—you get pissed off."

Definitions of the trance of counter-trance-ference generally put the onus on the client or patient. In other words, the implicit message is that the therapist or teacher is reacting to their client's or student's trance-ference. This eliminates the possibility that the therapist or teacher is in a parental and counter-trance-ference identity first, and at some level is asking the client/student to play their game and not question.

Some teachers I have worked with are in their teacher identity, and are in a constant state of trance-ference/counter-trance-ference with their clients and students. In this way they are in a characterological or integrated trance-ference. I call this characterological when therapists or teachers adapt a system which supports, reinforces and exalts counter-tranceference, i.e., being the unconditionally loving mommy or daddy. I define characterological as having little or no awareness of your process. Two people might be behaving in a power-tripping way (i.e., being manipulative). The first person is aware of what they are doing, feels bad about it, but cannot stop it. The second person is not aware of what they are doing, and hence, doesn't feel bad about it. The first person's process is not characterological because they feel bad and have awareness; the second person's is characterological because they not only feel no remorse, but they are unaware of their process. Not being aware and feeling no remorse are hallmarks of a characterological disorder.

TRANCE-FERENCE/COUNTER-TRANCE-FERENCE RELATIONSHIPS

At this point, I would like to expand the parameters of trance-ference/counter-trance-ference to include not only therapist/client, teacher/student or guru/disciple, but many of our other relationships.

Once again, we need to look back on our definition of trance-ference as an age-regressed state, with a lack of awareness by an individual. This causes him or her to move from the present-time to the past-time self and, consequently, relating to an internalized—rather than a present-time—other. The past-time self has associations, emotions and memories, and transfers them onto the present-time other. When this occurs awareness goes to sleep.

It should also be noted that most people are adults in present time but, at varying points or situations, they often become age-regressed. However, I have met integrated age-regressed people who are never adults in present time but are always acting and seeing the world as children. I saw a woman for therapy who always expected her husband and the universe (her husband-daddy-mommy) to "take care" of her. This so eclipsed her life that she would not work even though they had little money. This was an age-regressed trance-ference of parents on her husband and on the world. It is appropriate to expect your parents to provide for you, but the New Age "the universe (mom/dad) will provide" or "take care of me" is an integrated age-regressed philosophy. In India, we used to say, "It is true that the universe will take care of you, but it might not take care of you the way you want or imagine that you should be taken care of."

Why do some people become the age-regressed child while others the all-knowing adult? In one situation, the memory in the form of a picture of the child relating to the parent is fused with and they become the child, transferring the parent onto the other. This is trance-ference. In the other situation, the memory in the form of a picture of the child reacting to the parent, the parent is fused with trance-ferring the child onto another. This is counter-trance-ference.

This impacts us in many ways. If the fusion is with the child, she/he can get involved with "omniscient" teachers, therapists, politicians, or religious leaders since they trance-fer mom/dad onto the authority figure. In other words, just as the infant sees mom as a magical omniscient being who fulfills all their desires, so too does the adult operating out of a child identity sees a guru, teacher, or spiritual system as all knowing, all powerful and magical.

For example, in India, heaven is called Vaikunta. Vaikunta is seen as a place where, whenever a desire arises, it is magically filled. Notice how in this scenario, the magical trance-ference is placed onto the hereafter. Later on we will discuss how children create a hereafter or spiritualized trance-ference metaphor when their biological needs are not met.

QUANTUM PSYCHOLOGY PRINCIPLE:

If you subjectively see and experience yourself as a **TEACHER**, than you are probably in trance-ference/counter-trance-ference and being mom/dad and making or allowing the students/clients to act as children.

This principle does not preclude the fact that many people have something to share and teach which is valuable. However, there's a difference between being a **TEACHER** and simply presenting material and teaching another what you know. I remember, while being trained in Ericksonian Hypnosis, one trainer saw himself as my **TEACHER**. I explained to him that he was not my **TEACHER**, but rather that he was teaching me hypnosis. He did not understand the difference. In order to differentiate, if I teach you how to play guitar, I am your guitar teacher. But if I see myself as a **MASTER** and your **TEACHER**, then I could be in countertrance-ference/trance-ference with you. Unfortunately for everyone involved, all too often the teacher is fused with the **TEACHER**.

In Quantum Psychology, a true teacher has neither a subjective experience of being a **TEACHER**, nor do they really want to be one. It is just what is happening. From a Quantum Psychology perspective, the best a true teacher can do is to give you the tools to work on yourself. This is empowering another. But, on the other hand, if a therapist, teacher or guru believes they have the ultimate answer to your problems, or the answer to how to be in life if only you follow their example and do it their way, this is disempowering and counter-trance-ference.

T rue spirituality is the realization that everything is made of **THAT ONE SUBSTANCE**. Looking through the lens of developmental psychology might *possibly* give us hints on how awareness is unknowingly fixated—thus inhibiting our awareness of **THAT ONE SUBSTANCE.**

Stephen H. Wolinsky

THE TRANCE OF SPIRITUALIZATION REVISITED

We have discussed the many ways trance-ference and counter-trance-ference takes us out of present time and, hence, out of our humanity. In this section, I will explore the most insidious, unquestioned and deepest level of trance-ference: Spiritualization.

BEYOND IDEALIZATION

Most ego psychologists acknowledge the trance-ference of merger, twinship, mirroring and idealization. Idealization, as we all know, occurs when we idealize people, making them more than human so that as children we feel extra safe, more comfortable, and less threatened. This can be seen when young boys say things like, "My father can beat up your father," or "My mom's better than your mom." Ego psychology suggests, but does not go further into, the next level of trance-ference which Quantum Psychology calls spiritualization.

SPIRITUALIZATION

The deepest form of trance-ference is spiritualization which occurs when the trance-ference of idealization is solidified and moves to the next step.[1] In spiritualization, idealization is not resolved. In other words, mom and dad are not seen as human beings but instead are super-idealized and seen as gods, saints, or great teachers. This goes on to create what Quantum Psychology calls the god or guru trance.

Once in the early '70s and recently in Norway I knew people who had idealized his guru and kept on telling me how great he was—certainly much smarter than mine. I said to them, to point out his spiritualized trance, "My guru can beat up your guru." The spiritualization trance-ference is the next step after idealization.

---

[1] I discussed this in Chapter 14 of *The Dark Side of the Inner Child: the Next Step.*

DE-HYPNOSIS AND COUNTER-TRANCE-FERENCE

In *Trances People Live*, the process discussed is not hypnosis but de-hypnosis. In this case, unlike ego psychology, Quantum Psychology does not attempt to set up or create a "positive trance-ference" with the client. Quantum Psychology believes that the idea of using trance-ference was constructed by the therapist's own counter-trance-ference issues. What I am saying here needs to be emphasized since for many this is more than just controversial—it is **BLASPHEMOUS.**

Many therapists believe that trance-ference is beneficial and that by being the "good enough parent," they can guide the client through their developmental phases. Thus, they encourage trance-ference as part of the healing process. Quantum Psychology believes that this merely *psychologizing* and only justifies and serves the unresolved counter- trance-ference issues in the world of psychology.

QUANTUM PSYCHOLOGY PRINCIPLE:

Encouraging, allowing or supporting trance-ference only begets more dependency and trance-ference.

THE QUANTUM APPROACH TO TRANCE-FERENCE

BUST THE TRANCE-FERENCE FIRST

I would like to share my own experience of the most important intervention that I, as a student, ever experienced. I had lived in India about two years, and without realizing it, I had trance-ference issues with my Indian teachers/gurus. In other words, if I had a question like, "What should I do?" "Where should I live?" "Should I get married?" many gurus with counter-trance-ference issues would play the super-spiritualized, all-knowing parent and give me answers.

The spiritual identity I had taken on was, whatever the guru—i.e., Mom or Dad—said to do, you should "surrender" to and do. In other words, the spiritual as well as the family game was to do what your parents said, and everything would come to you and if you didn't do what they said, you'd never get rewards (enlightenment). I didn't know I had trance-ference issues with these teachers/gurus because almost every teacher-guru I had seen had their own personal counter-trance-ference issues which they "bought into" and "got off" on the power of.

In January 1979 I went to see Nisargadetta Maharaj and he said to me, "Are you willing to stay eight days and absorb the teachings?" I, thinking I was being a good disciple and not realizing I had trance-ference issues, replied as I had been trained, "Whatever Maharaj wants me to do, I'll do." He looked at me like I was a jerk. "Don't you understand? I don't play the guru/disciple game. If you want that, go someplace else. If you want to stay, stay; if you don't, then leave." Now, I was shocked. He had busted my trance-ference immediately as it came up. He didn't wait. He didn't enjoy it; he didn't play my game. "I" was disoriented and confused for weeks.

That was some twenty years ago and I have kept that understanding and philosophy with me. The shock I felt was caused by his not only refusing to go along with my trance-ference but also my narcissistic mirroring of him, in order to get him to merge with me. He did not need my mirroring, adoration or merger. His job was clear—*bust the trance-ference, bust the narcissism* so that I could be free from the concepts I was unknowingly operating out of.

Bust the Trance-ference, Bust the Narcissism

That is the presenting issue of all issues. Then, handle what comes up around it.

De-Idealizing—Breaking the Trance-ference

In the Quantum approach, once the trance-ference and narcissism are seen, they're confronted and dealt with. At each step during therapy, the therapist is asked to break the trance-ference of idealization. This can be accomplished by having the client place an image of the idealized other next to the therapist and notice the similarities and differences.[2] This leads to differentiating the past from the present.

---

[2]This is discussed in detail in *Trances People Live: Healing Approaches in Quantum Psychology.*

A major breakthrough in the Way of the Human is to realize that you, the therapist, and everyone else are human beings. This creates the experience of compassion and humanity. Without the dissolution of trance-ference and narcissism, and the trance-ference processes of merger, twinship, mirroring, idealization and spiritualization, there can be no freedom or humanity which only comes through de-idealizing of the other (not as a put down) and the realization of our own humanness.

How powerful is this experience of humanity? In the early 1980s, I realized that I was an incest survivor. At that time, there was only one Incest Survivors Anonymous group in New Mexico and sometimes I'd be the only one there. I can still recall the first time I went. There I was, totally therapy trained for years, a client for years, years of meditation, years of living in India—when I looked around the room, there was a secretary, a painter, an astrologer, and a housewife. I realized that I was the same as them—and all of my defenses vanished.

I instantly saw everyone there as the same. It was the most important "spiritual experience" I had ever had—it was a total connection to being human and to humanity.

THE PROBLEM OF SEPARATION: THE GLUE THAT HOLDS SPIRITUAL TRANCES TOGETHER

In guru/disciple, teacher/student, therapist/client and love relationships, separation is always a problem. If the guru/disciple, teacher/student or therapist/client is running trance-ference/ counter-trance-ference issues (narcissistic), then the teacher, guru or therapist (just like mom and dad) becomes threatened at the possible loss (separation) of a disciple, student or client. This is why they put them down when they attempt to individuate. Teachers, gurus or therapists say things like, "They are not surrendered," "They are resisting," or "They have some worldly karma to work out."

In love relationships, when one attempts to separate from another, the one being separated from tends to "put down" the other and make them into the anti-Christ (the one being left is the Christ).

I once had a client who said to me, "If the person I want doesn't want me, obviously they are assholes." This is because there is an age-regressed re-enactment of an incomplete earlier developmental process wherein they realized they were separate from mom. Johnson (1991) says it this way:

> Natural attempts at separation are blocked, causing parental anxiety, or are actively punished. At the same time, the child's natural abilities for empathic mirroring are overvalued and reinforced by parents who require merger with the child in order to feel secure or worthwhile. (p. 79)

This explains the narcissistic counter-trance-ference of the guru, teacher or therapist who cannot allow their disciple or student to leave. Why? Because it brings up the separation problem the guru or teacher or therapist did not resolve with their parents.

This is also why the guru reinforces and praises the false self that the disciple or student presents. This goes on for two reasons: First, because the guru/teacher wants the student to stay, and hence, resists completing their individualization process; and, second, disciples get unconsciously hooked into the system because it duplicates their own pre-verbal unresolved merger/separation and grandiosity issues with their mother. Johnson (1991) says:

> In analyzing this symptom constellation, it may help to remember that the natural libidinal self[3] of any individual desires contact and support in the expression of autonomy. . . . [The symbiotic character is forced to choose between contact and autonomy. Yet the contact . . . is not directed at the real libidinal individual, but rather at an idealized merger-object. When separation, individuation, autonomy, difference, adventure, etc., are repeatedly blocked, the individual internal-

---

[3]The libidinal self is that part of you which desires merging. It is often confused with sex but that is not accurate.

izes that block and copies the environment in doing to herself what was done to her. This self -restraint constitutes the antilibidinal self. (p. 158)

In other words, the proper self-other relationship in this model is one in which I give myself up and over to you to obtain the bliss of merger. It is also important to note that there is developmental arrest in this state and role-relationship model, such that the individual feels herself to be dependent, in need of supplies, and in need of an all-gratifying caretaker as would a small child. In this repressed state, the individual experiences these archaic feelings irrespective of the degree of adult autonomy she may have really attained. (p. 159)

Here again Johnson points to the causes of the re-enactment of the merger trance-ference with therapists, teachers and gurus.

EVEN MORE SPIRITUALIZED: THE TRANSFORMATIONAL MOTHER

THE MOTHER AS GURU

There is no question that developmental research demonstrates the overwhelming influence of the relationship between infant and mother. More interesting is how unresolved issues within this most basic area of our lives result in the over-seeking for transformation outside of ourselves rather than inside.

The child sees the mother as a transformational figure, meeting needs, handling hunger, cold, or loneliness. In this way, the mother as a transformational person, is trance-ferred onto the teacher, guru, therapist, or psycho-spiritual system, turning them into the transformational mother (object).

Noted psychoanalyst, Christopher Bollas (1987) says it this way:

I wish to identify the infant's first subjective experience of the object (mother) as a transformational object. . . . Not yet fully identified as the other, the mother is experienced as a process of transformation, and the future lives on in the form of object seeking in adult life, when the object (person) is sought for its function as a signifier of transformation. Thus, in adult life, the quest is not to process [digest] the object (person); rather the object is pursued in order to surrender to it as a medium that alters the self. The mother is an environmental transformer of the subject (child). The memory of this early object relation manifests itself in the person's search for an object (a person, place, event, or ideology) that promises to transform the self.

I think we have failed to take notice of the phenomenon in adult life of the wide-ranging collective search for an object (mother) that is identified with the metamorphosis of the self. In many religious faiths, for example, when the subject believes in the deity's actual potential to transform the total environment, he sustains the structure. (pp. 16-17)

This is the over-spiritual seeker identity looking for another to transform you rather than taking responsibility for your own transformation. Often in guru/disciple, teacher/student or therapist/client relationships, the guru, teacher or therapist becomes the transformational mother (object). In fact, many a teacher, guru or therapist has adopted a whole philosophy or system to re-enforce this age-regression. For example, one system has made statements like, "The guru is the root of all action," or "The guru takes responsibility for your spiritual unfoldment." These are classic "red flags" of the mother being trance-ferred as a transformational object by the disciple (child) onto the guru (mother), and the guru's counter-tranceference and narcissism placed back on the disciple. Furthermore, in many spiritual and psychological systems the technology, techniques or model of doing the work are given the transformational power rather then the one who is doing the practice. Christopher Bollas (1987) says:

> This anticipation of being transformed by an object (mother) . . . inspires the subject with a reverential attitude towards it, so that even though the transformation of the self will not take place on the scale it reached during early life, the adult subject tends to nominate such objects (mother or philosophies) as sacred. (pp. 16-17)

This also explains the use of sacred objects like statutes of saints and pictures of teachers or gurus, not to mention the arbitrary rules and regulations. Before I worked through and saw my own pre-verbal, pre-conscious beliefs, in India both I and others were engaged in daily ritual worship at precise times and in exact ways. We had attributed to statutes and pictures the spiritual power to transform us. We asked for blessings, grace, and forgiveness from an inanimate object—believing somehow that it had the power to transform us—rather than taking responsibility for our own transformation. Moreover, if we missed our ritual worship or did it the "wrong way", we believed, in some superstitious, intangible way, that something bad would happen to us and we'd never get transformed or enlightened. This is making something outside of yourself sacred rather than seeing yourself as responsible for your own transformation. It is like a person making a statue of a saint and worshipping the statue rather than realizing that they made the statue.

Gurdjieff, regarding rituals and ritual worship, suggested that to the degree to which the energy is lessening, dissipating, or beginning to die down within a spiritual system—such will be the degree to which a system or a teacher will get more into ritual worship. Actually, ritual worship should be a warning that there is not much energy left in the system.

According to Bollas (1987):

> The search for transformation and for the transformational object is perhaps the most pervasive archaic

object relation, and I want to emphasize that this search arises not out of desire for the object per se, or primarily out of craving or longing. It arises from the person's certainty that the object (mother/teacher, etc.) will deliver transformation; this certainty is based on the object's nominated capacity to resuscitate the memory of early ego transformation. In arguing this, I am maintaining that...the search for the transformational object, and nomination of the deliverer of environmental transformation, is an ego memory (reenactment). (p. 27).

I recall in India, before I realized my pre-verbal automatic structures, spending years looking for sacred objects to worship and trying to get them blessed by "sacred people." I remember there even being a process called prana-pratista which provided three ways of having a sacred object "enlivened," or made sacred so that you could worship it:

1. It could be done by the touch of a saint (a sacred person.)
2. It could be done by the seeker asking the energy or deity to sit inside the object so that you could worship it.
3. A Brahmin priest could perform a sacred ceremony to ask the deity to sit inside the object so that you could worship it.

In fact, you were even asked what it was you wanted from the statute so that you could get the health, wealth, or enlightenment you desired. This is certainly the ultimate in giving an inanimate object the power to make you healthy, wealthy and wise.

Bollas (1987) writes that:

Each aesthetic experience is transformational, so the search for what Krieger terms the 'aesthetic object' is a quest for the transformational object (mother). The transformational object seems to promise the beseeching subject an experience where self fragmentations will be integrated. (p. 33).

SPIRITUAL EXPERIENCES

What then are these spiritual experiences of union we are all seeking. Bollas (1987) again:

> In my view the aesthetic moment is an evocative resurrection of an early ego condition often brought on by a sudden and uncanny rapport with an object (mother), a moment when the subject is captured in an intense illusion of being selected by the environment for some deeply reverential experience. This holding experience sponsors a psycho-somatic memory of the holding environment. It is a pre-verbal, essentially pre- representational registration of the mother's presence. (p. 39).

> Transformational-object-seeking is an endless memorial search for something in the future that resides in the past. I believe that if we investigate many types of object relating we will discover that the subject is seeking the transformational object (mother) and aspiring to be matched in symbiotic harmony within an aesthetic frame that promises to metamorphose the self. (Bollas, 1987, p. 40).

CONCLUSION

As we continue to look at combinations of spiritual trances which prevent us from developing multi-dimensional awareness, we can begin to see their possible roots in past-time pre-conscious pre-verbal experiences. Few could deny the compelling desire for transformation, and yet, how amazing that the compulsion or obsession with transformation could sometimes lie in our pre-verbal past.

How are we to view all of this? For now, let us just consider that being human is a discovery that belongs uniquely to each of us. There are no formulas, rules, or people who can give it to us. Rather, it is an unfolding process whereby we discover who we are by discovering who we are not. I was once in Bombay with a "friend," "brother" and teacher of mine, Swami Prakashanda. He said to me, regarding mantra meditation, "Om Namah Shivaya [a mantra used in India], Om Namah Shivaya, you take it, use it, and then you throw it away. There are no formulas." Not only are there no formulas, we will also come to see that the seeker identity, which seeks—through rules, formulas or begging—for transformation and grace from another, must be explored, dismantled and discarded. Said another way, the desire to merge with a guru is not bad. However, if we are attempting to do it from an infantile identity, "we" will "get" nowhere. What will be demonstrated in Volume III is that we must let go of these infantile identities in order to enter into the last phase of multi-dimensional awareness—the **NOT I-I** prior to the **VOID**, or the Underlying Unity of Quantum Consciousness.

D evelopmental psychology is not the truth. It is a lens, useful or not we cannot say— either way it must also be discarded and gone beyond, to "know" the no state of **I AM** which has no frames of reference, no frames to frame.

Stephen H. Wolinsky

Question everything (especially lenses and maps, including developmental psychology).

Don't believe anything.

(Nisargadatta Maharaj)

Part III

THE SYMBIOTIC TRANCE

SYMBIOSIS: ATTACHMENT

Ego psychology states that between the ages of 5 and 12 months, a growing infant cannot tell the difference between her/his mother and himself.

> The earliest mental representations of self and object (mother), the undifferentiated self-object (mother) representation (image) or schema is characteristic at this stage. There is neither physical nor psychic differentiation (Horner, 1984, p. 27)

The infant experiences the mother as omnipotent and omniscient, and an undifferentiated or a barely differentiated unity with itself. Years later, this can lead to one or more spiritual trances: the first, in which one identifies with the omnipotent mother and thus feels both omniscient and omnipotent. The second phase is the trance-ference onto another, or what I call the teacher or guru trance, in which the internalized identity (infant) and the internalized omnipotent mother are trance-ferred onto a spiritual figure, making them both omnipotent and a transformational object.

Johnson (1987) says that:

> In the symbiotic period, the child has the beneficial illusion of control because he believes he shares or controls the mother's omnipotent power." (p. 18)

This could also explain the collapsing of the levels and infantile understanding in many "New Age" thinkers who believe they can create or co-create with the **ALL** that omniscient, omnipotent consciousness. Furthermore, it should also be noted that the anthropomorphic tendency, i.e., to trance-fer a nervous system onto **THAT UNDIFFERENTIATED CONSCIOUSNESS** or God, "as if" God or Undifferentiated Consciousness *wants* this or that or is trying to *teach lessons* also represents this infantile trance-ference.

PREMATURE DETACHMENT:
THE SCHIZOID PERSONALITY

In this spiritual trance, the schizoid prematurely detaches from his or her body and cannot feel. They could be called over-observers and are referred to by Palmer as the "Unenlightened Buddha" (see Volume II). They appear spiritual, but deep down they feel as though they have nothing and are nothing. (Small nothing as in a lack.) This premature detachment actually is a defense. In other words, they look detached, but it is a defense against feeling.

After living in India for six years and traveling and visiting with almost sixty teachers, ashrams, and gurus, I met many spiritual aspirants who were acting-out this schizoid process. They oftentimes had high cheekbones, a brittle bony structure and, in extreme cases, a film or coating over their eyes. When I looked into their eyes, even though they kept making lots of eye contact, I was unable to pierce through this covering. Very dissociative, and aloof, and appearing spiritual, the schizoid individual is terrified of engulfment, remaining very defensively detached as a defense against their underlying age-regressed fear; hence, to defend against feeling, they become over-observers.

A by-product of meditation is dis-association, but it can be used as a way of "spiritualizing dissociation, and using meditation as medication."

Dissociation or premature observation is an automatic defense that protects you during trauma. It occurs when you split-off from the experience of a painful event, refusing to feel the pain or fear or humiliation. Usually, we learn to dissociate as children, when we have few internal defenses to fall back upon. A child who is molested by her father cannot allow herself to fully feel the horror, so she "shuts down" part of her reaction by splitting-off from it. . . . The main characteristic of dissociation . . . is that it allows a person to not experience something. When a child dissociates from feelings of abandonment, for example, the split-off from feeling occurs automatically and unconsciously, as a way of protecting the child. . . .

The dis-association of Witnessing, by contrast, allows you to become aware of what is occurring. Witnessing is free of judgment, evaluation, significance and preference. When you are in the pure awareness of Witnessing you are beyond the observer-observed dyad (see Volume III, **NOT I-I**). By contrast, dissociation is a process that leaves you in resistance to experience.

Meditation, can certainly be misused as a way of attempting to dissociate from uncomfortable or threatening feelings. And it is certainly true that many abused people have found solace in meditation because the disidentification that is the goal of many Eastern approaches seems so similar to the patterns of dissociation underlying their own emotional lives.

> The schizoid's adaptation to an insufficiently nourishing, indeed punitive, environment is to internally migrate. The false, compensatory self of the schizoid person is characterized by distance rather than by grounded, accessible living. (Johnson, 1987, p. 19)

In Quantum Psychology, the schizoid must do lots of body work, such as Rolfing and Feldenkrais, coupled with an ongoing practice of yoga. This will enable them to feel their body first, before moving onto dismantling identities. In fact, in Quantum Psychology workshops, I always suggest that people get ongoing body work, as a way to integrate the Quantum work into a daily walking-around, integrative experience.

THE DESIRE FOR UNION

It is the resistance to the natural biological merger-separation process, particularly separation and individuation that causes the spiritualized trance of trying to return to unconscious union, often with the mother later spiritualized as God or a relationship (soulmate). This often gets confused with samadhi.[4] Notice too how many spiritual seekers stuck in the guru/ disciple trance are very dependent and find it painful to separate physically from the guru (mom/dad) and become individuals functioning in the world.

Samadhi is considered a no-me state. The no-me state available in present time is different from the drive to merge with mother, or in this case, the mother trance-ferred onto the universe, a teacher, a guru, or a relationship partner. However, to an individual stuck in this early trance, they seem the same—hence, they label dissociation as spiritual.

Furthermore, in many cases I have seen, the desire for union with God or the desire to merge with another person and lose oneself in relationship is the unconscious resistance to separation from their mother, and is therefore a re-enactment of the individuation-separation process.

Johnson 1987) says:

Paradise Lost—Moving from unconsciousness union to separation differentiation. According to Mahler's system occurs at approximately six months...(p. 22)

According to the developmental observers, the child is now grandiose, experiencing a sense of omnipotence due, in part, to the still retained belief of unity with the mother. The toddler still wishes to believe and apparently convinces himself that he owns his mother's magical powers[5] and can have absolute con-

---

[4]Samadhi is a deep absorption in meditation, an absorption so deep, in fact, that the self disappears. Samadhi is also considered the eighth or final step in Raja Yoga called the king of yogas and in many forms of Buddhist Yoga or eight-limbed yoga.
[5]They seem magical only to an infant.

trol over them.[6] He certainly must experience continual, and hopefully optimal, frustrating exceptions
to that illusion. Yet, while he is building the construct
of separateness, his cognitive inmaturity continues to
protect him from the full realization of his separateness and vulnerability. The manic high times of this
period, as well as involvement in developing autono-
mous functions and interacting with the newly experienced world, also protect him from becoming aware
of these unpleasant realities. . . . (pp. 25-26)

When his need to integrate his desires for independent expression and dependent unity is badly handled
and/or when his need for integrating grandiosity and
vulnerability is inappropriately dealt with--refusal to
accept the rapprochement with reality is often the result. Then, the infant regresses to the reassuring illusions of grandiosity and symbiotic unity [with Mom
later trance-ferred onto the teacher or guru] and becomes fixated at this developmental level. (pp. 26-27)

Here we have again the experience of a resistance to separation and a desire for dependent unity with the mother, or later an
imagined trance-ferred mother placed upon the universe or the guru/
teacher.

According to Althea Horner (1984):

this defensive stance also denies one of the primary
realities to be confronted during this sensitive time—
limitation.

Here we notice how the New Age promotes grandiosity with
its "You can have or create anything you want" philosophy. Developmental stuckness reinforces this myth. Often in workshops I tell

---

[6]As mentioned earlier this explains the developmental issue with believing the philosophy,
"I create it all," "I can create reality," etc. It is an age-regression of an infant who sees Mom
as magical, omnipotent and omniscient and now acts-out of that structure *believing* it is so.

groups that you cannot have everything you want. That expectation is infantile and negates reality. For example, many New Agers believe that there is "abundance" on the planet. They often say, "Don't come from scarcity." Unfortunately, there is a limited amount of gold, silver, oil, diamonds, etc. on the planet. This is a fact. For that reason, if some people have billions, many won't have anything. Furthermore, you cannot have all you want; you can have what you want given your IQ, genetics, natural abilities, looks, inheritance, external context, luck, etc. *The Way of the Human* at this level requires that you be honest with yourself and acknowledge and work with your limitations, rather than indulge your imagined grandiosity.

SPIRITUAL TRANCES

1. I Am One with the Mother. In India, people are frequently disciples of the Mother. Notice how this can be a re-enactment of the symbiotic relationship the child has with their mother.
2. I Am One. Here, differentiation at one level is incomplete, which means that the person feels no separation and in life fuses with everything and everyone.

The Way of the Human asks us to acknowledge all the dimensions of our humanness. To prematurely say, "I am one with everything," without the ability to hold your separateness and body boundaries also denotes a developmental regression. This regression and developmental delay must be looked at and taken apart. In this way, our true human nature and freedom at all dimensions of awareness can be stabilized.

I was giving a workshop in Florida a few years ago and a woman in her early 30's complained about how she felt afraid when her husband left for work. When we began to look at this more closely, what emerged was that she felt abandoned when her husband left. Abandonment, as mentioned earlier, can be a signal of a deep age-regression. Part of her presenting philosophy was that she was very spiritual and one with everything. But what she was feeling showed that developmentally she was stuck in a symbiotic union with her mother which she trance-ferred onto her husband as well as her spiritual system. Whenever she had to experience or acknowledge that her husband was separate from her, she would freak out and feel abandoned.

This inability to acknowledge differentiation between herself and the world showed her developmental arrest at age 5 to 12 months. Her spiritual premises also showed, by her inability to work, an expectation that God or the universe (i.e., the object mother, now her husband) would take care of her. There developed a deep confusion within her when this did not occur. I walked over to her, holding my hand near her head and asked, "Can you see a difference between my hand and your head?" "Yes," she said. "Can you feel a difference between my hand and your shoulder?" "No." In other words, she bad no boundaries. For homework I asked her to see a picture frame around her husband this week to hopefully begin the long process of creating clearer boundaries.

HATCHING

The hatching period is the time when the infant hatches out of symbiotic union with the mother and begins to differentiate her/himself from mom. This is the time of beginning to walk, talk, etc.

> The more the symbiotic partner helps the infant to become ready to hatch from the symbiotic orbit smoothly and gradually—that is, without undue strain upon his own resources—the better equipped the child becomes to separate out and to differentiate his self-representations from the hitherto fused symbiotic self- plus-object representations. (Mahler, 1968)

If, however, the hatching from this symbiotic merging with mom does not go smoothly, other internal trances can arise.

TRANCE I: THE PRIMA DONNA COMPLEX

Imagining that everything you say, think, do, experience is important and significant is what I call the "Prima Donna Complex."

This is the child that the parents overindulge. The parent who says, "What a genius," when the child says Da-Da or Ma-Ma. When the child walks, the parents can't believe it's possible. This child begins to think they are *so special* that they become prima donnas.

TRANCE II: SEEING THE WORLD THROUGH MOM'S EYES

Imagining others see you the way your mother saw you.

OR

Imagining you are the way your mother saw you. This reminds me of the song John Lennon wrote to Paul McCartney:

> "You lived with straights who told you were king, just like your mama would tell you anything. Those freaks were right when they said you were dead. . . . The one mistake you made was in your head. . . . How do you sleep at night?"

The developmental skill which needs to be learned during this phase is the ability to move from inward (internal) to outward (external world) and from outward to inward at choice. This can be likened to Gurdjieff's self-remembering, wherein your focus of attention is split 50-50, outward and inward.

This exercise suggests you can have both by splitting your attention inside and outside so that they are equally balanced. In the words of Ouspensky (1949) who was a student of Gurdjieff:

> I am speaking of the division of attention which is a characteristic feature of self-remembering.

> I represent it to myself in the following way:

> When I observe something, my attention is directed toward what I observe—a line with one arrowhead:

I—the observed phenomenon.

When, at the same time, I try to remind myself, my attention is directed both inward and outward, and a second arrowhead appears on the line:

I—the observed phenomenon

Having visualized the process in this manner, I saw that the problem consisted of directing attention on oneself without weakening or obliterating the attention directed on something else. (p. 119)

THE NEXT DEVELOPMENTAL PHASE
PRACTICING PHASE—10 MONTHS TO 16 MONTHS

This period marks the time of huge grandiosity, the feeling of "I can do anything." This is the time the child begins to walk and be independent and gets great joy from his or her accomplishments. This is the time of grandiosity. This is the place of developmental stuckness we see in seminar leaders who sell their workshops with "You can have anything you want." These seminar leaders could be viewed through the lens of developmental psychology as grandiose or psychopathic.

They're either grandiose because they believe "You can create it all" and are thus stuck in the practicing period. Or perhaps they're pathologically narcissistic and think they're the center of the universe and can do anything.Or they might know it's not true but care only about making money and being rich and famous, with no thought about the people they are taking advantage of.

SPIRITUAL TRANCE—"I CREATE MY REALITY"

In New Age circles, this is the cry of people who are developmentally arrested at this stage. They imagine that they are the center of the universe and that their beliefs or thoughts create their external world. In order to be clear, your beliefs do help to create your internal subjective experience. They do not create or control the external world or how or what the external world thinks of you.

If a New-Ager is walking down the street and someone yells out, "Asshole," they might say to themselves, "I wonder why I created that" or "I wonder if there are lessons to learn." This is both grandiose—i.e., "I create their actions"—and an age-regressed spiritual reframe—i.e., learning lessons, or some higher power (Mom/Dad, school, etc.) is teaching me for some divine growth reason. Quantum Psychology would say that you are not responsible for the person yelling out "asshole." But you are responsible for what you internally, subjectively create in response to their remark such as "Who cares," or "I'm going to kill them," or "I feel hurt."

To joke about this New Age grandiosity, noted New Age comedian Swami Beyondananda said, "Everyone now is so New Age, even muggers are New Age. I was walking down the street the other day. A mugger knocked me down, grabbed my wallet, and as he was running away said, 'Now, why did you create this in your life'?"

THE NEW AGE COMPLEX

Viewing through the lens of developmental psychology, I call this trance the "New Age Complex," because in this trance, to use the words of psychoanalytic developmental psychology, the child imagines "The world is your oyster." Here the child falls in love with their own grandiosity as they learn to walk and talk. They feel like they can create it all, do it all, accomplish anything. This does not appreciate the context in which we live.

QUANTUM PSYCHOLOGY PRINCIPLE:

The context is greater than the individual.

New Age and spiritual teachers suffer from this syndrome when they tell people that by taking their workshop or by doing a certain spiritual practice, they can have it all just by creating the image in their mind. This is one of the clearest demonstrations of developmental delay on the part of the teacher presenting the workshop and the student believing such seminar leaders.

This can be seen as the trance wherein people think their internal dreams and fantasies will come true. Or they might exhibit the cognitive distortion of emotional reasoning, namely, it feels right or it feels like it will happen; therefore, it will happen. Recently, I spoke to a spiritual teacher who had started receiving lots of money. She told me that as soon as she "opened up to the universe, money came." This narcissistic, grandiose trance made her believe that because she opened up internally, money came (externally)—"as if" she were in control of the money people gave her from the external.

WHAT IS A NARCISSIST?

There was a woman who was having dinner with a narcissistic man. For the first hour, the man talked about himself. After an hour or more, he looked at the woman and said, "Enough about me, now tell me what do you think of me?" This is the classic trance of someone stuck at the practicing phase.

THE GURU TRANCE

The teacher or guru who demands that he be the center of the universe might be both narcissistic and grandiose. First, they demonstrate their developmental delay by believing they have magical powers (magical mommy) or like gods, i.e., spiritualized mom. And second, by narcissistically expecting to always be the center of attention, suggesting you can be liberated (be one) if you (the age regressed infant) focus your attention on them (magical-omniscient mommy/dad) and they getting enraged when this does not occur.

THE DISCIPLE TRANCE

The disciple (who is stuck in this infantile trance) plays out the other side of this identity, imagining the teacher or guru (mother/ father) is omniscient and can see, feel, or know the disciple's innermost heart. In other words, the infant within the disciple transfers the omniscient mother onto the teacher or guru, and assumes the mother/ guru knows their deepest wishes and thoughts—because they are them.

RAPPROCHEMENT—18 MONTHS (THE CONFRONTATION WITH THE WORLD)

In the Rapprochement phase, identities begin to get more and more solidified. This occurs because the individual is now clearly separate from mom and begins to be confronted by the world. The child, however, still needs to idealize mom out of the fear of not being able to survive.

> To the extent that the issues of the rapprochement phase are not handled adequately, the individual may, in a very meaningful way, remain developmentally fixed in these patterns of archaic infantile consciousness--grandiosity, idealization, splitting the representations of self and others. (Johnson, 1987, pp. 27-28)

> The individual, perhaps for an entire lifetime, continues to look for his or her self in all the wrong places--in the fulfillment of the archaic grandiosity and/or in the fulfillment of the archaic idealization. (Ibid., p. 28).

> . . .With respect to the issue of grandiosity, the child needs repeated but supportive frustration of that illusion. He needs to learn repeatedly but gently that he is not omnipotent and that he cannot do or have anything he wants simply because he wants it. (Ibid., pp. 30-31.)

Unfortunately again, often teachers or gurus and spiritual systems do not allow this to occur. Even worse, their philosophy reinforces the infantile structure of premature merging by offering statements such as, "The guru and I are one."

What we must appreciate in this statement of oneness is that, yes, it's true, we are one. The problem is that we must acknowledge and appreciate our animal nature and psycho-emotional nature, along with our Quantum Nature. Otherwise, premature merging is based on arrested development and trances, with their accompanying infantile understandings which yield individual pain. *The Way of the Human* asks us to separate and be a mature individual. Then by becoming that individual human, one can stabilize their experience in the world as they move into **ESSENCE** and, ultimately, into Quantum Consciousness.

> It is at this difficult juncture when the individual first fully appreciates his separation, deals emotionally with the impact of that reality, and is called upon to integrate his magnificence with his vulnerability. This rapprochement with reality represents the individual's first attempt to reconcile an idealized dream, which includes the illusions of symbiosis and grandiosity, with the realities of existence, which include separateness and limitation (Ibid., p. 41)

> The narcissist's salvation is not in his accomplishments, specialness, or uniqueness. The "drama of the gifted child" (Miller, 1981) is in his discovery of his *human ordinariness*. In that *ordinariness is his ability to feel real human feelings* unaffected by his internalized (or externalized) parents' acceptance or rejection of his feelings. *Once his ordinariness is realized*, he can express his gift as just that--a gift. His gift is not who he is; but humanness is who he is. (Ibid. p. 49)

In Quantum Psychology, true spirituality is to be aware of the underlying unity, aware of your **ESSENCE**, aware of your psycho-emotional nature, aware of your animal nature and aware of the external world, etc. *The Way of the Human, therefore, is to realize and be aware of our humanness, ordinariness, vulnerability, and underlying connection to humanity, all simultaneously.*

THE TRANSITION PHASE

In the transition phase of development, the child is separate from Mom. However, to make this transition, the child might have a teddy bear, pillow, or a blanket. The child makes the inanimate object animate, and thus still feels connected, having not quite completely left the merger with Mom.

If a person does not complete this phase, then they are susceptible to a trance-itional spiritual object. For example, a mantra, prayer beads, a rabbit's foot, or a picture hung around the neck, all are re-enactments of the unfinished transition phase.

When separation from Mom is complete, the trance-itional objects can be given up. It must be understood that the child's/ disciple's desire for God could be a desire for their merging with mother, and that spiritual paraphernalia are a spiritualized re-enactment of teddy bears and blankets. Although they make the person feel more comfortable, when they can be seen for what they are, they can be given up. This yields greater freedom since your connection is directly with yourself and the world rather than using an intermediary step (mantra or prayer to reach yourself).

In the words of the Sufi poet-saint Rumi, "Prayer leads to trance." Why? Because it buffers us from experiencing present time.

When I say this in workshops, someone will usually become upset with me. My response regarding prayer is, If there is only one substance, then who is praying to something separate from themselves, and who is answering the prayer?

THE TRANCE OF DETACHMENT

Detachment is often sought after but sometimes it is the trance of detachment.

The trance of detachment looks like detachment but actually it is often times a defense against feeling. According to object-relations theory, the defensive detachment is the way the infant defends against the feeling of separation from Mom. In other words, in order to "not feel" the separation from mom, the child becomes prematurely detached. Unfortunately, this defensive premature detachment is sometimes labeled as acceptance, distancing, or more spiritual.

Recently, I did a demonstration in a workshop with a man who was having marital problems (i.e., not getting what he wanted from his wife). He said, "I accept her." I asked, "When you say accept, what do you feel in your body toward her?" He replied, "I distance myself." Later he realized this was distancing and defending was labeled acceptance which was not acceptance itself which brings about appreciation and more intimacy.

In "spiritual" groups, too, I have seen people who claimed detachment, when it was rather cutting-off and defending againt human feelings.

What then is the difference between premature detachment and true detachment which is Witnessing and beyond the observer-observed dyad. Premature mature detachment is a defense against separation. Witnessing is beyond the observer-observed dyad, and contains not resistance, defensiveness, judgement, evaluation, or significance. (see Volume III, the **NOT I-I**).

FINAL NOTE

Mis-perceived betrayal is the major ingredient in the creation of identities. It is mis-perceived betrayal (i.e., realizing mom is separate from you) which forms what is called in psychoanalytic developmental psychology the "narcissistic injury" (see Volume II).

Identities contain trances. Some of the deepest trances are spiritual trances. These spiritual trances are difficult to root out for three major reasons: 1) they are very early and pre-verbal; 2) they are never questioned; and 3) spiritual systems and teachers are often organized around them and reinforce and validate them.

CONCLUSION

Quantum Psychology has several statements regarding how this trance of transference is unfortunately "acted out," both with yourself, with others, and the observer:

1. Do unto yourself that which was done unto you.
2. Do unto others that which was done unto you.
3. How you observe "yourself" is how Mom and Dad observed you

Bollas (1987) also suggests that as you were treated as a child, so you will treat yourself, or as you were viewed by mom and dad as a child so shall you view yourself.

> One idiom of representation is the person's relation to the self as an object to be observed, and object relationships where the individual may objectify, imagine, analyze, and manage the self through identification with primary others who have been involved in that very task (p. 41). . . . It is my view that each person transfers elements of the parents' child care to his own handling of himself as an object (p. 59) (and, hence, observes him or herself through the eyes of Mom and Dad).

In other words, how your parents treated and observed you as a child will be internalized and you will treat and observe "yourself" (actually an age regressed you) the same way they did. I have worked with innumerable people who "beat themselves up" for behaving a certain way. In every situation, the client had an "internalized parent identity" and a "beaten child identity." They internalized a parent who was abusive, and then abused themselves. An **ESSENCE** or **I AM** prior to taking on Identities never beats themselves up. To repeat, "You will do unto yourself that which was done unto you."

In the above situation, the infant identifies with the beaten child identity and the abusive parent. The internalized parent then beats up the internalized child. It needs to be noted that when people say, "I have a critical part of myself," this needs to be challenged immediately. If a client says to me, "I have a critical part of myself," I respond with, "Who was critical of you as a child, your mother or father?" They might respond, "My mother." We must understand this is not a part of them but a part of mom which they took on, fused with and internalized—and which they now think is them. No infant or child is critical of himself. An external critical other is fused with and taken-on which they now think is a part of themselves--it is really a part of mom.

De-hypnosis and Quantum Psychology are all about "getting" that these parts or identities are not you—but are rather parts or identities of others which were taken-on as a child. De-hypnosis is about unfusing these parts or identities so that you can be *prior* to taking on anyone else's identities (i.e., who you are) before you took on any programming. As Nisargadatta Maharaj said, "What you know about yourself came from outside; therefore discard it."

The Way of the Human asks us not only to awaken to our own and other's trance-ference, but also to our own and others counter-trance-ference. It is only through becoming aware of, and looking objectively at, these primitive trances which dominate our interactions, that we can become free and recognize our full human potential.

APPENDIX
JUST FOR FUN

THE LIBERATION OF THE MINOTAUR

Part I

I n his theory of psychoanalysis, Freud used the Oedipus myth to describe both a psychological state and what he himself considered a sociological condition.

Quantum Psychology does not believe in myths.

MYTH:

> A traditional or legendary story usually concerning deities or demi-Gods; any invented story; an imaginary or fictitious thing or person (American College Dictionary, 1963, p. 8)

But often times myths, even if they are misunderstood, can describe through veiled symbology, powerful archtypes and psychological insights and situations which mirror the internal world. In this way, Quantum Psychology turns its attention to the myth of the Minotaur. Few myths or veiled characters have been so misunderstood and yet contain such a depth of psychological understanding.

The myth of the Minotaur with the head of a bull and the body of a man first appeared in ancient Minoan culture somewhere around 3000 B.C. It should be noted that this male Minotaur has also been depicted as a female by Picasso, Dali and Subraches. The Minotaur myth has existed since before the birth of Christ and 500 years before the birth of the Buddha.

Let us begin by telling the actual story of the Minotaur. Afterwards we can explore implications and application for relationships by taking apart each segment of the myth to discern its symbols as well as its powerful message.

THE MYTH OF THE MINOTAUR

King Minos of Crete invoked the wrath of Poseidon when he failed to sacrifice a magnificent white bull sent to him for that purpose. King minos instead sacrificed a different bull, trying to fool Poseidon. Poseidon's revenge was to cause Phasaphae, King Minos' wife, to fall in love with the animal. In order to attract the bull, Phasaphae asked Daedalus, chief architect at Knossos and all around handyman, to make her a hollow wooden cow structure. When she concealed herself inside, the bull found her irresistible. The outcome of their bizarre association was the hideous monster who was half-man and half-bull.

King Minos asked Daedalus to build a Labyrinth in which to confine the Minotaur and demanded that Athens pay an annual tribute of seven youths (virgins) and seven maidens (virgins) to satisfy the monster's huge appetite. Minos eventually found out that Daedalus had been instrumental in bringing about the union between his wife and the bull and threw the architect and his son into the Labyrinth. Daedalus made wings from feathers stuck together with wax and wearing these, father and son made their getaway. His son Icarus flew to close too the sun, the wax on the wings melted, and he plummeted into the sea off the Island of Ikaria.

Athenians meanwhile were enraged by the tribute demanded by Minos. The Athenian hero, Theseus, vowed to kill the Minotaur and sailed off the Crete posing as one of the sacrificial youths (virgins). On arrival he fell in love with Ariadne, the daughter of King

Minos, and she promised to help him if he would take her away with him afterward. She provided him with a ball of twine (string) and this he unwound on this way into the Labyrinth and used to retrace his steps after slaying the monster. Theseus fled Crete with Ariadne. The two married but Theseus abandoned Ariadne on the Island of Naxos on his way back to Athens.

On his return to Athens, Theseus forgot to unfold the white sail that he had promised to display to announce to his father that he was still alive. This prompted his distraught father, Angeus, to hurl himself to his death from the Acropolis. This . . . is how the Aegean Sea got its name. (Lonely Plant Travel survival kit, Greece, David Willette, Rosemary Hall, Paul Hellander, Kerry Kenchian, ©1994; Lonely Planet Publications, Austrialia, California, London, England)

THE MISUNDERSTOOD MINOTAUR: ITS SYMBOLS

Quantum Psychology sees the Minotaur and Minotaures not as monsters to be destroyed, but as manifestations and symbolic representations of both the biological and deep psychological processes of sexuality.

The first symbolic representation is Poseidon, the ruler of the ocean, who is a "personification" as opposed to what I call a "classical archetype." Quantum Psychology differentiates between an archetype and a personification in the following way: a personification is a creation which occurs when "not knowing" creates chaos. For example, for thousands of years no one knew what caused the wind to blow and this "not knowing" might create the internal experience of discomfort or chaos. To handle this chaos, people became anthropomorphic and might create a Wind God. They would then pray to and worship this new God (personification) created out of their unconscious desire to organize the chaos of "not knowing" the scientific facts about what wind is. This God, depicted as a person, is a personification and anthropromorphic.

Archetypes, on the other hand, come directly from the **EMPTINESS**. The Quantum field, or **UNDIFFERENTIATED CONSCIOUSNESS** which condenses down forming the COLLECTIVE (see Volume III). As it condenses further, energy patterns are formed and as it condenses still further, archetypes are created. An archetype is a condensation of the **EMPTINESS** or Quantum field, and originates in the collective. In short, a personification comes from the unconscious or conscious mind of an individual whereas an archetype is formed by the direct condensation of the **VOID OF UNDIFFERENTIATED CONSCIOUSNESS** which forms the COLLECTIVE (see Volume III, The Archetypes of the Collective).

The mind as a unified whole is symbolically represented by the ocean. In Buddhism, for example, there are specific Mudras (hand positions) which the Buddha is depicted in. Each hand position depicts a different understanding. For example, the most famous position of Buddha sitting touching (tapping) the earth represents Buddha's acknowledgment of the earth as the witness to his enlightenment. This Mudra depicts the earth as the impartial witness to all of our thoughts, feelings, emotions and actions. I personally have in my house a Buddha statue where Buddha's hand position depicts the calming of the ocean (or the mind).

Poseidon is a personification of the Greek God of the ocean or mind and he gives a beautiful Bull (representative of sexual energy and fertility) to King Minos (a King can be representative of the higher self). Poseidon (the whole universal mind) delivers this to Minos (the higher self) and asks Minos to destroy the Bull (sexuality.)

This demonstrates a major division made in the body/mind by Poseidon (universal mind) "as if" sex were not a part of the body/mind experience or the unified whole. This separation of body, mind and spirit demonstrates the imagined split between the body, the mind and the unified whole. It is interesting to note this since even Freud said that *the ego is body-centered*. This preconceived split is symbolically demonstrated by Poseidon's (the universal mind) dividing the whole universal mind into parts. This separation of body and mind from the unified whole makes sexuality (which is a body function) something to be destroyed. As mentioned throughout the book, this is a cornerstone understanding for various religions who see the body with its functions as bad and as something to be gone beyond, controlled or even destroyed (sacrificed) in order for enlightenment to come.

Minos (the higher self or **ESSENCE**) cannot destroy the Bull because he sees its beauty (his connection to sexuality). In order to outsmart Poseidon (the undivided mind), Minos (the higher self or **ESSENCE**) destroys an image of the bull (something that looks like sex) but not the Bull itself. Here we see how we misunderstand pure sexuality as a natural biological impulse and an expression of the unified whole. We confuse this natural biological impulse and believe that it's the same as our images or ideas about sex rather than seeing it as natural and part of the whole. In this way, through our images of sex we try to destroy it by labeling it as bad. Recently I met a guru wannabe who labeled sex as a trance rather than seeing her ideas about sex as a trance and sex as a natural biological function. Briefly stated, we create images of sexuality which are not sex. We then try to destroy our natural impulses because of the images we have created, causing further division within us.

In revenge, Poseidon causes Minos' wife Pasaphae to fall in love with the Bull. In other words, King Minos (**ESSENCE**) does not see a separation between himself and sexuality. He tries to outsmart the attempt of the mind to divide itself. Like all patterns in the mind which creates divisions and separations, this escalates and Pasaphae, the feminine archetype believes, in the separation which is proposed by the mind (Poseidon). She loses herself in her overwhelming desire because she sees sexuality as something separate from herself.

Phasaphae has the architect, Daedalus (an *image* builder) make her a Bull container that she can fit into so as to attract the Bull. This symbolizes how this works in our society. We do not understand the natural sexual impulse and so we divide and separate it from ourselves. Because of this separation, we create an *image* rather than allowing the pure natural biological attraction that people could have for sexuality. An image (container) is used to entice or seduce men (or women) and vice-versa. She must hide herself (her real feelings) and who she is, in or behind a container or mask in order for the (Bull) to want to have sex with her.

Here we see the lies. First, the separation from the unified whole mind. Next the separation of the body and the mind. Next the separation of sex from ourselves. Finally, the separation of male and female. All of this creates divisions (lies) forming images and masks (containers) which we present to the world as real or us, forgetting they are lies. One way to describe narcissism and the narcissistic trance is that you fall in love with the images you create about yourself. In this way, you lose yourself. Instead of examining the lies which create separation, contemporary psychology focuses on trying to change or have more choices over the images and personas (containers) we hide in or behind or make them better and more acceptable.

The Bull and Phasaphae have sex and from this the Minotaur is born. Minos (**ESSENCE**) falls into the trap of believing in separation and proclaims the Minotaur (Bastard) a monster after finding out about his wife's relationship with sexuality (the Bull).

IS THE MINOTAUR A MONSTER?

In family therapy, children are often labeled as symptom bearers, a representation of the problems that exist within the marriage. If the problem is separation (seeing sexuality as separate), something or someone has to be at fault. In this case, it is the Minotaur, the unwanted child born out of wedlock. At a deeper level, however, it is the problem of separation, i.e. imagining sex and the fruit of sex (the Minotaur) as separate from everything else (i.e., the underlying unity). Children born out of wedlock are called *bastards*, certainly a derogatory term. From a family therapy perspective to save the marriage, the Minotaur (the by-product of separation and sexuality) is considered an evil bastard and is sent by Minos (who now has fallen and experiences sexuality separate from himself and the underlying unity) to a Labyrinth (the symbol for the divided or unconscious mind). A Labyrinth (unconscious mind) is outside of the view of awareness and is a maze, which, once entered into is near impossible to "get out" of.

There, within the depths of the unconscious mind (Labyrinth), is placed the Minotaur (sexuality). Hidden from the world, Minos is now separate, obsessed (unconsciously) by the sexuality that the Minotaur represents, and unconsciously fixated on it. King Minos (who is now a fallen higher self or **ESSENCE**) believes in separation. He finds out that Daedalus (the architect) built the container (image) of the cow to attract the Bull and to punish him; he throws Daedalus (the image maker) and his son, Icarus, (a reflection and a creation of the image maker) into the Labrinyth of the unconscious mind.

Daedalus makes fake wings out of sticks and wax so that they can fly away. Here the image maker creates (automatically) (a False Self to overcome the False Core) more images, i.e., something *false* to get out of the unconscious mind. Here we see the newer psychology's false attempt to create a new image or presentation (False Self) to go beyond the unconscious (False Core) rather than going into it. The two try to escape by using this False Self vehicle. Icarus (the image of the image maker) flies too close to the sun (a symbolic representation of God), with the (false) wings of wax. The method (wings) doesn't work (melts) and he falls into the sea, the unified whole. From the point of view of the divided mind, at first glance this seems like death. However, from the point of view of the unified whole, there is no birth or death.

In reality, Icarus falls, into the unified whole. This fall is a symbolic representation of what occurs when a false method or means or path is used to get free of the mind. Since the method is false, it *appears* that it cannot carry you back to God (non-dual awareness). In this way at first you feel and think you are free, but sooner or later, the methods melt (are seen to be false) as it approaches the heat of the non-dual awareness of God (the Sun). In reality, however, everything is made of the same substance and is a unified whole. Externally from the point of view of the divided mind, it appears as though there is a "fall" because of a false method or false understanding. However, we all return to the unified whole mind (the ocean) at death. In this way, Icarus' false method is melted and destroyed, but he is freed from the illusion of separation (as are we all), at his death, when he is reabsorbed into the unified whole of consciousness. This can be viewed to illustrate how it is all **ONE SUBSTANCE**. Even though a person appears to be on the "wrong" path or using the wrong method, there are *no* mistakes. All roads at death lead to the unified whole which we all are, cannot escape from, and hopefully can recognize.

I once said to Nisargadetta Maharaj, "I had this experience that there was no such thing as choice—and that whatever is supposed to happen will happen. Is that true?" "Obviously," Nisargadetta replied.

Minos (the "fallen"[1] higher self) asks King Ageans of Athens, as a tribute from the loss of a war (here a war is a violent belief that there is separation, to send seven boys and seven maidens (both virgins) to be sacrificed (given over) to the Minotaur (sexuality). Here the virgins are supposedly eaten by the Minotaur, but Quantum Psychology says that they are *absorbed* and reunited with their own sexuality as a natural function and a part of the whole. From the point of view of separation, the seven virgins are destroyed (by sexuality). From the point of view of Quantum Psychology, they are reunited with their natural biological function, and the body (sex) mind separation disappears.

Buried deeply within the Labyrinth of the unconscious mind lies the Minotaur which is viewed as the monster (of sexuality) by the forces of separation and division. King Aegeus (Mr. Separation himself) cannot bear sending virgins to be destroyed (absorbed) by the Minotaur (sexuality). He sends his son Thesus (the son of Mr. Separation) disguised as a male virgin to the Labyrinth (unconscious mind) of the Minotaur (sexuality) to destroy the Minotaur (sexuality). Again King Aegeus does not want to look at the lie of his imagined separation from his own sexuality which also separates him from the unified whole. Instead he looks outside himself and *blames* others for his separation. He wants to destroy others rather than dissolve his separating concepts. If he looks at his separating concepts, he must face his own lies and pain and let go of his concepts.

Thesus sets off for Crete in a boat with black sails and he tells his father that if he is alive, upon his return, he will change the black sails to white. However, if the mission is a failure and he dies, the sails will remain black. Notice that traditionally black is bad, white is good. But here Thesus sails with black sails symbolizing an evil mission (a mission which continues to re-enforce the experience of separation from sexuality).

---

[1]Fallen is a relative term used to describe how he now sees himself and others as separate.

He sets forth for Crete where he meets King Minos' daughter, Aridane (the feminine) and they fall in love (become integrated) and get married. In this way, marriage means that the imagined separation between masculine and feminine has vanished and that these two forces are integrated as one. Aridane (the feminine) knows the way in and out of the Labyrinth (of the mind) where sexuality (Minotaur) is. She gives Thesues a twine of thread (string—a representation of the path) so that he may enter the Labyrinth and find his way back out safely. Theseus enters the Labyrinth, kills the Minotaur (sexuality) and escapes (the thread is the path into and out of the Labyrinth of the unconscious mind).

They flee Crete for Athens, but when Thesus reaches a small island, he abandons Adriane (the feminine who had showed him the path into and out of the unconsious mind). Quantum Psychology suggests that the loss of sexuality is the beginning of the end for "relationships." Notice in your life how when sexuality disappears from a relationship, the partner feels abandoned and the relationship is finished. Why? Because real sexuality and marriage are only satisfying when there is an integration, and when sexuality can aid in that end. If sexuality is abandoned (destroyed), then the natural biological integration is no more. *With* that, the masculine and feminine are two. This disintegration is so painful that it often signals the *end* of a marriage. This is a real life sequence. Men often abandon women who held the rope for them, i.e., women who held them together so that they could succeed. After abandoning this integration they become separate again by abandoning the feminine.

Theseus heads for Athens. But because of his killing of his own sexuality becoming separate and abandoning his feminine, he becomes unconscious (amnesic) and forgets to change the black sails to white. In other words, because he has separated and destroyed his sexuality, he goes into a trance. This also means that the evil mission of dividing and separating sexuality from the whole mind has been successful and he is flying black, the color of the "evil" separation. The sails are kept black also symbolizing his death (greater separation) and, hence, the black or dark forces have won—dark being the separating forces, light or white, the revealing forces. His father (Mr. Separateness) sees the black sails on the ship from a mountaintop.

He becomes so divided from himself after ordering the death of the Minotaur (sexuality) and thinking sexuality has won, and his son (images of himself) is dead and that he killed himself (by killing sexuality), that he throws himself into the sea—(the whole mind). Again, even though he struggles and has done "evil" (ordering even more separation) and suffers because of this, in the end, like all of us, he joins the whole unified field or the **VOID OF UNDIFFEREN- TIATED CONSCIOUSNESS**.

Part II

THE MINOTAUR COMPLEX

To best understand the Minotaur complex, it is important to look at its context, namely, society and religion's relationship to sexuality.

First, let us examine Quantum Psychology's relationship to sexuality, the body/mind, and the unified field. Quantum Psychology sees *no* separation between the **VOID OF UNDIFFERENTIATED CONSCIOUSNESS** or the unified field and the body. On the contrary, Quantum Psychology sees the spirit, the body and the mind as a condensation of **THAT ONE SUBSTANCE**.

According to Quantum Psychology theory, the more separate we feel from the **VOID OF UNDIFFERENTIATED CONSCIOUSNESS** and the more divisions we have between body, mind and spirit, the more pain we will experience. It is a bottom line division of imagined separate self against imagined separate self.

SYMPTOMS OF THE MINOTAUR COMPLEX

The symptoms of the Minotaur complex are rampant throughout the world, but they're most overtly apparent in our religious and spiritual groups.

SYMPTION 1

First, sexuality is seen as bad, and it is consciously hidden and repressed. This creates an unconscious fixation upon sexuality and an over-compensation for these hidden sexual urges. This over-compensation can manifest as projecting sexual feelings upon another and labeling the "other" as bad for having these feelings or as guilt for feeling your own biological (and survival) processes, since sexuality is part of the survival of the species.

This is especially manifested throughout our society in religions claiming sexuality as bad and in spiritual groups which claim that not only is sexuality bad, but if it is transformed (by not performing the act—abstinence), then it is easy to become enlightened (reunited with God). Somehow in this aspect of the Minotaur complex, the core distortion is that God and the **VOID of UNDIFFERENTIATED CONSCIOUSNESS** can be reached more readily through sexual abstinence and that for God (**VOID of UNDIFFERENTIATED CONSCIOUSNESS**) sex is **BAD**.

This distortion does not see the body or sexuality as a condensation of the **VOID OF UNDIFFERENTIATED CONSCIOUSNESS** but rather, due to unconscious repression, there is a fixation on sex, sex is seen as separate from the bodily functions and the **VOID OF UNDIFFERENTIATED CONSCIOUSNESS** and the unified whole. Simply stated, one does not see sex and the body as a condensation of **THAT ONE SUBSTANCE**.

SYMPTOM 2

The next symptoms in the Minotaur complex is the split that occurs between body, mind and spirit.

In Quantum Psychology, the body is the mind is the spirit is the unified whole. When there is a splitting, this pits the body, the mind, and the spirit against each other.

The manifestation of this is trying to overcome one for the other. In many religions and psychologies, the spirit or the mind is considered the most important.

Often in psychology the mind is placed above the body, possibly because most people depict the mind in the head which is on top of the body and try to change themselves through the mind, neglecting the body.

In spiritual circles, the mind is oftentimes seen as something which gets in the way of God (the unified field) and is thus considered bad for people. This split is manifested and leads us into a painful process whereby people see sex as something separate from themselves and from God, or the unified field.

SYMPTOM 3

One of the strongest issues in our society is having and appreciating sexuality as a vehicle for love, integration, and intimacy rather than as a tool for power and increasing self image, as it is often used. Sexuality should be considered as love and intimacy made manifest.

SYMPTOM 4

Seeing sex separate from yourself.

SYMPTOM 5

Utilizing philosophies, religions, Gods, Goddesses, or psychologies as a way to reinforce sexual repression.

CONCLUSION

We need to realize that our body is all part of the unified whole and made of **THAT ONE SUBSTANCE**, including sex and death. Realizing who you are is a process of realizing everything is made of **THAT ONE SUBSTANCE**. This understanding moves us beyond the Labyrinth of the dualistic mind and into the **VOID of UNDIFFERENTIATED CONSCIOUSNESS**

REFERENCES

Agneesens, C. (Forthcoming). *Fabric of Wholeness: Embodying Relational Gravity.*

Almaas, A. H. (1986). *The void.* York Beach: Samuel Weiner, Inc.

American College Dictionary. (1963). New York: Random House.

Arica Institute, Inc., The. (1989). *The Arican.* New York.

Bahirjit, B. B. (1963). *The Amritanubhava of Janadeva.* Bombay: Sirun Press.

Benbu, I. (1977). *Stalking the wild pendulum.* Rochester, Vermont: Destiny Books.

Blank, G. R., & Blank, R. *Ego psychology II: Psychoanalytic developmental psychology.* New York: Columbia University Press.

Bohm, D. (1951). *Quantum theory.* London: Constable.

Bohm, D. (1980). *Wholeness and the implicit order.* London: Ark Paperbacks.

Bohm, D. (1985). *Unfolding meaning.* London: Ark Paperbacks.

Bohm, D., & Peat, D. F. (1987)). *Science, Order and Creativity*. New York: Bantam Books.

Bollas, C. (1987). *The Shadow of the object: Psychoanalysis of the unthought known*. New York: Columbia University Press.

Bollas, C. (1989). *Furies of destine: Psychoanalysis and human idiom*. London: Free Association Books.

Bourland, D., & Johnson, P. (1991). *To be or not: An e-prime anthology*. San Francisco: International Society for General Semantics.

Buddhist Text Translation Society. (1980). *The heart sutra and commentary*. San Francisco: Buddhist Text Translation Society.

Capra, F. (1976). *The tao of physics*. New York: Bantam Books.

Edinger, E. (1992). *Ego and the archetype: Individualization and the religious function of the archetype*. Boston: Shambhalla.

Gleick, James. (1987). *Chaos*. New York: Penguin Books.

Godman, D. (1985). *The teaching of Ramana Maharishi*. Ankara, London.

Hawkins, S. (1988). *A brief history of time*. New York: Bantam Books.

Herbert, N. (1985). *Quantum reality*. New York: Anchor Press.

Horner, A. J. (1985). *Object relations and the developing ego in therapy*. Northridge, New Jersey: Jason Arunsun, Inc.

Hua, Master Tripitaka. (1980). *Shurangama sutra*. San Francisco: Buddhist Text Translation Society.

Ichazo, O. (1993). *The fourteen pillars of perfect recognition.* New York: The Arica Institute, Inc.

Isherwood, C., & Prahnavarla, Swami. (1953). *How to know God: The yoga of Patanjali.* CA: New American Library.

Johnson, S. M. (1987). *Humanizing the narcissistic style.* New York: The Arica Institute, Inc.

Johnson, S. M. (1991). *The symbiotic character.* New York/ London: W. W. Norton & Co.

Kaku, M. (1994). *Hyperspace.* New York: Anchor-Doubleday Volumes.

Kaku M. (1987). *Beyond Einstein: The cosmic quest for the theory of the universe.* New York: Bantam Volumes.

Korzybski, A. (1993). *Science and sanity.* Englewood, New Jersey: Institute for General Semantics.

Korzybski, A. (1962). *Selections from Science and Sanity.* Englewood, New Jersey: International Non-Aristotelian Library Publishing Company.

Irving J. L. (1941). *Language habits in human affairs.* England, New Jersey: International Society for General Semantics

Mahler, M. (1968). *On the human symbiosis and vicissitudes of individuation.* New York: International Universe Press.

Marshall, R. J., & Marshall, S. V. (1988). *The transference-counter-transference matrix: The emotional-cognitive dialogue in psychotherapy, psychoanalysis and supervision.* New York: Columbia University Press.

Mckay, M. D. M., & Fanning, P. (1981). *Thoughts and feelings: The art of cognitive stress intervention.* Oakland, CA: Harbinger Publications.

Miller, H. (1961). *Tropic of Cancer.* New York: Grove Press.

Miller, H. (1961). *Tropic of Capricorn.* New York: Grove Press.

Muktananda, Swami. (1974). *Play of consciousness.* Ganeshpuri: Shree Gurudev Ashram.

Muktananda, Swami. (1978). *I am that: The science of hamsa.* New York: S.Y.D.A. Foundation.

Mookerjit, Ajit. (1971). *Tantra asana. A way to self-realization.* Basel, Paris, New Delhi: Ravi Kumar.

Naranjo, E. (1990). *Enneatype structures: Self analysis for the seeker.* CA: Gateways IDHHB, Inc.

Nicoll, M. (1984). *Psychological commentaries on the teaching of Gurdjieff and Ouspensky.* Vol. 1. Boulder/London: Shambhala.

Nisargadatta, Majaraj. *I am that.* 1994. Durham, NC: Acorn Press

Ouspensky, P. D. (1949). *In search of the miraculous.* New York: Harcourt, Brace and World, Inc.

Palmer, H. (1988). *The Enneagram.* CA: Harper & Row.

Peat, D. F. (1987). *The bridge between matter and mind.* New York: Bantam Books.

Peat, D. F. (1988). *Superstrings and the search for the theory of everything.* Chicago: Contemporary Books.

Peat, D. F., & Briggs, J. (1989). *The turbulent mirror: An illustrated guide to chaos theory & the science of wholeness.* New York: Harper & Row, 1989.

Peat, D. F. (1990). *Einstein's moon: Bell's theorem and the curious quest for quantum reality.* Chicago: Contemporary Books.

Peat, D. F. (1991). *The philosopher's stone: Chaos, synchronicity, and the hidden order of the world.* New York: Bantam Books.

Postnieks, Diana. Conversations with the author.

Reich, W. (1942). *The function of the orgasm. The discovery of the orgone.* New York: World Publishing.

Riso, D. R. (1987). *Personality types: Using the Enneagram for self-discovery.* Boston: Houghton Mifflin Company.

Riso, D. R. (1988). *Understand the Enneagram.* Massachusetts: Houghton Mifflin Company.

Riso, D. R. (1987). *Humanizing the narcissistic style.* New York/ London: W.W. Norton & Co.

Shah, I. (1978). *Learning how to learn: Psychology and spirituality in the Sufi Way.* London: Octagon Press

Shah, I. (1978). *A perfumed scorpion: The way to the way.* San Francisco: Harper & Row

Shakaran, R. (1991). *The spirit of homeopathy.* Bombay: Homeopathic Medical Publishers.

Singh, J. (1963). *Pratyabhijnahrdeyam: The secret of self recognition.* Delhi: Motilal Banarsidass.

Singh, J. (1979). *Siva Sutra, the yoga of Supreme Identity.* Delhi: Motilal Banarsidass.

Singh, J. (1979). *Vijnanabhairava or diving consciousness*. Delhi: Motilal Banarsidass.

Singh, J. (1980). *Spanda Karikas*. Delhi: Motilal Banarsidass.

Suzuki, S. *Zen mind, beginner's mind*. New York: Weatherhill, 1970.

Talbot, M. (1981). *Mysticism and the new physics*. New York: Bantam Books.

Talbot, M. (1987). *Beyond the quantum*. New York: Bantam Books.

Talbot, M. (1991). *The holographic universe*. New York: Harper Collins.

Vithoukas, G. (1980). *The science of homeopathy*. New York: Grove Press.

Weinberg, H. L. (1959). *Levels of knowing and existence: Studies in general semantics*. Englewood, New Jersey: Institute of General Semantics.

Wolinsky, S. H. (1993). *The dark side of the inner child*. Norfolk, CT: Bramble Co.

Wolinsky, S. H. (1991). *Trances people live: Healing approaches to quantum psychology*. Norfolk, CT: Bramble Co.

Wolinsky, S. H. (1993). *Quantum consciousness*. Norfolk, Connecticut: Bramble Books.

Wolinsky, S. H. (1994). *The tao of chaos: Quantum consciousness*. Vol. II. Norfolk, CT: Bramble Books.

Wolinsky, S. H. (1995). *Hearts on Fire* Capitola, CA